Special Finance Applications in Microsoft Dynamics 365 for Finance and Operations

Special Finance Applications in Microsoft Dynamics 365 for Finance and Operations

A Guide to Mastering Commonly Experienced Complex Financial Applications in Microsoft

Dynamics 365 for Finance and Operations

Ludwig Reinhard, PhD

Copyright

Piracy of copyright material on the internet is an ongoing problem across all media. If you come across any illegal copies of our works on the internet in any form, please provide us with the location address or website name immediately so that we can pursue a remedy. Please contact us at lreinhard7@live.de with a link to the suspected pirated material.

ISBN 13: 9781792855214

Table of Contents

Preface

What This Book Covers

As the title of the book indicates, the main focus of this book is on special finance application scenarios that people often come across when using Microsoft Dynamics 365 for Finance and Operations (MSDyn365FO).

That is, the book does not cover all finance-related functionalities available in the standard MSDyn365FO application, as other books do. It rather focuses on a few selected complex finance scenarios and details how one can incorporate them in the standard MSDyn365FO application without making system modifications. The book is thereby not industry-specific but rather applies to a number of different industries.

After describing what this book covers, let's briefly focus on how it is arranged. The first chapter focuses on fixed asset related parallel-accounting scenarios. This chapter is followed by a chapter that demonstrates how to create maturity-structure-based financial reports. Thereafter, the lower-of-cost-or-net-realizable-value principle is introduced (in chapter three), and it is explained how this principle can be incorporated into MSDyn365FO. The next chapter provides a deep dive on different ways one can import journals in MSDyn365FO, and the last chapter concludes with some case management related issues.

What You Need for This Book

All examples illustrated are processed on the Microsoft Dynamics 365 for Finance and Operations Fall 2018 (version 8.1, platform update 20) demo machine, available for download for example through Lifecycle Services (LCS). No specific software add-ons or code modifications are required to replicate and follow the illustrations and explanations.

Who This Book Is For

This book is intended for application consultants, financial controllers, finance managers, and accountants, as well as other professionals who are involved in the setup of Microsoft Dynamics 365 for Finance and Operations. A basic knowledge of financial terms and concepts and Microsoft Dynamics 365 for Finance and Operations terminology is required.

Conventions

In this book, you will find a number of text styles that distinguish among the different kinds of information.

Warnings and important notes are indicated by the following symbol:

Best-practice recommendations from the author are indicated by the following symbol:

Reader Feedback

Feedback from our readers is always welcome. Let us know what you think about this book—what you like or dislike. Reader feedback is important for us, as it helps us develop titles that you really get the most out of. To send us general feedback, simply email lreinhard7@live.de.

Errata

Although we have taken utmost care to ensure the accuracy of our content, mistakes do happen. If you find a mistake, we would be grateful if you would report this to us. By doing so, you can save other readers from frustration and help us improve subsequent versions of this book. If you find any errata, please report them by emailing lreinhard7@live.de.

Abbreviations

BS	Balance sheet
CM	Case management
CR	Credit
DR	Debit
ER	Electronic-report or electronic-reporting
FIFO	First in, first out
GAAP	Generally accepted accounting principles
GL	General ledger
IAS	International accounting standards
ID	Identifier
IFRS	International financial reporting standards
IS	Income statement
LIFO	Last in, first out
LoCoM	Lower of cost or market; Lower of cost or net realizable value
MS	Microsoft
MSDyn365FO	Microsoft Dynamics 365 for Finance and Operations
NRV	Net-realizable value
P&L	Profit and loss
USGAAP	US generally accepted accounting principles
SEC	Section
SLA	Service-level agreement

1.   Parallel Accounting

1.1.   What Is Parallel Accounting?

International operating companies are often required to prepare financial statements that follow multiple accounting regulations, the so-called generally accepted accounting principles (GAAP).

As an example, most companies listed on stock exchanges in Europe have to prepare financial reports that follow international accounting regulations (IAS/IFRS). Those companies are also regularly required to prepare financial statements that are in line with the accounting regulations applicable in their home countries (local-GAAP). Finally, tax authorities commonly ask for a third set of financial statements that follow tax regulations. Therefore, international listed companies often end up preparing three different kinds of financial reports.

Preparing financial reports that follow three different financial accounting standards can involve a lot of work. To reduce the amount of work required for preparing those reports, MSDyn365FO provides users with different tools and instruments. The way those tools and instruments are applied depends on the approach that is selected for parallel accounting. The next table summarizes the four approaches that are generally available for parallel accounting.

	Ledger Approach	Posting layer Approach
Full Posting Approach	A	B
Delta Posting Approach	C	D

Figure 1.1 *Parallel accounting approaches*

1

Figure 1.1 differentiates between a ledger and a posting-layer approach. The difference between both approaches is that the first one uses valuation-specific ledger accounts, whereas the second one uses so-called posting-layers to differentiate between the valuations required for the different accounting standards.

The second criteria for differentiating the parallel accounting approaches shown in figure 1.1 refers to the full and delta posting approaches. The main difference between those approaches is whether postings are duplicated in order to incorporate the various accounting regulations (full posting approach) or whether only difference—so-called delta—postings are made. Expressed differently, the full posting approach records a transaction multiple times—either on separate ledger accounts or on posting-layers—whereas the delta posting approach records the difference in the valuation required only.

The combination of the ledger or posting-layer approach and the full or delta posting approach results in four different options—identified by the letters a to d in figure 1.1—that companies can select from when it comes to parallel accounting.

In practice, the full posting approaches (*a* and *b*) are hardly used because they double or triple the number of transactions recorded. For that reason, a focus is made on the last two approaches (*c* and *d*) in the following.

1.2. Parallel Accounting in MSDyn365FO

1.2.1. Ledger Approach

The aforementioned ledger approach makes use of separate ledger accounts to incorporate the different accounting regulations. Let us investigate a simplified example, where a company acquires another one and records a goodwill in its financial statements because of this acquisition. The next table details the fair-market values of the assets and liabilities of the acquired company according to the different valuation principles.

Element	IFRS value	Local GAAP value	Tax GAAP value
Fixed Assets	$ 690	$ 600	$ 510
Inventory	$ 210	$ 200	$ 190
Accounts Receivable	$ 600	$ 600	$ 600
Cash	$ 100	$ 100	$ 100
Accounts Payable	-$ 500	-$ 500	-$ 500
Fair market value	**$ 1,100**	**$ 1,000**	**$ 900**

Figure 1.2 *Fair-market value calculations*

Assuming that a price of $1,500 is agreed upon for the acquisition of the company, a goodwill of $400 has to be recorded according to IFRS ($1,500 purchase price minus the IFRS fair-market value). For the local-GAAP financial statements, a goodwill of $500—and for the tax-GAAP a goodwill of $600—has to be recorded.

The next figure shows how the goodwill-related transactions are posted in MSDyn365FO according to the different accounting standards by following the delta-posting-ledger approach.

Date	Account DR	Account Name DR	Posting Layer	Amount DR	Account CR	Account Name CR	Posting Layer	Amount CR
Aug-18	170151	Goodwill (IFRS)	Current	$ 400	200101	Accounts Payable (IFRS)	Current	$ -500
Aug-18	180101	Fixed Assets (IFRS)	Current	$ 690	200111	Other Payables (IFRS)	Current	$ -1,500
Aug-18	140101	Inventory (IFRS)	Current	$ 210				
Aug-18	130101	Accounts Receivable (IFRS)	Current	$ 600				
Aug-18	110181	Cash (IFRS)	Current	$ 100				

Date	Account DR	Account Name DR	Posting Layer	Amount DR	Account CR	Account Name CR	Posting Layer	Amount CR
Sep-18	170152	Goodwill (Local)	Current	$ 100	200102	Accounts Payable (Local)	Current	$ -
Sep-18	180102	Fixed Assets (Local)	Current	$ -90	200112	Other Payables (Local)	Current	$ -
Sep-18	140102	Inventory (Local)	Current	$ -10				
Sep-18	130102	Accounts Receivable (Local)	Current	$ -				
Sep-18	110182	Cash (Local)	Current	$ -				

Date	Account DR	Account Name DR	Posting Layer	Amount DR	Account CR	Account Name CR	Posting Layer	Amount CR
Oct-18	170153	Goodwill (Tax)	Current	$ 200	200103	Accounts Payable (Tax)	Current	$ -
Oct-18	180103	Fixed Assets (Tax)	Current	$ -180	200113	Other Payables (Tax)	Current	$ -
Oct-18	140103	Inventory (Tax)	Current	$ -20				
Oct-18	130103	Accounts Receivable (Tax)	Current	$ -				
Oct-18	110183	Cash (Tax)	Current	$ -				

Figure 1.3 *Delta-posting-ledger approach for the acquisition of the new company with goodwill*

For reasons of simplicity, all transactions are recorded in a single general ledger accounting journal. No transactions are recorded in any of the subledgers, such as accounts payable, accounts receivable, fixed assets, and so on.

Please note that the delta-posting-ledger approach makes use of separate accounts that are used for the different accounting standards. As an example, the IFRS goodwill amount ($400) is recorded on account 170151. The local-GAAP goodwill amount ($500) can be identified by the sum of the amounts posted on accounts 170151 and 170152, where the amount posted on account 170152 only accounts for the difference in the goodwill between IFRS and the local-GAAP. The same applies to the tax-GAAP goodwill amount of $600, which can be calculated by adding the amounts posted on accounts 170151 and 170153.

In summary, the local-GAAP and tax-GAAP results are calculated by adding the local-GAAP-specific or tax-GAAP-specific accounts to the IFRS-specific accounts. As the IFRS transactions are always needed to calculate the local-GAAP and tax-GAAP results, the IFRS results or transactions are often referred to as the leading accounting standard from which the other ones are derived. The next figure exemplifies this principle by illustrating the financial statements for the transactions recorded according to IFRS, local-GAAP, and tax-GAAP.

For the Ten Months Ending Wednesday, October 31, 2018

Balance Sheet (IFRS)		Liabilities	
		Accounts Payable (200101)	500.00
Current Assets		**Total Accounts Payable**	**500.00**
Cash (110181)	€100.00		
Cash Equivalents		Tax Payable	
Total Cash and Cash Equivalents	**100.00**	**Total Tax Payable**	
Accounts Receivable (130101)	600.00	Other current liabilities (200111)	1,500.00
Total Accounts Receivable	**600.00**	**Total Other Current Liabilities**	**1,500.00**
Prepaid Expenses		Long term Bank Loans	
Total Other Current Assets		Notes Payable	
		Long term Interest Payable	
Raw Materials and Finished Goods Inventory (140101)	210.00	**Total Long Term Liabilities**	
Total Physical Inventory	**210.00**	**Total Liabilities**	**2,000.00**
WIP - All		Capital Stock	
Total Project		Additional Paid-in Capital	
Total Current Assets	**910.00**	Common Dividends	
		Other Income	
Fixed Assets		Retained Earnings (Local and Tax GAAP accounts)	
		Net Income (300160)	
Intangible Assets (170151)	400.00	**Total Shareholder Equity**	
Amortization - Intangible Fixed Assets			
Total Intangible Assets	**400.00**		
		Liabilities & Shareholder Equity	**€2,000.00**
Tangible Fixed Assets (180101)	690.00		
Accumulated Depreciation - Tangible Fixed Assets			
Other Assets			
Total Tangible Assets	**690.00**		
Total Fixed Assets	**1,090.00**		
Total Assets	**€2,000.00**		

Figure 1.4 *Financial statements using the delta-posting-ledger approach—IFRS*

For the Ten Months Ending Wednesday, October 31, 2018

Balance Sheet (Local GAAP)		Liabilities	
		Accounts Payable (200101, 200102)	500.00
Current Assets		**Total Accounts Payable**	**500.00**
Cash (110181, 110182)	€100.00		
Cash Equivalents		Tax Payable	
Total Cash and Cash Equivalents	**100.00**	**Total Tax Payable**	
Accounts Receivable (130101, 130102)	600.00	Other current liabilities (200111, 200112)	1,500.00
Total Accounts Receivable	**600.00**	**Total Other Current Liabilities**	**1,500.00**
Prepaid Expenses		Long term Bank Loans	
Total Other Current Assets		Notes Payable	
		Long term Interest Payable	
Raw Materials and Finished Goods Inventory (140101, 140102)	200.00	**Total Long Term Liabilities**	
Total Physical Inventory	**200.00**	**Total Liabilities**	**2,000.00**
WIP - All		Capital Stock	
Total Project		Additional Paid-in Capital	
Total Current Assets	**900.00**	Common Dividends	
		Other Income	
Fixed Assets		Retained Earnings	
		Net Income	
Intangible Assets (170151, 170152)	500.00	**Total Shareholder Equity**	
Amortization - Intangible Fixed Assets			
Total Intangible Assets	**500.00**		
		Liabilities & Shareholder Equity	€2,000.00
Tangible Fixed Assets (180101, 180102)	600.00		
Accumulated Depreciation - Tangible Fixed Assets			
Other Assets			
Total Tangible Assets	**600.00**		
Total Fixed Assets	**1,100.00**		
Total Assets	**€2,000.00**		

Figure 1.5 *Financial statements using the delta-posting-ledger approach—local-GAAP*

For the Ten Months Ending Wednesday, October 31, 2018

Balance Sheet (Tax GAAP)		Liabilities	
		Accounts Payable (200101, 200103)	500.00
Current Assets		**Total Accounts Payable**	**500.00**
Cash (110181, 110183)	€100.00		
Cash Equivalents		Tax Payable	
Total Cash and Cash Equivalents	**100.00**	**Total Tax Payable**	
Accounts Receivable (130101, 130103)	600.00	Other current liabilities (200111, 200113)	1,500.00
Total Accounts Receivable	**600.00**	**Total Other Current Liabilities**	**1,500.00**
Prepaid Expenses		Long term Bank Loans	
Total Other Current Assets		Notes Payable	
		Long term Interest Payable	
Raw Materials and Finished Goods Inventory (140101, 140103)	190.00	**Total Long Term Liabilities**	
Total Physical Inventory	**190.00**	**Total Liabilities**	**2,000.00**
WIP - All		Capital Stock	
Total Project		Additional Paid-in Capital	
Total Current Assets	**890.00**	Common Dividends	
		Other Income	
Fixed Assets		Retained Earnings	
		Net Income	
Intangible Assets (170151, 170153)	600.00	**Total Shareholder Equity**	
Amortization - Intangible Fixed Assets			
Total Intangible Assets	**600.00**		
		Liabilities & Shareholder Equity	**€2,000.00**
Tangible Fixed Assets (180101, 180103)	510.00		
Accumulated Depreciation - Tangible Fixed Assets			
Other Assets			
Total Tangible Assets	**510.00**		
Total Fixed Assets	**1,110.00**		
Total Assets	**€2,000.00**		

Figure 1.6 *Financial statements using the delta-posting-ledger approach—tax-GAAP*

Note In practice, companies would only create delta-posting-ledger accounts if transactions needed to be recorded on those accounts. As an example, the ledger accounts 110182 and 110183 used in this example do not record an amount and could therefore be relinquished.

When it comes to parallel accounting, special considerations need to be made in regards to the profit or loss that is posted at the end of the year with the year-end closing transactions. To illustrate those special considerations that need to be made, the following depreciation transactions for the company's goodwill are recorded for the three accounting standards used. Please see figure 1.7 for details.

Date	Account DR	Account Name DR	Posting Layer	Amount DR	Account CR	Account Name CR	Posting Layer	Amount CR
Nov-18	618701	Goodwill impairment (IFRS)	Current	$ 16	170151	Goodwill (IFRS)	Current	$ -16

Date	Account DR	Account Name DR	Posting Layer	Amount DR	Account CR	Account Name CR	Posting Layer	Amount CR
Nov-18	618702	Goodwill impairment (Local)	Current	$ 2	170152	Goodwill (Local)	Current	$ -2

Date	Account DR	Account Name DR	Posting Layer	Amount DR	Account CR	Account Name CR	Posting Layer	Amount CR
Nov-18	681703	Goodwill impairment (Tax)	Current	$ 4	170153	Goodwill (Tax)	Current	$ -4

Figure 1.7 *Delta-posting-ledger approach—depreciation of goodwill*

Running the year-end closing process with those additional transactions posted results in the following year-end closing voucher.

View subledger journal   Transaction origin   Transactions   Audit trail   Posted sales tax   Original document   Accounting source explorer   Related vouchers   ⌕

Voucher transactions

Overview   General

✓	Journal number	Voucher ▽	Date ↑	Ledger account	Account name	Description	Currency	Amount in transaction currency
	DE1-000011	YE2018-CL1	1/1/2019	140103--	Inventory (Tax)		EUR	-20.00
	DE1-000011	YE2018-CL1	1/1/2019	180103--	Fixed Assets (Tax)		EUR	-180.00
	DE1-000011	YE2018-CL1	1/1/2019	170153--	Goodwill (Tax)		EUR	196.00
✓	DE1-000011	YE2018-CL1	1/1/2019	140102--	Inventory (Local)		EUR	-10.00
✓	DE1-000011	YE2018-CL1	1/1/2019	180102--	Fixed Assets (Local)		EUR	-90.00
✓	DE1-000011	YE2018-CL1	1/1/2019	170152--	Goodwill (Local)		EUR	98.00
	DE1-000011	YE2018-CL1	1/1/2019	200111--	Other Payables (IFRS)		EUR	-1,500.00
	DE1-000011	YE2018-CL1	1/1/2019	200101--	Accounts Payable (IFRS)		EUR	-500.00
	DE1-000011	YE2018-CL1	1/1/2019	110181--	Cash (IFRS)		EUR	100.00
	DE1-000011	YE2018-CL1	1/1/2019	130101--	Accounts Receivable (IFRS)		EUR	600.00
	DE1-000011	YE2018-CL1	1/1/2019	140101--	Inventory (IFRS)		EUR	210.00
	DE1-000011	YE2018-CL1	1/1/2019	180101--	Fixed Assets (IFRS)		EUR	690.00
	DE1-000011	YE2018-CL1	1/1/2019	170151--	Goodwill (IFRS)		EUR	384.00
	DE1-000011	YE2018-CL1	1/1/2019	300160--	Retained Earnings		EUR	22.00

Figure 1.8 *Year-end closing voucher—delta-posting-ledger approach*

The year-end closing voucher shown in figure 1.8 shows a total profit of $22, which is posted on the ledger account for retained-earnings (300160). This total profit is made up by the profit or loss according to IFRS and the profit-or-loss difference according to the other accounting standards. The following formula details the amount posted on the retained-earnings account.

$$
\begin{aligned}
\text{Retained-Earnings} &= \text{Profit/Loss (IFRS)} + \text{Profit/Loss Difference (Local-GAAP)} \\
&\quad + \text{Profit/Loss Difference (Tax-GAAP)} \\
&= \$16 + \$2 + \$4 \\
&= \$22
\end{aligned}
\tag{1}
$$

Incorporating this total profit or loss in the financial statements shown previously would result in a wrong representation of the company's profit according to the different accounting standards because of double- or triple-counting effects. The next figure aims to illustrate those double- or triple-counting effects.

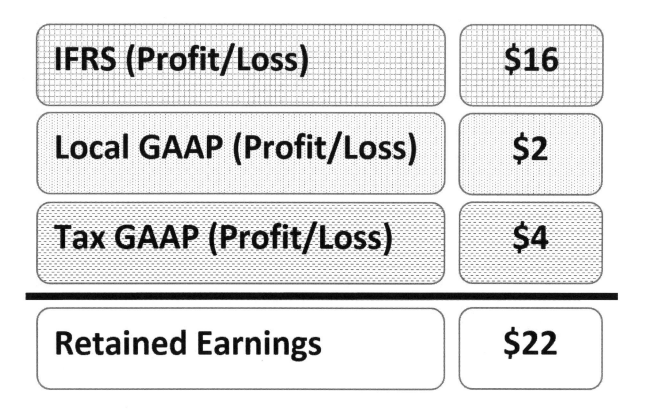

Figure 1.9 *Double- or triple-counting effects on retained-earnings—delta-posting-ledger approach*

The correct representation of the IFRS result consequently requires a correction of the profit or loss that is related to the other accounting standards. The next figure illustrates the required correction.

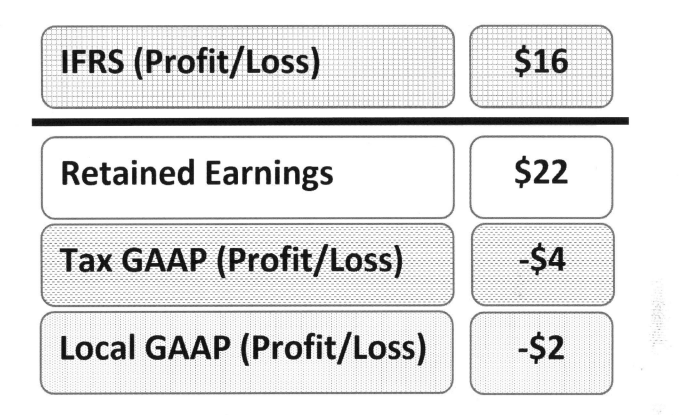

Figure 1.10 *Profit-or-loss correction—IFRS*

Figure 1.10 shows that the amount posted on the retained-earnings account needs to be corrected by the profit or loss that can be assigned to the tax-GAAP and local-GAAP accounting regulations to arrive at the IFRS profit or loss. This correction can be taken care of by including a corrective position in the financial-report designer that is shown in figure 1.11 below.

For reasons of simplicity, the corrective position is included in the financial reporting line 2230 for the retained-earnings in figure 1.11.

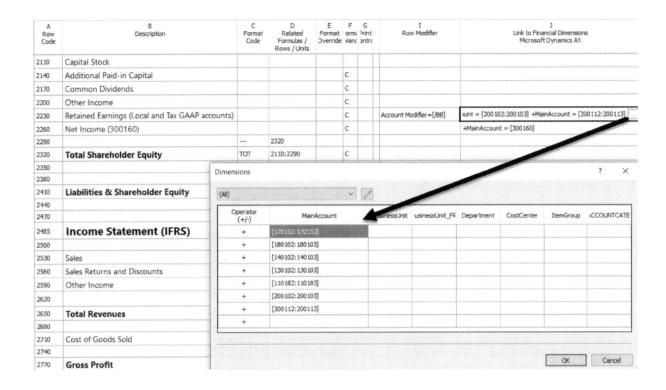

Figure 1.11 *Corrective position financial-report designer—IFRS*

With this corrective financial reporting line, the profit or loss according to the IFRS accounting regulations is presented correctly in the financial statements. Please see figure 1.12 for details.

Note
The corrective financial reporting line shown in figure 1.11 does not only show the main accounts included in this line but also a row modifier that filters for the beginning balance transactions. This row modifier is required to avoid transactions other than the ones included in the year-end closing voucher for the local-GAAP or tax-GAAP affecting the IFRS result.

For the One Month Ending Thursday, January 31, 2019

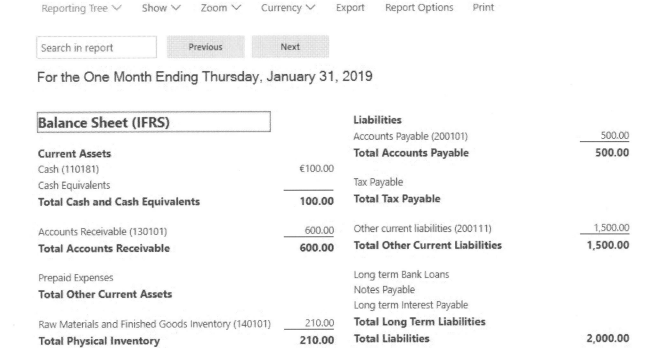

Figure 1.12 *Financial statements using the delta-posting-ledger approach with corrective position—*

IFRS

What has been said for the IFRS result also applies to the other accounting standards used. That is, a correction to the profit or loss shown on the retained-earnings account is required. Different from the correction that is required for IFRS, the profit-or-loss correction that is required for the local-GAAP needs an adjustment for the tax-GAAP-related profit-or-loss difference only.

The underlying reason for this slightly different correction principle is the delta posting approach, which allows calculating the local-GAAP result by adding the profit or loss of the IFRS and local-GAAP accounts.

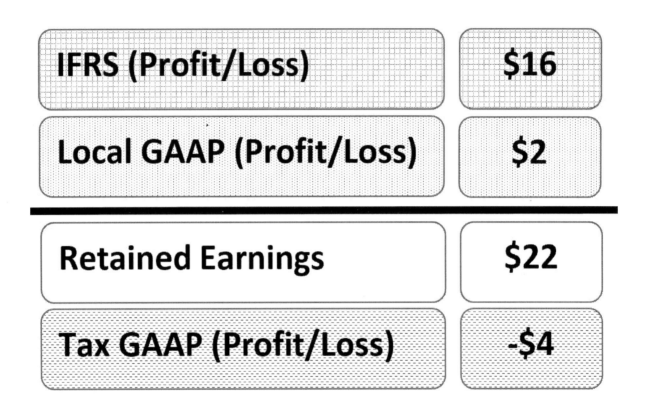

Figure 1.13 *Profit-or-loss correction—local-GAAP*

In line with what has been said above for the profit correction, an adjustment line in the financial report designer is required also for the local-GAAP result. This adjustment line holds all tax-GAAP-specific accounts and filters only those tax-GAAP transactions that are included in the year-end closing voucher. Please see figure 1.14 for details.

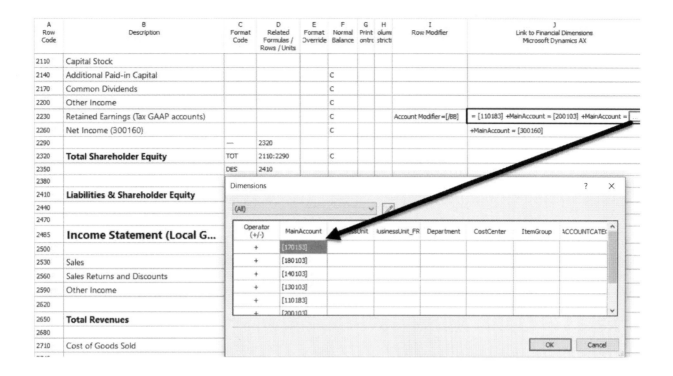

Figure 1.14 *Corrective position financial-report designer—local-GAAP*

The resulting financial statement for the local-GAAP can be identified in figure 1.15.

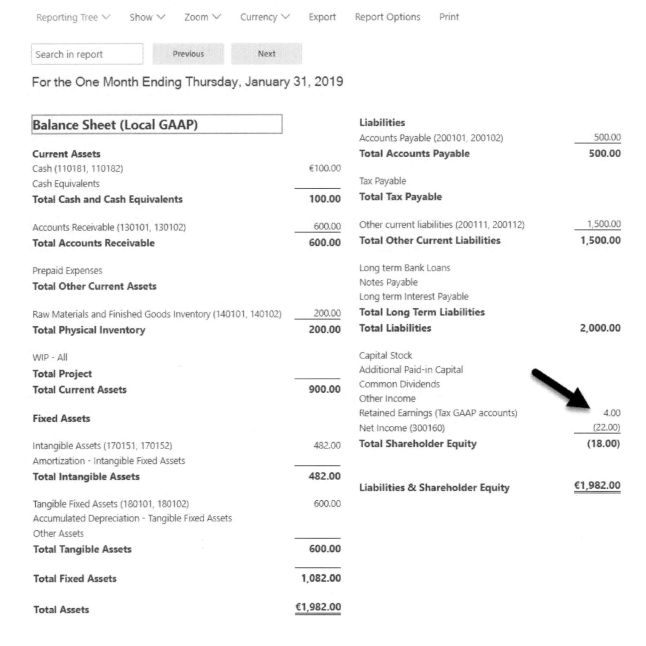

For the One Month Ending Thursday, January 31, 2019

Balance Sheet (Local GAAP)

Current Assets	
Cash (110181, 110182)	€100.00
Cash Equivalents	
Total Cash and Cash Equivalents	**100.00**
Accounts Receivable (130101, 130102)	600.00
Total Accounts Receivable	**600.00**
Prepaid Expenses	
Total Other Current Assets	
Raw Materials and Finished Goods Inventory (140101, 140102)	200.00
Total Physical Inventory	**200.00**
WIP - All	
Total Project	
Total Current Assets	**900.00**
Fixed Assets	
Intangible Assets (170151, 170152)	482.00
Amortization - Intangible Fixed Assets	
Total Intangible Assets	**482.00**
Tangible Fixed Assets (180101, 180102)	600.00
Accumulated Depreciation - Tangible Fixed Assets	
Other Assets	
Total Tangible Assets	**600.00**
Total Fixed Assets	**1,082.00**
Total Assets	**€1,982.00**

Liabilities	
Accounts Payable (200101, 200102)	500.00
Total Accounts Payable	**500.00**
Tax Payable	
Total Tax Payable	
Other current liabilities (200111, 200112)	1,500.00
Total Other Current Liabilities	**1,500.00**
Long term Bank Loans	
Notes Payable	
Long term Interest Payable	
Total Long Term Liabilities	
Total Liabilities	**2,000.00**
Capital Stock	
Additional Paid-in Capital	
Common Dividends	
Other Income	
Retained Earnings (Tax GAAP accounts)	4.00
Net Income (300160)	(22.00)
Total Shareholder Equity	**(18.00)**
Liabilities & Shareholder Equity	**€1,982.00**

Figure 1.15 *Financial statements using the delta-posting-ledger approach with corrective position—*

local-GAAP

Finally, a profit correction is also required for the tax-GAAP result. This profit correction follows the same principles that have been outlined above. For that reason, reference is made to what has been mentioned previously.

Figure 1.16 *Corrective position financial-report designer—tax-GAAP*

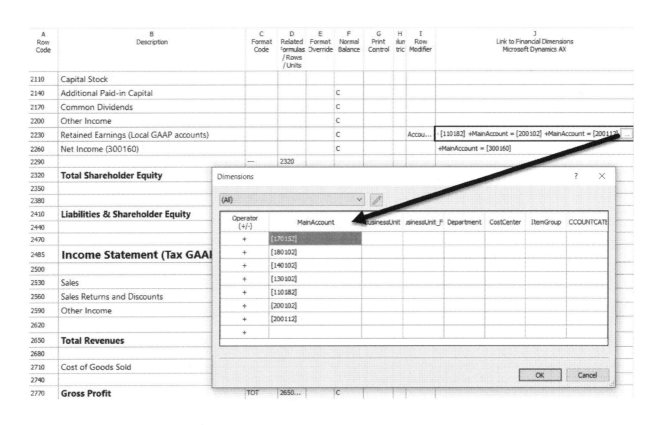

Figure 1.17 *Corrective position financial-report designer—tax-GAAP*

With this corrective financial reporting line in place, the profit or loss according to the tax-GAAP accounting regulation can be identified in figure 1.18.

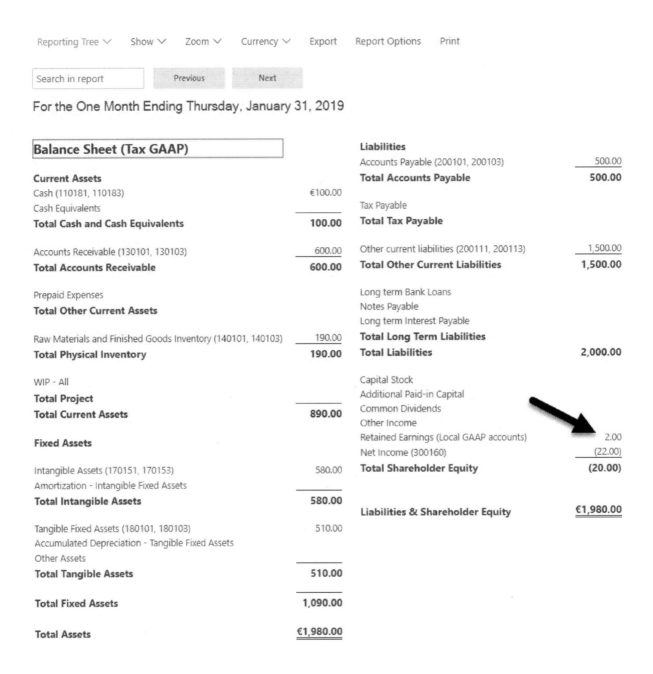

Figure 1.18 *Financial statements using the delta-posting-ledger approach with corrective position—*

tax-GAAP

1.2.2.   Posting-Layer Approach

After investigating the delta-posting-ledger approach, let us now have a look at the delta-posting-layer approach. To illustrate the difference between both approaches in a straightforward manner, a new company account has been created in which the following transactions for the acquisition of the new company were posted.

Date	Account DR	Account Name DR	Posting Layer	Amount DR	Account CR	Account Name CR	Posting Layer	Amount CR
Aug-18	170150	Goodwill	Current	$ 400	200100	Accounts Payable	Current	$ -500
Aug-18	180100	Fixed Assets	Current	$ 690	200110	Other Payables	Current	$ -1,500
Aug-18	140100	Inventory	Current	$ 210				
Aug-18	130100	Accounts Receivable	Current	$ 600				
Aug-18	110180	Cash	Current	$ 100				

Date	Account DR	Account Name DR	Posting Layer	Amount DR	Account CR	Account Name CR	Posting Layer	Amount CR
Sep-18	170150	Goodwill	Operations	$ 100	200100	Accounts Payable	Operations	$ -
Sep-18	180100	Fixed Assets	Operations	$ -90	200110	Other Payables	Operations	$ -
Sep-18	140100	Inventory	Operations	$ -10				
Sep-18	130100	Accounts Receivable	Operations	$ -				
Sep-18	110180	Cash	Operations	$ -				

Date	Account DR	Account Name DR	Posting Layer	Amount DR	Account CR	Account Name CR	Posting Layer	Amount CR
Oct-18	170150	Goodwill	Tax	$ 200	200100	Accounts Payable	Tax	$ -
Oct-18	180100	Fixed Assets	Tax	$ -180	200110	Other Payables	Tax	$ -
Oct-18	140100	Inventory	Tax	$ -20				
Oct-18	130100	Accounts Receivable	Tax	$ -				
Oct-18	110180	Cash	Tax	$ -				

Figure 1.19 *Delta-posting-layer approach for the acquisition of the new company with goodwill*

A comparison of the transactions shown in figure 1.19 with the ones in figure 1.3 shows that all transactions are now recorded on the same ledger account. As an example, the goodwill for the IFRS, local-GAAP, and tax-GAAP is posted on ledger account 170150.

A second major difference from the ledger-posting approach shown in figure 1.3 is that the transactions for the different accounting standards are separated by referring to a posting-layer. That is, the IFRS-related transactions are recorded with the current posting-layer, the local-GAAP-related transactions are recorded with the operations posting-layer, and the tax-GAAP-related transactions are recorded with the tax posting-layer.

Note Recording transactions on different posting-layers cannot be realized in a single journal but requires the set up of separate so-called journal names that refer to the different posting-layers. Figure 1.20 exemplifies this setup.

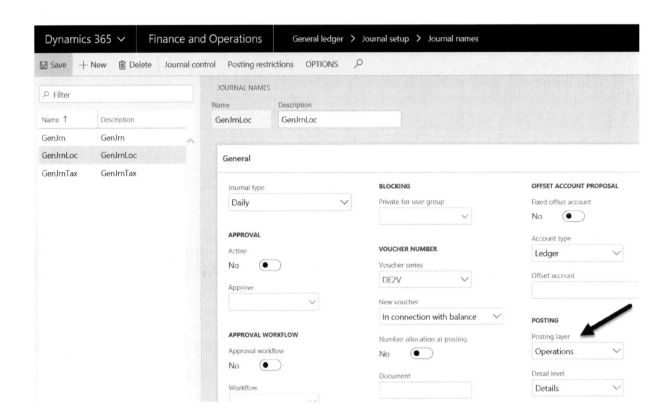

Figure 1.20 *Journal-name setup for postings on different posting-layers*

A third major difference between the ledger and the posting-layer approach relates to the setup of the financial statements in the financial-report designer. That is, when applying the posting-layer approach, one has to differentiate between the various accounting standards by making use of a row-modifier attribute that establishes a link to the aforementioned posting-layers. Figure 1.21 exemplifies the necessary setup for the tax-GAAP balance sheet report, where the amounts of the current and tax posting-layer are summarized.

A Row Code	B Description	C Format Code	D Related Formulas / Rows / Units	E Format Override	F orma lanc	G Print ontro	I Row Modifier	J Link to Financial Dimensions Microsoft Dynamics AX
50	**Balance Sheet (Tax GAAP)**							
75								
100	**Current Assets**							
130	Cash (110180)						e=[Current:Current], Buchungsebene=[Tax:Tax] ...	+MainAccount = [110...
160	Cash Equivalents							
190								
220	**Total Cash and Cash Equivalents**							
250								
430	Accounts Receivable (130100)						=[Current:Current], Bu...	+MainAccount = [130...
460								
490	**Total Accounts Receivable**							
520								
550	Prepaid Expenses							
580								
610	**Total Other Current Assets**							

Figure 1.21 *Tax-GAAP financial-report setup—delta-posting-layer-approach*

Incorporating those minor financial-report design changes ensures that the financial reports for the different accounting standards show the same results that have been reported when applying the delta-posting-ledger approach. For details, please compare the financial results presented in figure 1.22 to figure 1.24 with the data reported in figure 1.4 to figure 1.6.

For the Ten Months Ending Wednesday, October 31, 2018

Balance Sheet (IFRS)		Liabilities	
		Accounts Payable (200100)	500.00
Current Assets		**Total Accounts Payable**	**500.00**
Cash (110180)	€100.00		
Cash Equivalents		Tax Payable	
Total Cash and Cash Equivalents	**100.00**	**Total Tax Payable**	
Accounts Receivable (130100)	600.00	Other current liabilities (200110)	1,500.00
Total Accounts Receivable	**600.00**	**Total Other Current Liabilities**	**1,500.00**
Prepaid Expenses		Long term Bank Loans	
Total Other Current Assets		Notes Payable	
		Long term Interest Payable	
Raw Materials and Finished Goods Inventory (140100)	210.00	**Total Long Term Liabilities**	
Total Physical Inventory	**210.00**	**Total Liabilities**	**2,000.00**
WIP - All		Capital Stock	
Total Project		Additional Paid-in Capital	
Total Current Assets	**910.00**	Common Dividends	
		Other Income	
Fixed Assets		Retained Earnings	
		Net Income (300160)	
Intangible Assets (170150)	400.00	**Total Shareholder Equity**	
Amortization - Intangible Fixed Assets			
Total Intangible Assets	**400.00**	**Liabilities & Shareholder Equity**	**€2,000.00**
Tangible Fixed Assets (180100)	690.00		
Accumulated Depreciation - Tangible Fixed Assets			
Other Assets			
Total Tangible Assets	**690.00**		
Total Fixed Assets	**1,090.00**		
Total Assets	**€2,000.00**		

Figure 1.22 *Financial statements using the delta-posting-layer approach—IFRS*

For the Ten Months Ending Wednesday, October 31, 2018

Balance Sheet (Local GAAP)			Liabilities		
			Accounts Payable (200100)		500.00
Current Assets			**Total Accounts Payable**		**500.00**
Cash (110180)	€100.00				
Cash Equivalents			Tax Payable		
Total Cash and Cash Equivalents		**100.00**	**Total Tax Payable**		
Accounts Receivable (130100)	600.00		Other current liabilities (200110)		1,500.00
Total Accounts Receivable		**600.00**	**Total Other Current Liabilities**		**1,500.00**
Prepaid Expenses			Long term Bank Loans		
Total Other Current Assets			Notes Payable		
			Long term Interest Payable		
Raw Materials and Finished Goods Inventory (140100)	200.00		**Total Long Term Liabilities**		
Total Physical Inventory		**200.00**	**Total Liabilities**		**2,000.00**
WIP - All			Capital Stock		
Total Project			Additional Paid-in Capital		
Total Current Assets		**900.00**	Common Dividends		
			Other Income		
Fixed Assets			Retained Earnings		
			Net Income (300160)		
Intangible Assets (170150)	500.00		**Total Shareholder Equity**		
Amortization - Intangible Fixed Assets					
Total Intangible Assets		**500.00**			
			Liabilities & Shareholder Equity		**€2,000.00**
Tangible Fixed Assets (180100)	600.00				
Accumulated Depreciation - Tangible Fixed Assets					
Other Assets					
Total Tangible Assets		**600.00**			
Total Fixed Assets		**1,100.00**			
Total Assets		**€2,000.00**			

Figure 1.23 *Financial statements using the delta-posting-layer approach—local-GAAP*

For the Ten Months Ending Wednesday, October 31, 2018

Balance Sheet (Tax GAAP)

Current Assets		**Liabilities**	
Cash (110180)	€100.00	Accounts Payable (200100)	500.00
Cash Equivalents		**Total Accounts Payable**	**500.00**
Total Cash and Cash Equivalents	**100.00**		
		Tax Payable	
Accounts Receivable (130100)	600.00	**Total Tax Payable**	
Total Accounts Receivable	**600.00**		
		Other current liabilities (200110)	1,500.00
Prepaid Expenses		**Total Other Current Liabilities**	**1,500.00**
Total Other Current Assets			
		Long term Bank Loans	
Raw Materials and Finished Goods Inventory (140100)	190.00	Notes Payable	
Total Physical Inventory	**190.00**	Long term Interest Payable	
		Total Long Term Liabilities	
WIP - All		**Total Liabilities**	**2,000.00**
Total Project			
Total Current Assets	**890.00**	Capital Stock	
		Additional Paid-in Capital	
Fixed Assets		Common Dividends	
		Other Income	
Intangible Assets (170150)	600.00	Retained Earnings	
Amortization - Intangible Fixed Assets		Net Income (300160)	
Total Intangible Assets	**600.00**	**Total Shareholder Equity**	
Tangible Fixed Assets (180100)	510.00	**Liabilities & Shareholder Equity**	**€2,000.00**
Accumulated Depreciation - Tangible Fixed Assets			
Other Assets			
Total Tangible Assets	**510.00**		
Total Fixed Assets	**1,110.00**		
Total Assets	**€2,000.00**		

Figure 1.24 *Financial statements using the delta-posting-layer approach—tax-GAAP*

Another aspect that needs to be taken into account when it comes to parallel accounting according to the delta-posting-layer approach is the treatment of the profit or loss that is recorded with the year-end closing process. To demonstrate this treatment, the goodwill-impairment transactions that have been recorded for the delta-posting-ledger approach (see figure 1.7) have also been recorded for the delta-posting-layer approach. Figure 1.25 illustrates those transactions.

Date	Account DR	Account Name DR	Posting Layer	Amount DR	Account CR	Account Name CR	Posting Layer	Amount CR
Nov-18	618700	Goodwill impairment	Current	$ 16	170150	Goodwill	Current	$ -16

Date	Account DR	Account Name DR	Posting Layer	Amount DR	Account CR	Account Name CR	Posting Layer	Amount CR
Nov-18	618700	Goodwill impairment	Operations	$ 2	170150	Goodwill	Operations	$ -2

Date	Account DR	Account Name DR	Posting Layer	Amount DR	Account CR	Account Name CR	Posting Layer	Amount CR
Nov-18	618700	Goodwill impairment	Tax	$ 4	170150	Goodwill	Tax	$ -4

Figure 1.25 *Delta-posting-layer approach—depreciation of goodwill*

With those additional expense-related transactions recorded, the following year-end voucher results.

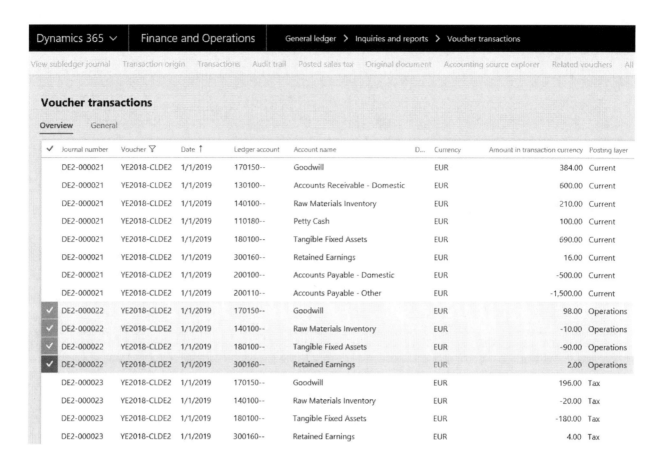

Figure 1.26 *Year-end closing voucher—delta-posting-layer approach*

Comparing the year-end closing vouchers in figure 1.26 and figure 1.8 shows that the delta-posting-layer approach separates the profit or loss for the different accounting standards by referring to the posting-layer used. As a result, no corrective adjustment position is required in the financial reports. Instead, only a reference to the difference posting-layers is required. Figure 1.27 demonstrates this for the tax-GAAP balance sheet report.

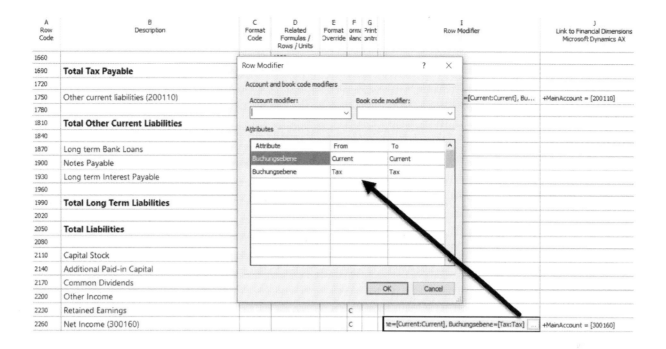

A Row Code	B Description	C Format Code	D Related Formulas / Rows / Units	E Format Override	F orm> ilanc	G Print ontre	I Row Modifier	J Link to Financial Dimensions Microsoft Dynamics AX
1660								
1690	**Total Tax Payable**							
1720								
1750	Other current liabilities (200110)						=[Current:Current], Bu...	+MainAccount = [200110]
1780								
1810	**Total Other Current Liabilities**							
1840								
1870	Long term Bank Loans							
1900	Notes Payable							
1930	Long term Interest Payable							
1960								
1990	**Total Long Term Liabilities**							
2020								
2050	**Total Liabilities**							
2080								
2110	Capital Stock							
2140	Additional Paid-in Capital							
2170	Common Dividends							
2200	Other Income							
2230	Retained Earnings				C			
2260	Net Income (300160)				C		1e=[Current:Current], Buchungsebene=[Tax:Tax]	+MainAccount = [300160]

Figure 1.27 *Tax-GAAP financial-report setup for the year-end result—delta-posting-layer approach*

Making a link between the retained-earnings account 300160 and the posting-layers used ensures a correct representation of the financial results for the different accounting standards. This can be verified by comparing the financial reports presented in the next three figures with the ones shown in figure 1.12, figure 1.15, and figure 1.18.

For the One Month Ending Thursday, January 31, 2019

Balance Sheet (IFRS)		Liabilities	
		Accounts Payable (200100)	500.00
Current Assets		**Total Accounts Payable**	**500.00**
Cash (110180)	€100.00		
Cash Equivalents		Tax Payable	
Total Cash and Cash Equivalents	**100.00**	**Total Tax Payable**	
Accounts Receivable (130100)	600.00	Other current liabilities (200110)	1,500.00
Total Accounts Receivable	**600.00**	**Total Other Current Liabilities**	**1,500.00**
Prepaid Expenses		Long term Bank Loans	
Total Other Current Assets		Notes Payable	
		Long term Interest Payable	
Raw Materials and Finished Goods Inventory (140100)	210.00	**Total Long Term Liabilities**	
Total Physical Inventory	**210.00**	**Total Liabilities**	**2,000.00**
WIP - All		Capital Stock	
Total Project		Additional Paid-in Capital	
Total Current Assets	**910.00**	Common Dividends	
		Other Income	
Fixed Assets		Retained Earnings	
		Net Income (300160)	(16.00)
Intangible Assets (170150)	384.00	**Total Shareholder Equity**	**(16.00)**
Amortization - Intangible Fixed Assets			
Total Intangible Assets	**384.00**		
		Liabilities & Shareholder Equity	**€1,984.00**
Tangible Fixed Assets (180100)	690.00		
Accumulated Depreciation - Tangible Fixed Assets			
Other Assets			
Total Tangible Assets	**690.00**		
Total Fixed Assets	**1,074.00**		
Total Assets	**€1,984.00**		

Figure 1.28 *Financial statements using the delta-posting-layer approach—IFRS*

For the One Month Ending Thursday, January 31, 2019

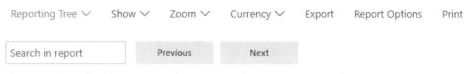

Balance Sheet (Local GAAP)

Current Assets	
Cash (110180)	€100.00
Cash Equivalents	
Total Cash and Cash Equivalents	**100.00**
Accounts Receivable (130100)	600.00
Total Accounts Receivable	**600.00**
Prepaid Expenses	
Total Other Current Assets	
Raw Materials and Finished Goods Inventory (140100)	200.00
Total Physical Inventory	**200.00**
WIP - All	
Total Project	
Total Current Assets	**900.00**
Fixed Assets	
Intangible Assets (170150)	482.00
Amortization - Intangible Fixed Assets	
Total Intangible Assets	**482.00**
Tangible Fixed Assets (180100)	600.00
Accumulated Depreciation - Tangible Fixed Assets	
Other Assets	
Total Tangible Assets	**600.00**
Total Fixed Assets	**1,082.00**
Total Assets	**€1,982.00**

Liabilities	
Accounts Payable (200100)	500.00
Total Accounts Payable	**500.00**
Tax Payable	
Total Tax Payable	
Other current liabilities (200110)	1,500.00
Total Other Current Liabilities	**1,500.00**
Long term Bank Loans	
Notes Payable	
Long term Interest Payable	
Total Long Term Liabilities	
Total Liabilities	**2,000.00**
Capital Stock	
Additional Paid-in Capital	
Common Dividends	
Other Income	
Retained Earnings	
Net Income (300160)	(18.00)
Total Shareholder Equity	**(18.00)**
Liabilities & Shareholder Equity	**€1,982.00**

Figure 1.29 *Financial statements using the delta-posting-layer approach—local-GAAP*

For the One Month Ending Thursday, January 31, 2019

Balance Sheet (Tax GAAP)

Current Assets			**Liabilities**	
Cash (110180)	€100.00		Accounts Payable (200100)	500.00
Cash Equivalents			**Total Accounts Payable**	**500.00**
Total Cash and Cash Equivalents	**100.00**			
			Tax Payable	
			Total Tax Payable	
Accounts Receivable (130100)	600.00			
Total Accounts Receivable	**600.00**		Other current liabilities (200110)	1,500.00
			Total Other Current Liabilities	**1,500.00**
Prepaid Expenses				
Total Other Current Assets			Long term Bank Loans	
			Notes Payable	
Raw Materials and Finished Goods Inventory (140100)	190.00		Long term Interest Payable	
Total Physical Inventory	**190.00**		**Total Long Term Liabilities**	
			Total Liabilities	**2,000.00**
WIP - All				
Total Project			Capital Stock	
Total Current Assets	**890.00**		Additional Paid-in Capital	
			Common Dividends	
Fixed Assets			Other Income	
			Retained Earnings	
Intangible Assets (170150)	580.00		Net Income (300160)	(20.00)
Amortization - Intangible Fixed Assets			**Total Shareholder Equity**	**(20.00)**
Total Intangible Assets	**580.00**			
			Liabilities & Shareholder Equity	**€1,980.00**
Tangible Fixed Assets (180100)	510.00			
Accumulated Depreciation - Tangible Fixed Assets				
Other Assets				
Total Tangible Assets	**510.00**			
Total Fixed Assets	**1,090.00**			
Total Assets	**€1,980.00**			

Figure 1.30 *Financial statements using the delta-posting-layer approach—tax-GAAP*

1.2.2.1. General Considerations

When it comes to fixed asset accounting, MSDyn365FO generally uses a full posting approach. That is, all fixed asset transactions that are made for the different accounting regulations are either made on separate ledger accounts or on separate posting-layers with the full amount posted on each account or posting-layer.

Companies that generally apply a delta posting approach—either by making use of separate ledger accounts or by making use of posting-layers as demonstrated in chapter 1.2.1. and 1.2.2.—face the issue that the full and delta posting approaches are mixed.

In other words, those companies apply either accounting approaches *a* and *c* or accounting approaches *b* and *d* (see figure 1.1). A consequence of this mixed accounting approach is that the identification and separation of the annual results becomes complex. The next example aims to illustrate the complexity involved in the identification and separation of the annual results for the different accounting standards.

Date	Description	Account DR	Account Name DR	Posting Layer	Amount DR	Account CR	Account Name CR	Posting Layer	Amount CR
				Postings 2018					
Jan 18	Investor puts money in	110130	Bank	Current	$ 5,000,000	300110	Capital Stock	Current	$ -5,000,000
Feb 18	Sales of services	130100	Accounts Receivable	Current	$ 800,000	401300	Other revenues	Current	$ -800,000
Apr 18	Purchase first fixed asset	180101	Fixed Assets (IFRS)	Current	$ 250,000	200101	Accounts Payable	Current	$ -250,000
		180102	Fixed Assets (Local)	Current	$ 250,000	200102	Accounts Payable	Current	$ -250,000
		180103	Fixed Assets (Tax)	Current	$ 250,000	200103	Accounts Payable	Current	$ -250,000
Jun 18	Bad debt reserve	618171	Bad debt expense (IFRS)	Current	$ 8,000	218171	Provision (IFRS)	Current	$ -8,000
		618172	Bad debt expense (Local)	Current	$ -500	218172	Provision (Local)	Current	$ 500
		618173	Bad debt expense (Tax)	Current	$ -3,000	218173	Provision (Tax)	Current	$ 3,000
Dez 18	Accum. Depreciation first fixed asset 2018	607251	Depr. expense (IFRS)	Current	$ 25,000	180251	Accum. Depr. (IFRS)	Current	$ -25,000
		607252	Depr. expense (Local)	Current	$ 12,500	180252	Accum. Depr. (Local)	Current	$ -12,500
		607253	Depr. expense (Tax)	Current	$ 8,500	180253	Accum. Depr. (Tax)	Current	$ -8,500

Figure 1.31 *Sample data–ledger approach*

Figure 1.31 shows sample transactions for the year 2018 that are recorded in MSDyn365FO by applying the ledger approach. That is, differences in accounting standards are recorded on separate ledger accounts.

For the non fixed asset related transactions, such as the bad-debt expense posted in June 2018, one can identify the delta posting approach for the three accounting regulations used. As an example, the bad-debt expense according to IFRS is $8,000, whereas the bad debt expense according to local-GAAP is $7,500 ($8,000 recorded on the IFRS-specific bad-debt expense account 618171 minus $500 recorded on the local-GAAP-specific bad-debt expense account 618172).

The fixed asset related postings that are made in April 2018 and December 2018, however, record the full amount for each accounting standard. As an example, the depreciation expense according to IFRS is $25,000 and is recorded on account 607251. The local-GAAP and tax-GAAP depreciation amounts are $12,500 and $8,500 and are recorded on accounts 607252 and 607253 respectively. That is, for the fixed asset related transactions, no accumulation of the posted transactions is necessary.

The complexity that this mixed accounting approach involves can be identified by comparing the profit or loss that results from the sample transactions (see figure 1.32) and the year-end closing voucher that MSDyn365FO generates (see figure 1.33).

	IFRS	Local GAAP	Tax GAAP
Revenue (401300)	$ -800,000	$ -800,000	$ -800,000
Bad debt expense (61817*)	$ 8,000	$ 8,000	$ 8,000
		$ -500	$ -3,000
Depreciation expense (60725*)	$ 25,000	$ 12,500	$ 8,500
Profit/loss 2018	$ -767,000	$ -780,000	$ -786,500

Figure 1.32 *Profit or loss for the different accounting standards*

Note The asterisks in figure 1.32 serve as placeholders for the different ledger accounts and accounting standards. For example, the abbreviation *61817** represent the accounts 618171, 618172, and 618173 used in figure 1.31.

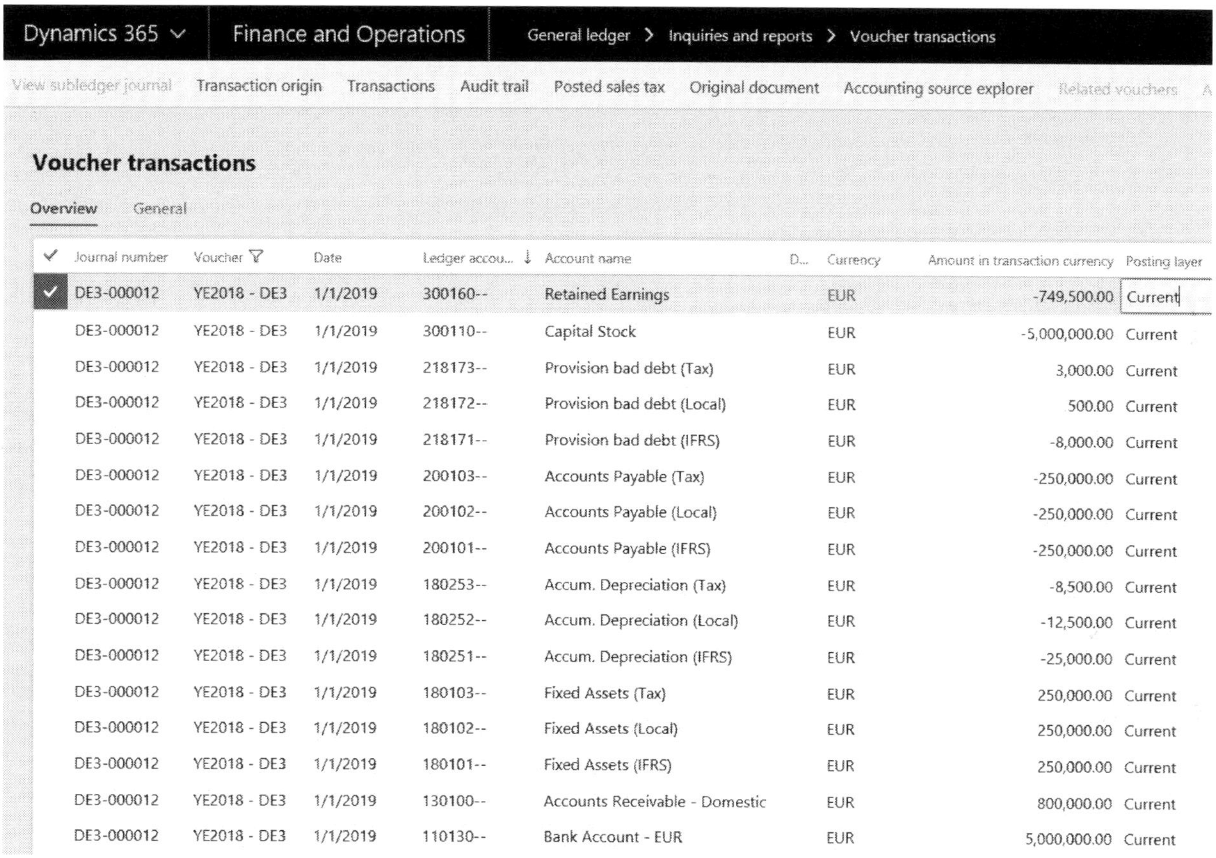

Journal number	Voucher	Date	Ledger accou...	Account name	D...	Currency	Amount in transaction currency	Posting layer
DE3-000012	YE2018 - DE3	1/1/2019	300160--	Retained Earnings		EUR	-749,500.00	Current
DE3-000012	YE2018 - DE3	1/1/2019	300110--	Capital Stock		EUR	-5,000,000.00	Current
DE3-000012	YE2018 - DE3	1/1/2019	218173--	Provision bad debt (Tax)		EUR	3,000.00	Current
DE3-000012	YE2018 - DE3	1/1/2019	218172--	Provision bad debt (Local)		EUR	500.00	Current
DE3-000012	YE2018 - DE3	1/1/2019	218171--	Provision bad debt (IFRS)		EUR	-8,000.00	Current
DE3-000012	YE2018 - DE3	1/1/2019	200103--	Accounts Payable (Tax)		EUR	-250,000.00	Current
DE3-000012	YE2018 - DE3	1/1/2019	200102--	Accounts Payable (Local)		EUR	-250,000.00	Current
DE3-000012	YE2018 - DE3	1/1/2019	200101--	Accounts Payable (IFRS)		EUR	-250,000.00	Current
DE3-000012	YE2018 - DE3	1/1/2019	180253--	Accum. Depreciation (Tax)		EUR	-8,500.00	Current
DE3-000012	YE2018 - DE3	1/1/2019	180252--	Accum. Depreciation (Local)		EUR	-12,500.00	Current
DE3-000012	YE2018 - DE3	1/1/2019	180251--	Accum. Depreciation (IFRS)		EUR	-25,000.00	Current
DE3-000012	YE2018 - DE3	1/1/2019	180103--	Fixed Assets (Tax)		EUR	250,000.00	Current
DE3-000012	YE2018 - DE3	1/1/2019	180102--	Fixed Assets (Local)		EUR	250,000.00	Current
DE3-000012	YE2018 - DE3	1/1/2019	180101--	Fixed Assets (IFRS)		EUR	250,000.00	Current
DE3-000012	YE2018 - DE3	1/1/2019	130100--	Accounts Receivable - Domestic		EUR	800,000.00	Current
DE3-000012	YE2018 - DE3	1/1/2019	110130--	Bank Account - EUR		EUR	5,000,000.00	Current

Figure 1.33 *Year-end closing voucher for 2018—ledger approach*

Figure 1.33 shows the year-end closing voucher for the year 2018, which shows a total profit of $749,500 posted to the retained-earnings account 300160. This amount is different from the profit-or-loss amounts that have been calculated for the three accounting standards in figure 1.32. The underlying reason for this difference is that all amounts that affect a company's profit or loss—irrespective of the accounting standard used—are simply accumulated in the year-end closing voucher. The next equation details this accumulation.

Retained-earnings 2018 ledger approach =

Revenue

+ Bad-debt expense (IFRS)

+ Bad-debt expense difference (local-GAAP)

+ Bad-debt expense difference (tax-GAAP)

$$(2)$$

+ Depreciation expense (IFRS)

+ Depreciation expense (local-GAAP)

+ Depreciation expense (tax-GAAP)

Retained-earnings 2018 ledger approach =

-\$800,000 + \$8,000 - \$500 - \$3,000 + \$25,000 + \$12,500 + \$8,500

$$(3)$$

= -\$749,500

The previous two equations show a double respectively triple-counting effect of the depreciation expense. This double respectively triple-counting effect is illustrated in the next figure.

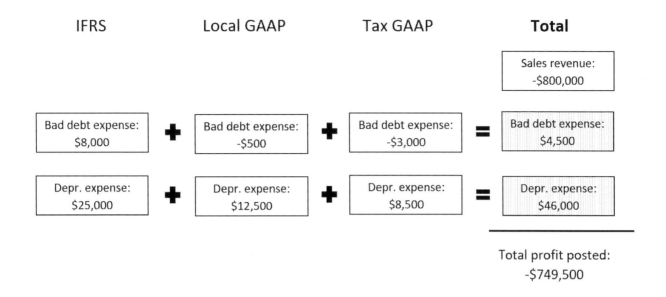

Figure 1.34 *Total profit ledger approach*

Note The profit amount of -$749,500 has a negative sign because of the accounting identity in MSDyn365FO where revenues are recorded as credit transactions with a negative sign. Costs are recorded as debit transactions with a positive sign.

Based on the illustration shown in figure 1.34, one can calculate the profit that can be assigned to the IFRS accounting standard simply by correcting the total profit by the amounts that can be assigned to the local-GAAP and tax-GAAP accounting standards. The next figure illustrates this principle.

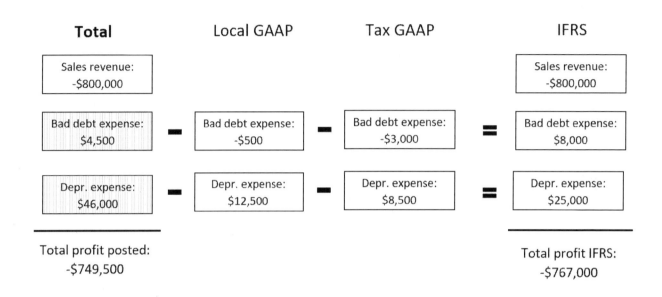

Figure 1.35 *Correction of total-profit-ledger approach—IFRS*

A similar correction calculation can be made to calculate the local-GAAP and tax-GAAP results.

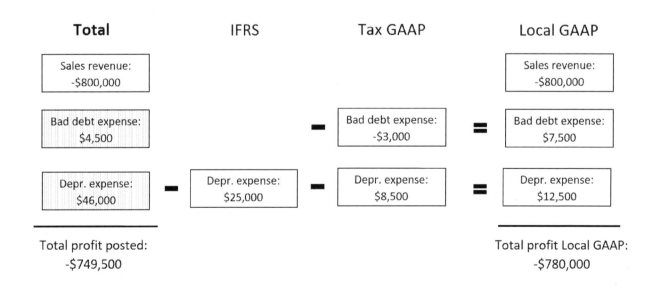

Figure 1.36 *Correction of total-profit-ledger approach—local-GAAP*

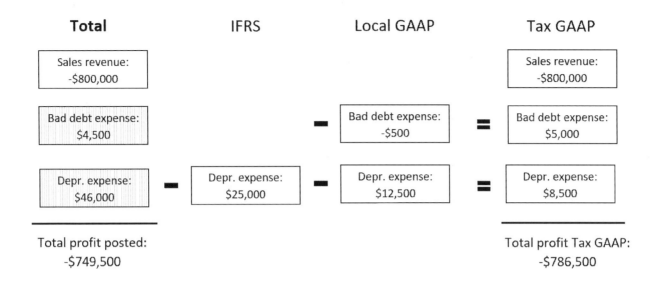

Figure 1.37 *Correction of total-profit-ledger approach—tax-GAAP*

A comparison of the correction calculations for IFRS, local-GAAP, and tax-GAAP in figure 1.35, figure 1.36, and figure 1.37 highlights that the correction calculations required for local-GAAP and tax-GAAP differ from the correction that is required for IFRS. The reason for this difference is the delta posting approach that is applied to the non fixed asset related bad-debt expense transactions only.

After investigating the complexities that the mixture of a delta posting approach and a full posting approach incorporates for companies that use separate ledger accounts for differentiating between accounting standards, let us now have a look at companies that follow the posting-layer approach instead.

To illustrate the difference in both approaches, the sample transactions that were used for demonstrating the complexities of the ledger approach have been adjusted correspondingly (see figure 1.38) and posted in a new company account in MSDyn365FO.

Date	Description	Account DR	Account Name DR	Posting Layer	Amount DR	Account CR	Account Name CR	Posting Layer	Amount CR
				Postings 2018					
Jan 18	Investor puts money in	110130	Bank	Current	$ 5,000,000	300110	Capital Stock	Current	$ -5,000,000
Feb 18	Sales of services	130100	Accounts Receivable	Current	$ 800,000	401300	Other revenues	Current	$ -800,000
Apr 18	Purchase fixed asset	180100	Fixed Assets	Current	$ 250,000	200100	Accounts Payable	Current	$ -250,000
		180100	Fixed Assets	Operations	$ 250,000	200100	Accounts Payable	Operations	$ -250,000
		180100	Fixed Assets	Tax	$ 250,000	200100	Accounts Payable	Tax	$ -250,000
Jun 18	Bad debt reserve	618170	Bad debt expense	Current	$ 8,000	218170	Provision	Current	$ -8,000
		618170	Bad debt expense	Operations	$ -500	218170	Provision	Operations	$ 500
		618170	Bad debt expense	Tax	$ -3,000	218170	Provision	Tax	$ 3,000
Dez 18	Accum. Depreciation first fixed asset 2018	607250	Depr. expense	Current	$ 25,000	180250	Accum. Depreciation	Current	$ -25,000
		607250	Depr. expense	Operations	$ 12,500	180250	Accum. Depreciation	Operations	$ -12,500
		607250	Depr. expense	Tax	$ 8,500	180250	Accum. Depreciation	Tax	$ -8,500

Figure 1.38 *Sample data-posting-layer approach*

The difference in the sample transactions illustrated in figure 1.31 and figure 1.38 relate to the different main accounts and posting-layers used.

Running the year-end closing process with those transactions recorded results in the following voucher.

View subledger journal   Transaction origin   Transactions   Audit trail   Posted sales tax   Original document   Accounting source explorer   Related vouchers   All

Voucher transactions

Overview   General

✓	Journal number	Voucher ▽	Date	Ledger accou... ↓	Account name	D...	Currency	Amount in transaction currency	Posting layer
✓	DE4-000023	YE2018-DE4	1/1/2019	300160--	Retained Earnings		EUR	5,500.00	Tax
✓	DE4-000022	YE2018-DE4	1/1/2019	300160--	Retained Earnings		EUR	12,000.00	Operations
✓	DE4-000021	YE2018-DE4	1/1/2019	300160--	Retained Earnings		EUR	-767,000.00	Current
	DE4-000021	YE2018-DE4	1/1/2019	300110--	Capital Stock		EUR	-5,000,000.00	Current
	DE4-000021	YE2018-DE4	1/1/2019	218170--	Provision bad debt		EUR	-8,000.00	Current
	DE4-000023	YE2018-DE4	1/1/2019	218170--	Provision bad debt		EUR	3,000.00	Tax
	DE4-000022	YE2018-DE4	1/1/2019	218170--	Provision bad debt		EUR	500.00	Operations
	DE4-000023	YE2018-DE4	1/1/2019	200100--	Accounts Payable - Domestic		EUR	-250,000.00	Tax
	DE4-000021	YE2018-DE4	1/1/2019	200100--	Accounts Payable - Domestic		EUR	-250,000.00	Current
	DE4-000022	YE2018-DE4	1/1/2019	200100--	Accounts Payable - Domestic		EUR	-250,000.00	Operations
	DE4-000021	YE2018-DE4	1/1/2019	180250--	Accum. Depreciation		EUR	-25,000.00	Current
	DE4-000022	YE2018-DE4	1/1/2019	180250--	Accum. Depreciation		EUR	-12,500.00	Operations
	DE4-000023	YE2018-DE4	1/1/2019	180250--	Accum. Depreciation		EUR	-8,500.00	Tax
	DE4-000023	YE2018-DE4	1/1/2019	180100--	Tangible Fixed Assets		EUR	250,000.00	Tax
	DE4-000022	YE2018-DE4	1/1/2019	180100--	Tangible Fixed Assets		EUR	250,000.00	Operations
	DE4-000021	YE2018-DE4	1/1/2019	180100--	Tangible Fixed Assets		EUR	250,000.00	Current
	DE4-000021	YE2018-DE4	1/1/2019	130100--	Accounts Receivable - Domestic		EUR	800,000.00	Current
	DE4-000021	YE2018-DE4	1/1/2019	110130--	Bank Account - EUR		EUR	5,000,000.00	Current

Figure 1.39 *Year-end closing voucher for 2018—posting-layer approach*

An investigation of the year-end closing voucher shown in figure 1.39 highlights that a profit of -$767,000 is posted on the retained-earnings account 300160 with the current posting-layer. This profit represents the profit for the IFRS accounting standard and is in line with the profit shown in figure 1.32.

The profit or loss for the other accounting standards, however, cannot easily be inferred from the IFRS result by accumulating the amounts posted on the retained-earnings account with the other posting-layers.

As an example, the local-GAAP profit of -$780,000 (see figure 1.32 above) is different from the sum of the retained-earnings amounts that have been posted on the current (-$767,000) and operations ($12,000) posting-layers. The reason for this outcome is a double-counting effect related to the depreciation expense recorded on the current posting-layer. The following two figures highlight this double-counting effect and illustrate the necessary corrections for the local-GAAP and tax-GAAP accounting regulations.

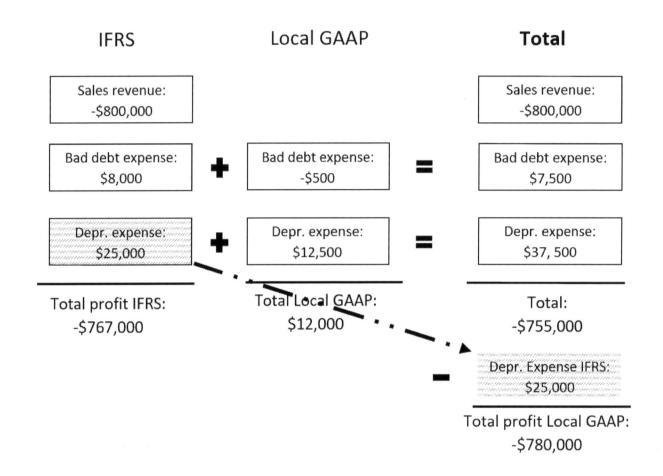

Figure 1.40 *Correction of total-profit-posting-layer approach—local-GAAP*

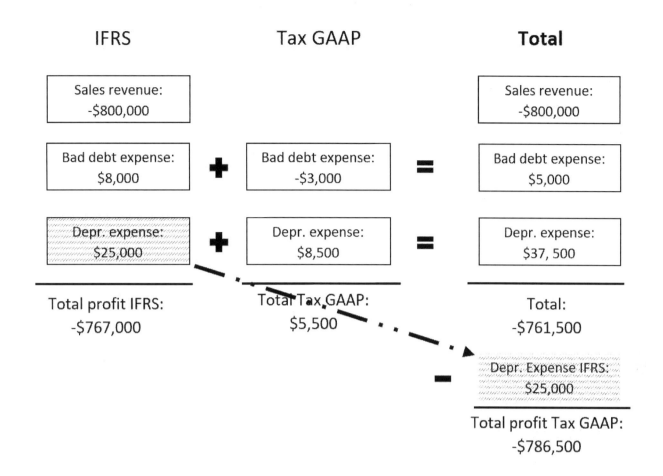

Figure 1.41 *Correction of total-profit-posting-layer approach—tax-GAAP*

As one can identify from figure 1.40 and figure 1.41, a simple correction of the accumulated profit from the different posting-layers by the IFRS depreciation-expense amount ensures a correct representation of the company's profit according to local-GAAP and tax-GAAP.

1.2.2.2.   Solution Approach: Fixed Asset Accounting with Delta-Posting-Ledger Accounting

After analyzing the corrections that need to be made to present the financial results for the different accounting standards used correctly, a question arises: How can those corrections be incorporated in MSDyn365FO?

When it comes to the delta-posting-ledger approach, this incorporation is straightforward and does not differ from the approach that has been applied in chapter 1.2.1. for the delta ledger postings without fixed assets. That is, for the IFRS-related financial reports, a correction position that takes care of the local-GAAP- and tax-GAAP-related valuation accounts needs to be included in the financial-report designer. Please see figure 1.35 for the correction approach and figure 1.42 for the implementation in the financial-report designer.

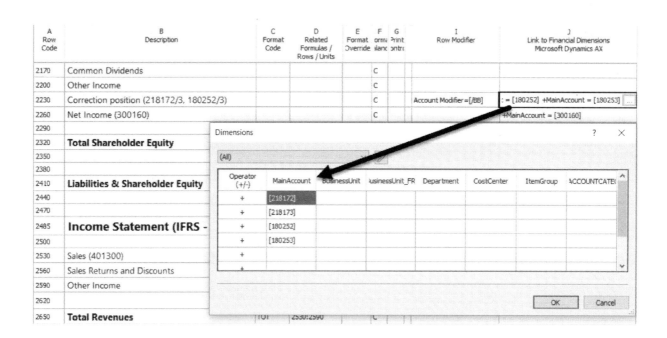

Figure 1.42 *Correction position in the financial-report designer—IFRS*

Similar corrective positions are required for the local-GAAP and tax-GAAP financial reports, as illustrated in the next two figures.

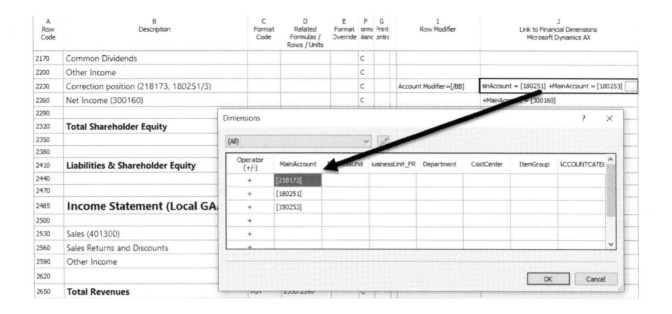

Figure 1.43 *Correction position in the financial-report designer—local-GAAP*

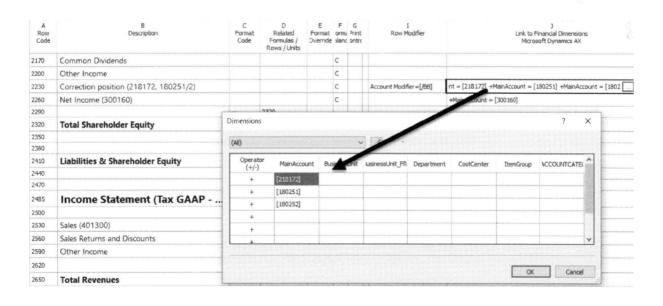

Figure 1.44 *Correction position in the financial-report designer—tax-GAAP*

With those corrective positions in place, the financial statements for the three accounting standards show the expected profit or loss. The following financial statements for the IFRS, local-GAAP, and tax-GAAP accounting standards prove this.

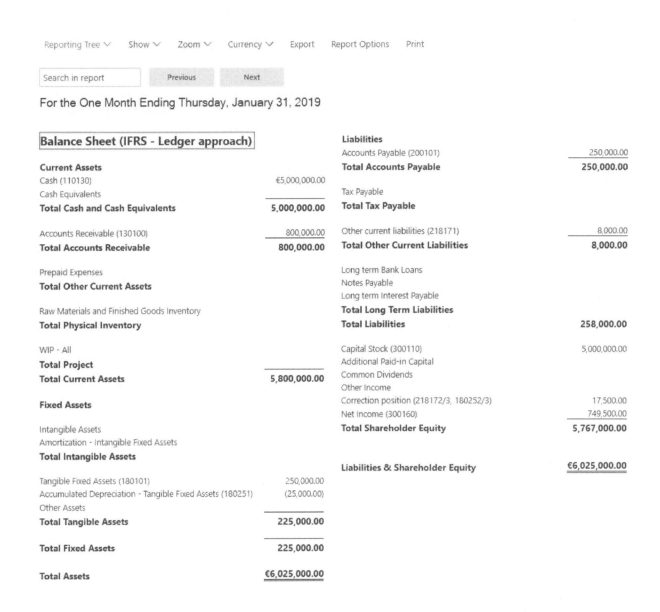

Figure 1.45 *Financial statements using the delta-posting-ledger approach with corrective position—*

IFRS

For the One Month Ending Thursday, January 31, 2019

Balance Sheet (Local GAAP - Ledger Approach)		Liabilities	
		Accounts Payable (200102)	250,000.00
Current Assets		**Total Accounts Payable**	**250,000.00**
Cash (110130)	€5,000,000.00		
Cash Equivalents		Tax Payable	
Total Cash and Cash Equivalents	**5,000,000.00**	**Total Tax Payable**	
Accounts Receivable (130100)	800,000.00	Other current liabilities (218171, 218172)	7,500.00
Total Accounts Receivable	**800,000.00**	**Total Other Current Liabilities**	**7,500.00**
Prepaid Expenses		Long term Bank Loans	
Total Other Current Assets		Notes Payable	
		Long term Interest Payable	
Raw Materials and Finished Goods Inventory		**Total Long Term Liabilities**	
Total Physical Inventory		**Total Liabilities**	**257,500.00**
WIP - All		Capital Stock (300110)	5,000,000.00
Total Project		Additional Paid-in Capital	
Total Current Assets	**5,800,000.00**	Common Dividends	
		Other Income	
Fixed Assets		Correction position (218173, 180251/3)	30,500.00
		Net Income (300160)	749,500.00
Intangible Assets		**Total Shareholder Equity**	**5,780,000.00**
Amortization - Intangible Fixed Assets			
Total Intangible Assets			
		Liabilities & Shareholder Equity	**€6,037,500.00**
Tangible Fixed Assets (180102)	250,000.00		
Accumulated Depreciation - Tangible Fixed Assets (180252)	(12,500.00)		
Other Assets			
Total Tangible Assets	**237,500.00**		
Total Fixed Assets	**237,500.00**		
Total Assets	**€6,037,500.00**		

Figure 1.46 *Financial statements using the delta-posting-ledger approach with corrective position—*

local-GAAP

For the One Month Ending Thursday, January 31, 2019

Balance Sheet (Tax GAAP - Ledger Approach)

		Liabilities	
		Accounts Payable (200103)	250,000.00
Current Assets		**Total Accounts Payable**	**250,000.00**
Cash (110130)	€5,000,000.00		
Cash Equivalents		Tax Payable	
Total Cash and Cash Equivalents	**5,000,000.00**	**Total Tax Payable**	
Accounts Receivable (130100)	800,000.00	Other current liabilities (218171, 218173)	5,000.00
Total Accounts Receivable	**800,000.00**	**Total Other Current Liabilities**	**5,000.00**
Prepaid Expenses		Long term Bank Loans	
Total Other Current Assets		Notes Payable	
		Long term Interest Payable	
Raw Materials and Finished Goods Inventory		**Total Long Term Liabilities**	
Total Physical Inventory		**Total Liabilities**	**255,000.00**
WIP - All		Capital Stock (300110)	5,000,000.00
Total Project		Additional Paid-in Capital	
Total Current Assets	**5,800,000.00**	Common Dividends	
		Other Income	
Fixed Assets		Correction position (218172, 180251/2)	37,000.00
		Net Income (300160)	749,500.00
Intangible Assets		**Total Shareholder Equity**	**5,786,500.00**
Amortization - Intangible Fixed Assets			
Total Intangible Assets		**Liabilities & Shareholder Equity**	**€6,041,500.00**
Tangible Fixed Assets (180103)	250,000.00		
Accumulated Depreciation - Tangible Fixed Assets (180253)	(8,500.00)		
Other Assets			
Total Tangible Assets	**241,500.00**		
Total Fixed Assets	**241,500.00**		
Total Assets	**€6,041,500.00**		

Figure 1.47 *Financial statements using the delta-posting-ledger approach with corrective position—*

tax-GAAP

1.2.2.3. Solution Approach: Fixed Asset Accounting with Delta-Posting-Layer Accounting

When the posting-layer accounting approach is applied, the financial results for the different accounting standards can be identified by filtering for the posting-layers in the financial-report designer. The next screenshot illustrates this for the IFRS result that is recorded on the current posting-layer.

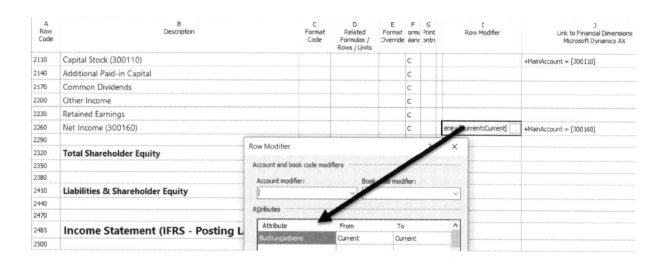

Figure 1.48 *Financial-report designer—IFRS*

Note The posting-layer filter that is applied to retained-earnings account 300160 for the IFRS accounting standard is identical to what has been used previously in chapter 1.2.2.

For the local-GAAP and tax-GAAP results, the approach that is illustrated in figure 1.48 cannot be used because of the previously shown double-counting effect of the IFRS depreciation expense, which needs a separate correction. This separate correction is accounted for by including an additional row in the financial-report designer that eliminates the aforementioned double-counting effect. Please see figure 1.49 and figure 1.50 for details.

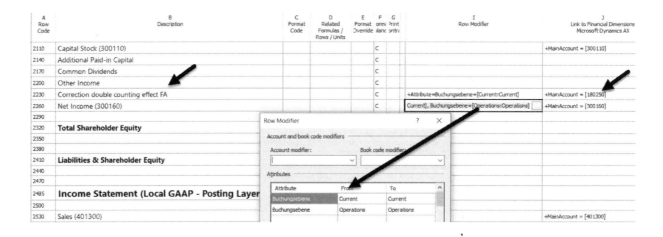

Figure 1.49 *Correction position for financial-report designer—local-GAAP*

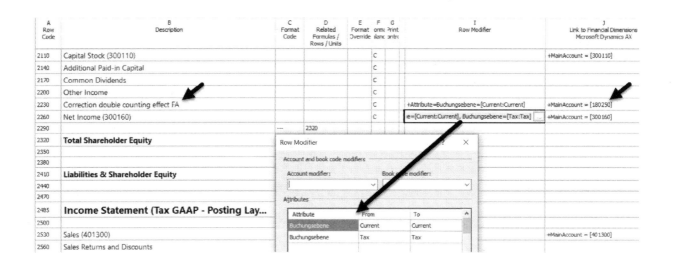

Figure 1.50 *Correction position for financial-report designer—local-GAAP*

With those correction positions in place, the financial reports for the three accounting standards used result in the same outcome that has been identified for the posting-ledger approach. Please see and compare the financial results presented in figure 1.51 to figure 1.53 with those presented in figure 1.45 to figure 1.47.

For the One Month Ending Thursday, January 31, 2019

Balance Sheet (IFRS - Posting Layer Approach)		Liabilities	
		Accounts Payable (200100)	250,000.00
Current Assets		**Total Accounts Payable**	**250,000.00**
Cash (110130)	€5,000,000.00		
Cash Equivalents		Tax Payable	
Total Cash and Cash Equivalents	**5,000,000.00**	**Total Tax Payable**	
Accounts Receivable (130100)	800,000.00	Other current liabilities (218170)	8,000.00
Total Accounts Receivable	**800,000.00**	**Total Other Current Liabilities**	**8,000.00**
Prepaid Expenses		Long term Bank Loans	
Total Other Current Assets		Notes Payable	
		Long term Interest Payable	
Raw Materials and Finished Goods Inventory		**Total Long Term Liabilities**	
Total Physical Inventory		**Total Liabilities**	**258,000.00**
WIP - All		Capital Stock (300110)	5,000,000.00
Total Project		Additional Paid-in Capital	
Total Current Assets	**5,800,000.00**	Common Dividends	
		Other Income	
Fixed Assets		Retained Earnings	
		Net Income (300160)	767,000.00
Intangible Assets		**Total Shareholder Equity**	**5,767,000.00**
Amortization - Intangible Fixed Assets			
Total Intangible Assets			
		Liabilities & Shareholder Equity	**€6,025,000.00**
Tangible Fixed Assets (180100)	250,000.00		
Accumulated Depreciation - Tangible Fixed Assets (180250)	(25,000.00)		
Other Assets			
Total Tangible Assets	**225,000.00**		
Total Fixed Assets	**225,000.00**		
Total Assets	**€6,025,000.00**		

Figure 1.51 *Financial statements using the delta-posting-layer approach with corrective position—*

IFRS

For the One Month Ending Thursday, January 31, 2019

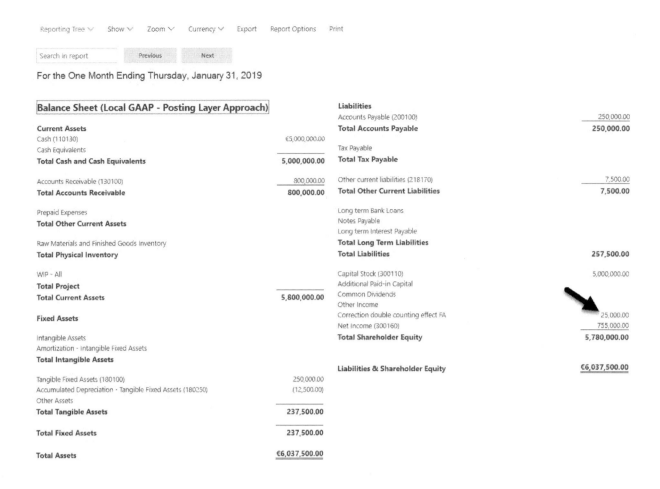

Balance Sheet (Local GAAP - Posting Layer Approach)		Liabilities	
Current Assets		Accounts Payable (200100)	250,000.00
Cash (110130)	€5,000,000.00	**Total Accounts Payable**	**250,000.00**
Cash Equivalents			
Total Cash and Cash Equivalents	**5,000,000.00**	Tax Payable	
		Total Tax Payable	
Accounts Receivable (130100)	800,000.00	Other current liabilities (218170)	7,500.00
Total Accounts Receivable	**800,000.00**	**Total Other Current Liabilities**	**7,500.00**
Prepaid Expenses		Long term Bank Loans	
Total Other Current Assets		Notes Payable	
		Long term Interest Payable	
Raw Materials and Finished Goods Inventory		**Total Long Term Liabilities**	
Total Physical Inventory		**Total Liabilities**	**257,500.00**
WIP - All		Capital Stock (300110)	5,000,000.00
Total Project		Additional Paid-in Capital	
Total Current Assets	**5,800,000.00**	Common Dividends	
		Other Income	
Fixed Assets		Correction double counting effect FA	25,000.00
		Net Income (300160)	755,000.00
Intangible Assets		**Total Shareholder Equity**	**5,780,000.00**
Amortization - Intangible Fixed Assets			
Total Intangible Assets		**Liabilities & Shareholder Equity**	**€6,037,500.00**
Tangible Fixed Assets (180100)	250,000.00		
Accumulated Depreciation - Tangible Fixed Assets (180250)	(12,500.00)		
Other Assets			
Total Tangible Assets	**237,500.00**		
Total Fixed Assets	**237,500.00**		
Total Assets	**€6,037,500.00**		

Figure 1.52 *Financial statements using the delta-posting-layer approach with corrective position—*

local-GAAP

For the One Month Ending Thursday, January 31, 2019

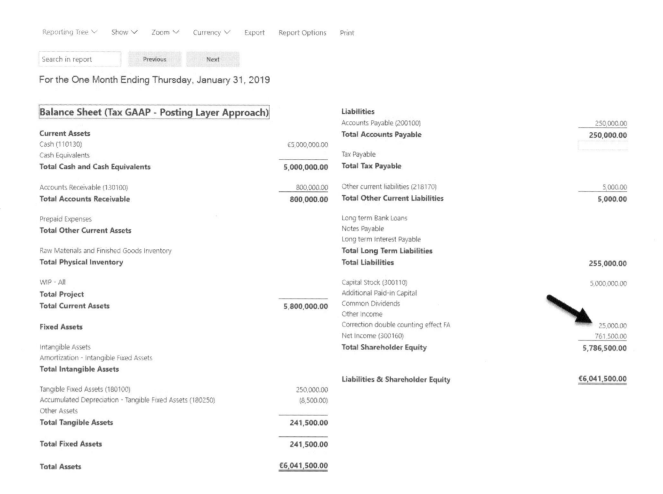

Figure 1.53 *Financial statements using the delta-posting-layer approach with corrective position—*

tax-GAAP

Note In the example presented, a single fixed asset transaction type that affects the company's profit—depreciation expenses—has been used. In practice, companies also record other fixed asset transactions that affect a company's profit, such as fixed asset revaluations, fixed asset depreciation adjustments, fixed asset sales, and so on. To ensure that the company's profit is presented correctly, if those posting types are also used, additional accounts need to be included in the corrective financial report designer position shown in figure 1.49 and figure 1.50.

Irrespective of the accounting approach used—ledger or posting-layer approach—the illustrated financial report modifications are in general sufficient to present a company's profit or loss in line with the different accounting standards.

Yet there is an important difference between the ledger and the posting-layer approach when it comes to analyzing the company's profit or loss in reports or inquiry forms in MSDyn365FO.

That is, if the ledger approach is used, companies can identify the profit or loss for the respective accounting standard (IFRS, local-GAAP, or tax-GAAP) in MSDyn365FO simply by filtering for the accounts that belong to this accounting standard. Figure 1.54 demonstrates this for the IFRS result, which can be identified from the trial balance by filtering for the accounting-standard-specific accounts.

Note The IFRS accounting-standard-specific accounts can be identified by the selected and highlighted lines in figure 1.54.

If the amounts recorded on the non-IFRS-specific accounts—the ones not highlighted in figure 1.54—are summarized, the correct profit or loss for the IFRS accounting standard can be identified (-$767,000).

	MainAccount	Name	Opening balance	Debit	Credit	Closing balance
✓	110130	Bank Account - EUR	5,000,000.00	0.00	0.00	5,000,000.00
✓	130100	Accounts Receivable - Domestic	800,000.00	0.00	0.00	800,000.00
✓	180101	Fixed Assets (IFRS)	250,000.00	0.00	0.00	250,000.00
	180102	Fixed Assets (Local)	250,000.00	0.00	0.00	250,000.00
	180103	Fixed Assets (Tax)	250,000.00	0.00	0.00	250,000.00
✓	180251	Accum. Depreciation (IFRS)	-25,000.00	0.00	0.00	-25,000.00
	180252	Accum. Depreciation (Local)	-12,500.00	0.00	0.00	-12,500.00
	180253	Accum. Depreciation (Tax)	-8,500.00	0.00	0.00	-8,500.00
✓	200101	Accounts Payable (IFRS)	-250,000.00	0.00	0.00	-250,000.00
	200102	Accounts Payable (Local)	-250,000.00	0.00	0.00	-250,000.00
	200103	Accounts Payable (Tax)	-250,000.00	0.00	0.00	-250,000.00
✓	218171	Provision bad debt (IFRS)	-8,000.00	0.00	0.00	-8,000.00
	218172	Provision bad debt (Local)	500.00	0.00	0.00	500.00
	218173	Provision bad debt (Tax)	3,000.00	0.00	0.00	3,000.00
✓	300110	Capital Stock	-5,000,000.00	0.00	0.00	-5,000,000.00
	300160	Retained Earnings	-749,500.00	0.00	0.00	-749,500.00

Figure 1.54 *Trial balance form—profit or loss, IFRS—using the ledger approach*

For the identification of the local-GAAP and tax-GAAP results, the same calculation approach can be applied. However, because of the full posting approach that is used for the fixed asset related transactions and the delta posting approach that is used for the non-fixed asset related transactions, other accounts need to be summarized. Figure 1.55 exemplifies this for the local-GAAP accounting standard.

	MainAccount	Name	Opening balance	Debit	Credit	Closing balance
✓	110130	Bank Account - EUR	5,000,000.00	0.00	0.00	5,000,000.00
✓	130100	Accounts Receivable - Domestic	800,000.00	0.00	0.00	800,000.00
	180101	Fixed Assets (IFRS)	250,000.00	0.00	0.00	250,000.00
✓	180102	Fixed Assets (Local)	250,000.00	0.00	0.00	250,000.00
	180103	Fixed Assets (Tax)	250,000.00	0.00	0.00	250,000.00
	180251	Accum. Depreciation (IFRS)	-25,000.00	0.00	0.00	-25,000.00
✓	180252	Accum. Depreciation (Local)	-12,500.00	0.00	0.00	-12,500.00
	180253	Accum. Depreciation (Tax)	-8,500.00	0.00	0.00	-8,500.00
	200101	Accounts Payable (IFRS)	-250,000.00	0.00	0.00	-250,000.00
✓	200102	Accounts Payable (Local)	-250,000.00	0.00	0.00	-250,000.00
	200103	Accounts Payable (Tax)	-250,000.00	0.00	0.00	-250,000.00
✓	218171	Provision bad debt (IFRS)	-8,000.00	0.00	0.00	-8,000.00
✓	218172	Provision bad debt (Local)	500.00	0.00	0.00	500.00
	218173	Provision bad debt (Tax)	3,000.00	0.00	0.00	3,000.00
✓	300110	Capital Stock	-5,000,000.00	0.00	0.00	-5,000,000.00
	300160	Retained Earnings	-749,500.00	0.00	0.00	-749,500.00

Figure 1.55 *Trial balance form—profit or loss, local-GAAP—using the ledger approach*

When using the posting-layer approach, such a simple identification of the profit or loss related to the different accounting standards cannot be realized because there is no functionality available that allows excluding specific posting-layer and account combinations in standard reports or standard inquiry forms. Figure 1.56 demonstrates this for the local-GAAP result, which cannot simply be identified by adding the current and operations posting-layers.

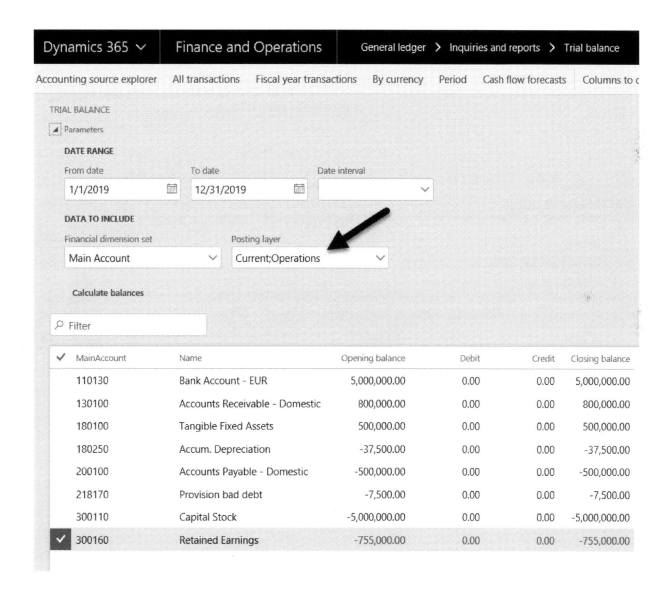

Figure 1.56 *Trial balance form—profit or loss, local-GAAP—posting-layer approach*

Figure 1.56 shows that the bad-debt reserve that is recorded on ledger account 218170 is in line with what has been presented further above. That is, the recorded IFRS and local-GAAP amounts are correctly summarized. The same, however, does not apply to the depreciation expense that is recorded on the accumulated depreciation account 180250 and the fixed asset acquisition amount that is recorded on account 180100, where the aforementioned double-counting effects can be identified.

A result of this double-counting effect is that reports other than the financial-report-designer reports shown previously cannot be used for analyzing the profit or loss for the other accounting standards when the posting-layer accounting approach is applied. This disadvantage can, however, be overcome by making use of corrective fixed asset books, which are presented next.

1.2.2.4.   Corrective Fixed Asset Books

The previous chapters showed that reports created with the help of the financial-report designer can help isolate the profit or loss that can be assigned to the different accounting standards irrespective of the accounting approach applied (ledger or posting-layer).

Apart from this outcome, the major disadvantage that was identified when using the posting-layer approach was that the MSDyn365FO standard reports and standard inquiry forms—other than the ones created with the help of the financial-report designer—could not be used for identifying the results of the derived financial-accounting standards (local-GAAP and tax-GAAP).

To allow MSDyn365FO users making use of those other standard reports and inquiry forms, corrective fixed asset books have to be used for recording adjustment transactions. The following three figures explain the concept of those corrective fixed asset books and adjustment transactions for the local-GAAP accounting standard by starting with the data that are presented in figure 1.56 above.

The data presented in figure 1.57 are identical to the ones in figure 1.56 except for how those data are presented.

	Current	Operations	Current + Operations
Assets			
Tangible Fixed Assets	$ 250,000	$ 250,000	$ 500,000
Accum. Depreciation	$ -25,000	$ -12,500	$ -37,500
Accounts Receivable	$ 800,000		$ 800,000
Cash	$ 5,000,000		$ 5,000,000
	$ 6,025,000	$ 237,500	$ 6,262,500
Liabilities & Shareholders Equity			
Capital Stock	$ -5,000,000		$ -5,000,000
Retained Earnings (Profit/loss)	$ -767,000	$ 12,000	$ -755,000
Accounts Payable	$ -250,000	$ -250,000	$ -500,000
Provision bad debt	$ -8,000	$ 500	$ -7,500
	$ -6,025,000	$ -237,500	$ -6,262,500

Figure 1.57 *Profit or loss, local-GAAP—posting-layer approach*

Figure 1.57 illustrates in a balance sheet like format that a simple addition of the data recorded on the current and operations layers results in a wrong representation of the company's profit. That is, the illustrated profit of -$755,000 is not in line with the profit that one would expect (-$780,000). Please see figure 1.32 for details.

If one wants to make use of the standard MSDyn365FO reports and inquiry forms other than the ones created by the financial-report designer, additional corrective transactions need to be recorded on the operations posting-layer. Figure 1.58 shows those corrective transactions in the gray highlighted column.

Everything presented in regards to the corrective books for the operations layer also applies to the tax layer. However, for reasons of brevity, only the corrections required for the operations layer are presented in the following.

	Current	Operations		Current + Operations
		Books	Corrective book	
Assets				
Tangible Fixed Assets	$ 250,000	$ 250,000	$ -250,000	$ 250,000
Accum. Depreciation	$ -25,000	$ -12,500	$ 25,000	$ -12,500
Accounts Receivable	$ 800,000			$ 800,000
Cash	$ 5,000,000			$ 5,000,000
	$ 6,025,000	$ 237,500		$ 6,037,500
Liabilities & Shareholders Equity				
Capital Stock	$ -5,000,000			$ -5,000,000
Retained Earnings (Profit/loss)	$ -767,000	$ 12,000	$ -25,000	$ -780,000
Accounts Payable	$ -250,000	$ -250,000	$ 250,000	$ -250,000
Provision bad debt	$ -8,000	$ 500		$ -7,500
	$ -6,025,000	$ -237,500		$ -6,037,500

Figure 1.58 *Profit or loss, local-GAAP—posting-layer approach—with corrective book*

With those additional corrective-book transactions, users can simply summarize the data recorded with the current and operations posting-layers to identify the local-GAAP result, which is shown in the last column in figure 1.58.

An important question when it comes to corrective fixed asset books is how one can create the additional transactions required on the operations posting-layer in an automated way without having to record those correction transactions manually. The next figure aims to answer this question by showing how a fixed asset acquisition and a fixed asset depreciation transaction need to be recorded on the different fixed asset books to allow a simple summary of the different books.

	Current	Operations		Current + Operations
	IFRS book	Local GAAP book	Corrective Local GAAP book	
Acquisition	$250,000	$ 250,000	$ -250,000	$ 250,000
Depreciation	$ 25,000	$ 12,500	$ -25,000	$ 12,500

Figure 1.59 *Corrective book—local-GAAP*

As one can identify from figure 1.59, the task of the corrective (local-GAAP) book is reversing the fixed asset transactions that have been recorded on the current posting-layer.

Note From an accounting perspective, the reversal transactions convert the full posting approach that is applied to the fixed asset transactions in MSDyn365FO to a delta-posting approach.

Applied to MSDyn365FO, this reversal can be achieved with the following three setup steps.

Step 1: Setup of corrective fixed asset books

Figure 1.60 exemplifies the setup of the corrective local-GAAP book (CORLOC LAY) that is linked to the operations posting-layer.

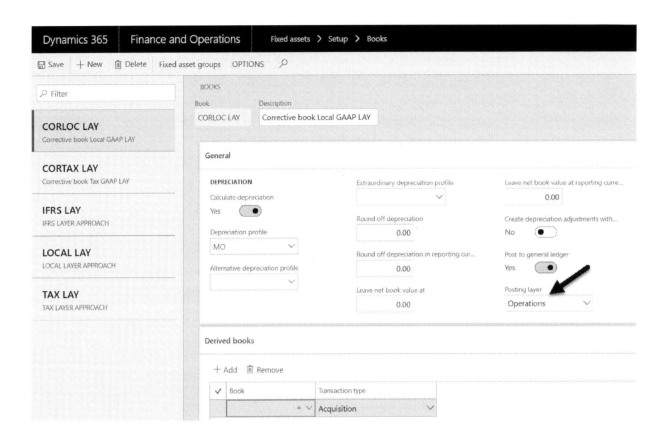

Figure 1.60 *Setup of corrective fixed asset book—local-GAAP*

Note A similar corrective book for the tax-GAAP (CORTAX LAY) can be identified in figure 1.60.

Step 2: Link to the leading IFRS accounting-standard book

The previously set up corrective books need to be linked to the leading IFRS accounting-standard-respective book by means of the standard fixed asset derived book functionality. This linkage is illustrated in figure 1.61 and shows how the IFRS book (IFRS LAY) links to the corrective books (CORLOC LAY and CORTAX LAY) for the different fixed asset transaction types.

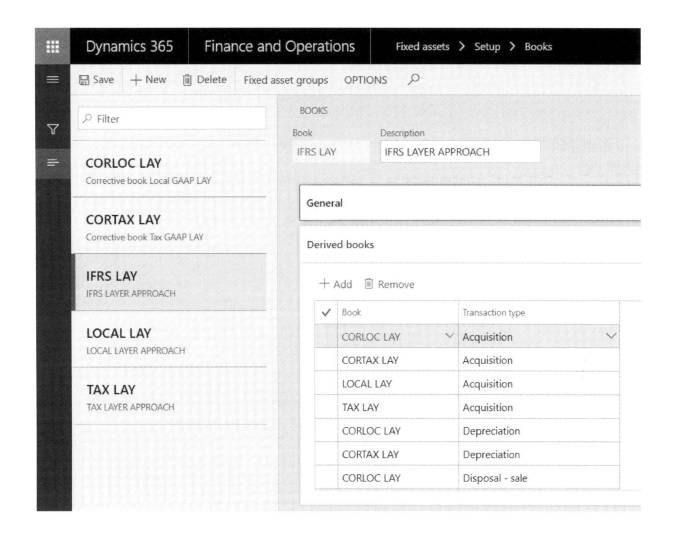

Figure 1.61 *Setup and linkage—IFRS book*

Note

Please note that the corrective fixed asset books have to be linked with the IFRS book for each fixed asset transaction type used to ensure that the IFRS-specific fixed asset postings are reversed at the operations posting-layer.

Step 3: Setup of the fixed_asset posting profile

With the previous setups made, two fixed asset book transactions are made, both on the operations and tax posting-layers; the first one with the local-GAAP- and tax-GAAP-specific books

(LOCAL LAY and TAX LAY) and a second one with the corrective books (CORLOC LAY and CORTAX LAY).

A key consideration with the fixed asset book transactions for the corrective fixed asset books is that the corrective books need to reverse the transactions recorded on the current posting-layer. This reversal can be achieved by making use of the same accounts that are used for the local-GAAP and tax-GAAP books but in reverse order. Figure 1.62 details the respective setup in the fixed asset posting profile.

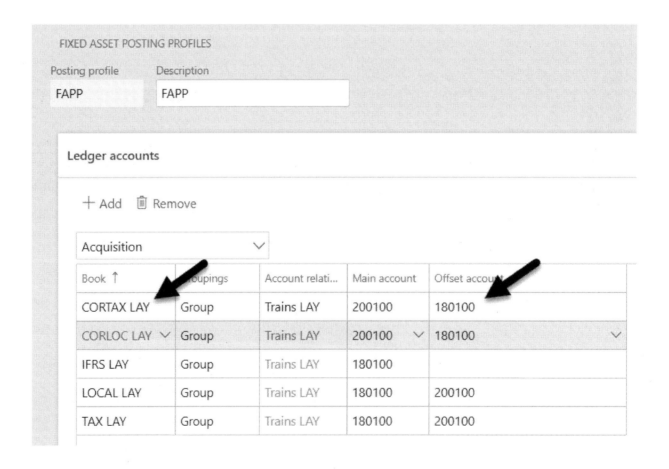

Figure 1.62 *Additional fixed asset posting lines with corrective fixed asset books*

To prove the functionality of the corrective fixed asset books, all fixed asset transactions shown in figure 1.38 have been entered once again in a new company account before the year-end closing was processed. The resulting year-end-closing voucher is shown in figure 1.63.

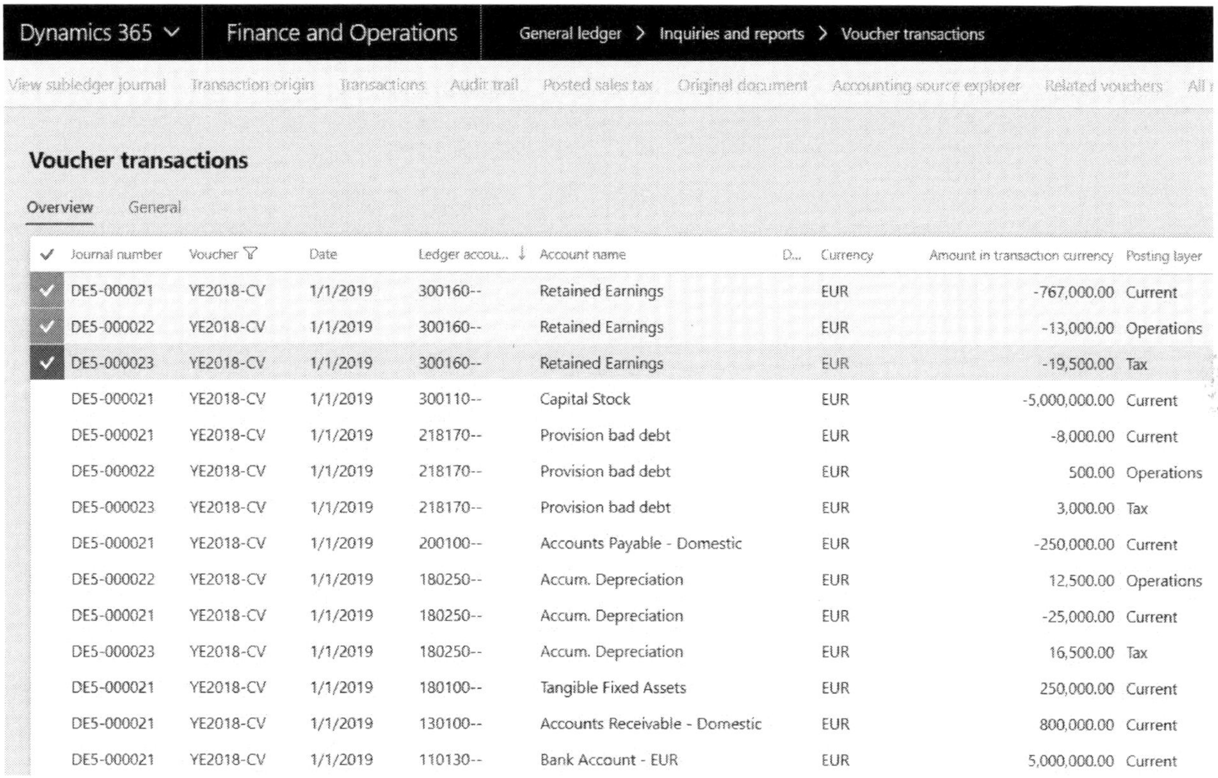

Dynamics 365 Finance and Operations General ledger > Inquiries and reports > Voucher transactions

Voucher transactions

Overview General

Journal number	Voucher	Date	Ledger account	Account name	D...	Currency	Amount in transaction currency	Posting layer
DE5-000021	YE2018-CV	1/1/2019	300160--	Retained Earnings		EUR	-767,000.00	Current
DE5-000022	YE2018-CV	1/1/2019	300160--	Retained Earnings		EUR	-13,000.00	Operations
DE5-000023	YE2018-CV	1/1/2019	300160--	Retained Earnings		EUR	-19,500.00	Tax
DE5-000021	YE2018-CV	1/1/2019	300110--	Capital Stock		EUR	-5,000,000.00	Current
DE5-000021	YE2018-CV	1/1/2019	218170--	Provision bad debt		EUR	-8,000.00	Current
DE5-000022	YE2018-CV	1/1/2019	218170--	Provision bad debt		EUR	500.00	Operations
DE5-000023	YE2018-CV	1/1/2019	218170--	Provision bad debt		EUR	3,000.00	Tax
DE5-000021	YE2018-CV	1/1/2019	200100--	Accounts Payable - Domestic		EUR	-250,000.00	Current
DE5-000022	YE2018-CV	1/1/2019	180250--	Accum. Depreciation		EUR	12,500.00	Operations
DE5-000021	YE2018-CV	1/1/2019	180250--	Accum. Depreciation		EUR	-25,000.00	Current
DE5-000023	YE2018-CV	1/1/2019	180250--	Accum. Depreciation		EUR	16,500.00	Tax
DE5-000021	YE2018-CV	1/1/2019	180100--	Tangible Fixed Assets		EUR	250,000.00	Current
DE5-000021	YE2018-CV	1/1/2019	130100--	Accounts Receivable - Domestic		EUR	800,000.00	Current
DE5-000021	YE2018-CV	1/1/2019	110130--	Bank Account - EUR		EUR	5,000,000.00	Current

Figure 1.63 *Year-end closing voucher with corrective fixed asset books*

The most striking difference between the year-end closing voucher that was recorded by the company that made use of the corrective fixed asset books (figure 1.63) and the one that was recorded in the company that did not make use of those corrective books (figure 1.39) is that the profit recorded on the retained-earnings accounts for the three different posting-layers respectively accounting standards matches the expected results shown in figure 1.32.

That is, adding the local-GAAP profit of -\$13,000 (recorded on retained-earnings account 300160 with the operations posting-layer) to the IFRS profit of -\$767,000 (recorded on the retained-earnings account with the current posting-layer) results in the expected local-GAAP profit of -$780,000. The same applies to the tax-GAAP profit of -$786,500, which can be identified as the sum of the profit on the tax posting-layer (-$19,500) and the profit of the current posting-layer (-$767,000).

The following three figures summarize the aforementioned by showing the amounts that can be identified from the trial balance form.

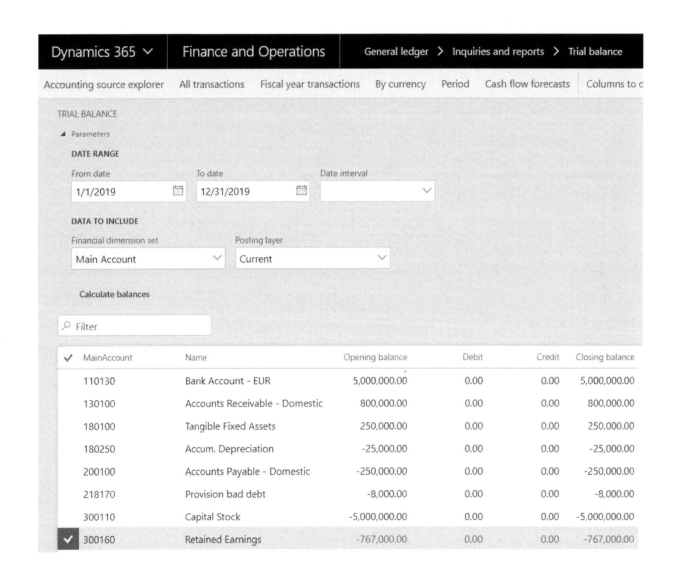

Figure 1.64 *Trial balance form—profit or loss, IFRS—posting-layer approach with corrective books*

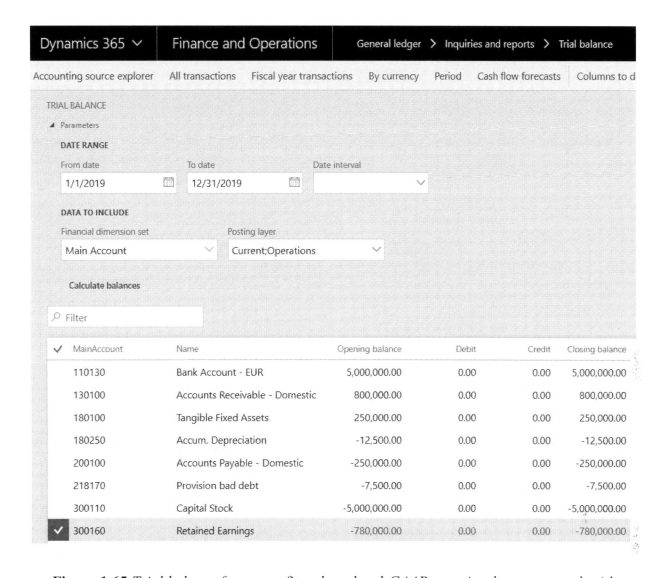

Figure 1.65 *Trial balance form—profit or loss, local-GAAP—posting-layer approach with*

corrective books

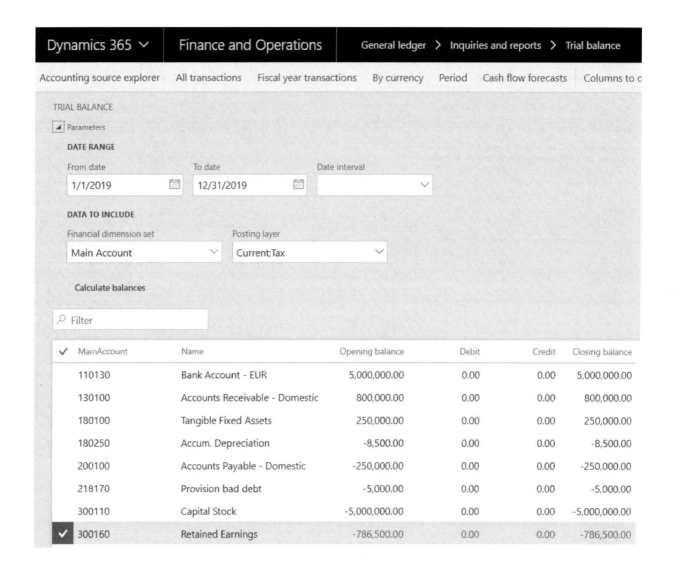

Figure 1.66 *Trial balance form—profit or loss, tax-GAAP—posting-layer approach with*

corrective books

1.2.3. Summary

The previous sections demonstrated the different approaches that companies can apply when they have to comply with different accounting standards at the same time.

From a conceptual perspective, the ledger accounting approach that uses valuation-specific ledger accounts seems to be the preferable one, because the profit or loss of the different accounting standards can be identified in all forms and reports. This advantage comes, however, at the price of having to create additional GAAP-specific accounts, which make the setup of the fixed asset posting profile more complex.

The alternative posting-layer approach seems to overcome this disadvantage, because the same ledger accounts can be used for all accounting standards. However, when it comes to recording fixed asset related transactions for the different accounting standards, the advantage of using the same ledger accounts for all accounting standards becomes a disadvantage, mainly because of the necessity of setting up additional corrective fixed asset books.

In summary, both parallel accounting approaches have advantages and disadvantages that one needs to be aware of before making a decision for one or the other. The main aim of this chapter was making those advantages and disadvantages transparent so that MSDyn365FO users can make an informed decision about what approach to use.

2. Maturity-Structure-Based Financial Reports

2.1. Legislative Background

Accounting standards often contain special regulations when it comes to reporting on the maturity-structure of specific financial positions. As an example, the German Commercial Code specifies that companies have to provide a breakdown of their short-term and long-term receivables and payables. (For details, please see sections 268 and 286 of the German Commercial Code.) Companies that follow international accounting standards are subject to similar regulations, especially when it comes to reporting on leases and financial instruments. (For example, see IAS1, IAS17, and IFRS7.)

As the various accounting standards do not specify in detail how maturity-structure-based financial reports have to be designed, a variety of different reporting formats can be found in practice. The following three figures provide examples of those reports and illustrate how companies report on the maturity-structure of their financial instruments in their annual financial reports.

The Company's contractual obligations as of December 31, 2017 are as follows:

Payments Due by Period

($ in millions)	Total		2018		2019—2020		2021—2022		Thereafter
Purchase obligations [1]	$ 2,226	$	715	$	892	$	478	$	141
Loans payable and current portion of long-term debt [2]	3,074		3,074		—		—		—
Long-term debt	21,400		—		3,200		4,589		13,611
Interest related to debt obligations	8,206		675		1,200		1,011		5,320
Unrecognized tax benefits [3]	67		67		—		—		—
Transition tax related to the enactment of the TCJA [4]	5,057		545		853		1,194		2,465
Operating leases	852		255		301		158		138
	$ 40,882	$	5,331	$	6,446	$	7,430	$	21,675

Figure 2.1 *Maturity-structure contractual obligations—Merck*

Source: https://investors.merck.com/financials/annual-reports-and-proxy/default.aspx

in € million	31.12.2017			
	Maturity within one year	Maturity between one and five years	Maturity later than five years	Total
Deferred income	2,427	4,276	471	7,174
Advance payments from customers	934	122	–	1,056
Other taxes	934	–	–	934
Deposits received	505	346	5	856
Payables to other companies in which an investment is held	744	–	–	744
Payables to subsidiaries	129	–	–	129
Social security	75	23	–	98
Other	5,031	160	7	5,198
Other liabilities	10,779	4,927	483	16,189

Figure 2.2 *Other liabilities—BMW Group*

Source: https://www.bmwgroup.com/content/dam/bmw-group-websites/bmwgroup_com/ir/

downloads/en/2018/Geschäftsbericht/BMW-GB17_en_Finanzbericht_ONLINE.pdf

Other current and non-current financial liabilities

Figures in millions of euros

	2017		2016	
	up to 1 year	more than 1 year	up to 1 year	more than 1 year
Bonds	51	3,298	809	3,351
Promissory loans		1,652	65	1,651
Liabilities to banks	619	117	550	575
Loans	87	22	98	27
Derivative financial liabilities	75	10	147	7
Finance lease obligations	6	18	6	22
Other financial liabilities	714	83	1,008	69
	1,552	5,200	2,683	5,702

Figure 2.3 *Other current and noncurrent financial liabilities—Bosch*

Source: https://www.bosch.com/explore-and-experience/annual-report/

2.2.   Implementation in MSDyn365FO

After investigating details of maturity-structure-based financial reports that can be found in practice, a question arises: How can one set up and operate MSDyn365FO in a way that those reports are created in an automated way?

An important consideration in this respect is that, for example, a bank loan that is classified as long-term today might need to be classified as short-term tomorrow. Therefore, making use of ledger accounts that summarize long-term and short-term loans without an additional separation of the individual bank loans does not make sense, because a part of the transactions recorded on those summary accounts require permanent adjustments. Therefore, what is needed is a functionality that allows an individual identification of the different financial instruments so that they can be classified correctly into the company's maturity-structure whenever needed.

MSDyn365FO ships with a couple of instruments that allow this individual identification. As an example, one might think of using descriptive texts or reason codes for the identification of different bank loans. Those two instruments, however, are not appropriate, because the information held in those fields gets lost when year-end closing transactions are processed. In addition, the use of descriptive texts or reason codes cannot be enforced. As a result, there is a risk that transactions are recorded incorrectly.

What is needed, therefore, is an instrument that is carried forward in the year-end closing process. In addition, one must be able to enforce the usage of this instrument to ensure that users do not forget to enter the information that is required for creating maturity-structure-based financial reports.

At this moment, there are only two instruments available that fulfill those criteria. First, ledger accounts; second, financial dimensions. In other words, companies can either use ledger accounts or financial dimensions to separate their financial instruments to generate maturity-structure-based financial reports. The next chapters exemplify those two approaches based on an example that is detailed in the next subchapter.

2.2.1. Sample Data

For reasons of simplicity and illustration, a focus on a single line—bank loans—of a maturity-structure-based financial report is made in the following. Figure 2.4 details the elements—the bank loans—that make up this maturity-structure-based reporting line.

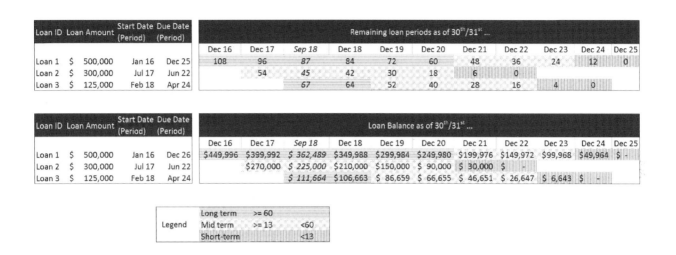

Figure 2.4 *Sample data for maturity-based financial reporting*

As one can identify from figure 2.4, three different bank loans (loan 1, loan 2, and loan 3) are used in the example. Details of the bank loan amounts, the periods when the loans were issued, and the periods when they have to be repaid can be found in the left section of figure 2.4. In the right section, one can find information on the remaining loan periods and the remaining loan amounts at the end of a given period or year for each of the loans used. As an example, on December 31, 2016, loan 1 had 108 remaining loan periods until it had to be repaid and had an open amount of $449,996.

The gray highlighted cells in figure 2.4 aim to illustrate the maturity-structure of the different loans based on the information provided in the legend, which can be found at the bottom of the figure.

Note
To keep the example and transactions recorded as simple and straightforward as possible, it is assumed that the company borrows and repays the different loans as is. That is, it is assumed that the interest rate for each of the loans is 0%.

2.2.2. Ledger Account Approach

As mentioned above, one of the available instruments that can be used for creating maturity-based financial reports are ledger accounts that need to be set up first. Figure 2.5 illustrates the respective setup of the ledger accounts that are used for the three sample bank loans.

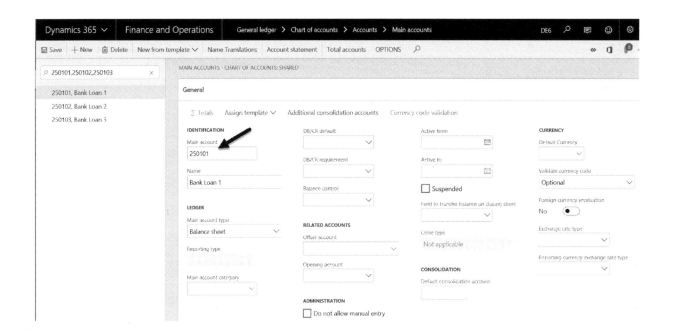

Figure 2.5 *Setup of financial-instrument-specific ledger accounts*

After those ledger accounts are set up, one can record financial transactions against them. Figure 2.6 details this by showing that each transaction for the different bank loans is made with a reference to the ledger account that has specifically been set up for the corresponding loan.

Figure 2.6 *Financial transactions for bank loans—ledger account approach*

Once all transactions in a given period are recorded, maturity-structure-based financial reports can be created. The creation of those reports is straightforward and necessitates the setup of a row- and column-structure. Figure 2.7 and figure 2.8 exemplify the setup of those structures.

A Row Code	B Description	C Format Code	D Related Formulas / Rows / Units	H Column estrictio	I o\ di	J Link to Financial Dimensions
100	**Maturity Structure - Ledger Account Approach**					
130						
160	Bonds					
190	Promissory Loans					
310	Liabilities to Banks					
340	**Loans**	TOT	347:361			
347	*- Loan 1*					+MainAccount = [250101]
354	*- Loan 2*					+MainAccount = [250102]
361	*- Loan 3*					+MainAccount = [250103]
370	Derivative Financial Liabilities					
400	Finance Lease Obligations					
430	Other Financial Liabilities					
460		---				
490	**Total**	CAL	@340			

Figure 2.7 *Maturity-structure-based financial report—row structure*

73

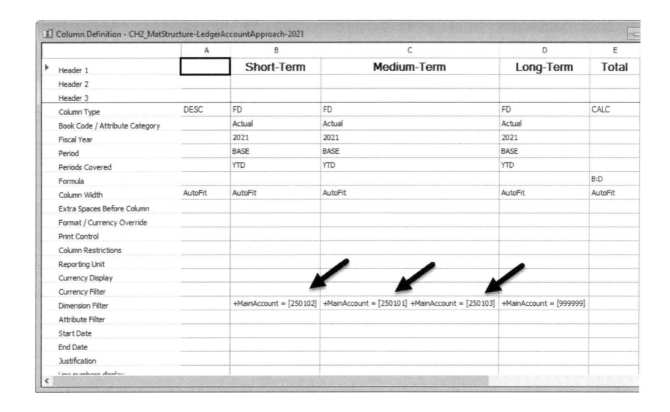

Figure 2.8 *Maturity-structure-based financial report—column structure*

Please note that a reference to the different ledger accounts used is made in the row and the column structure of the report. The first reference (in the row structure) is made to show each of the bank loans used in a separate reporting line. From a financial reporting perspective, this separation is not needed (see, for example, figure 2.3). The reference is made nevertheless for illustrative purposes, to allow the reader an easy and straightforward identification of the different bank loans.

The second reference of the ledger accounts is made in the report-column-structure form that is shown in figure 2.8. As one can identify from this figure, the loans are manually assigned to the different report columns, which differentiate between short-term, medium-term, and long-term financial instruments. As time progresses and the maturity-structure of the financial instruments changes, an update to this reference is necessary. In other words, the reference to the ledger accounts that is shown in figure 2.8 needs to be updated permanently to correctly represent the maturity-structure of the company's financial instruments.

After setting up the rows and columns of the maturity-structure-based financial report, the report can be generated by processing the transactions recorded in MSDyn365FO. The output of the report for the period ending in September 2018 is shown in figure 2.9.

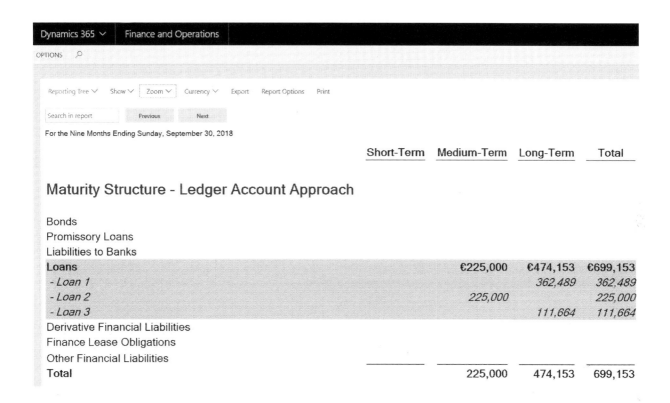

Figure 2.9 *Sample maturity-structure-based financial report for September 2018*

2.2.3. Financial Dimension Approach

The second approach that can be used for creating maturity-structure-based financial reports is the financial dimension approach. This approach makes use of separate financial dimensions rather than ledger accounts to distinguish between the different financial instruments.

Figure 2.10 shows the setup of three financial dimension values that are used for differentiating between the three bank loans used.

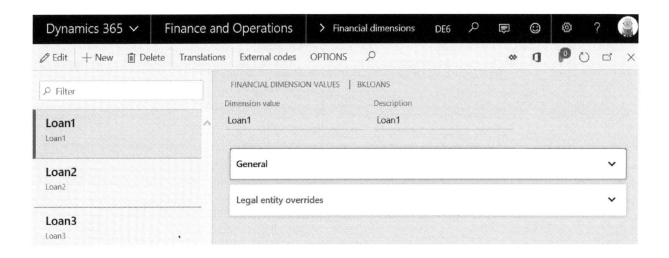

Figure 2.10 *Setup of financial-instrument-specific financial dimensions*

Once the financial dimension are set up, they need to be incorporated into the account structure that is used by the company. Incorporating the new financial dimension into the company's account structure can be done, for example, by making use of an advanced rule structure that is shown in figure 2.11.

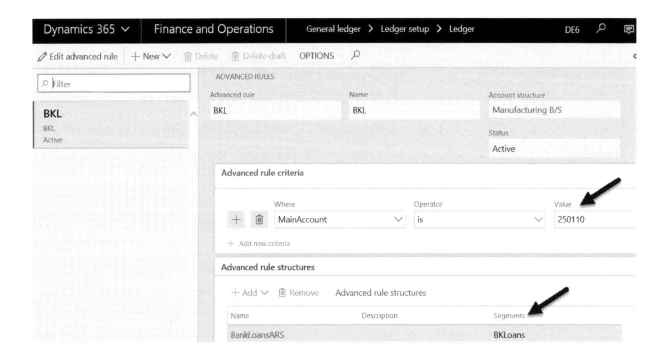

Figure 2.11 *Setup of advanced rule structure for financial-instrument-specific financial dimension*

The advanced rule structure that is shown in figure 2.11 specifies that one has to enter a financial dimension value from the BKLoans segment, whenever a transaction is recorded on the general bank loan account no. 250110. Figure 2.12 demonstrates this for the recording of the principal amounts of the three bank loans.

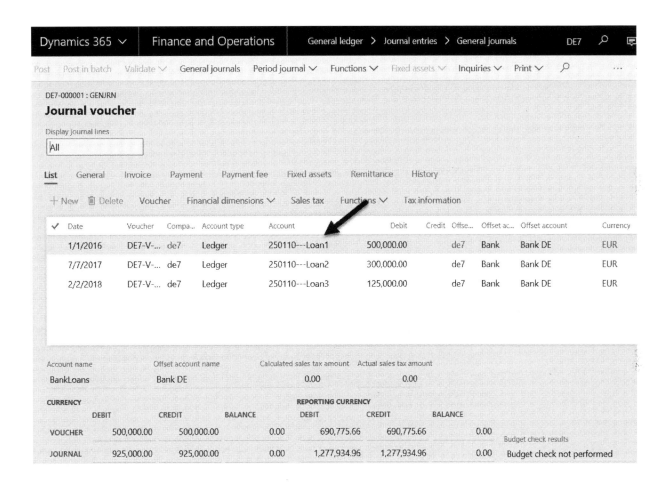

Figure 2.12 *Financial transactions for bank loans—financial dimension approach*

As with the ledger account approach shown in the previous chapter, a row- and column-structure must also be set up for the financial report that is used when making use of the financial dimensions approach. The next two figures detail this setup for the sample bank loan data used.

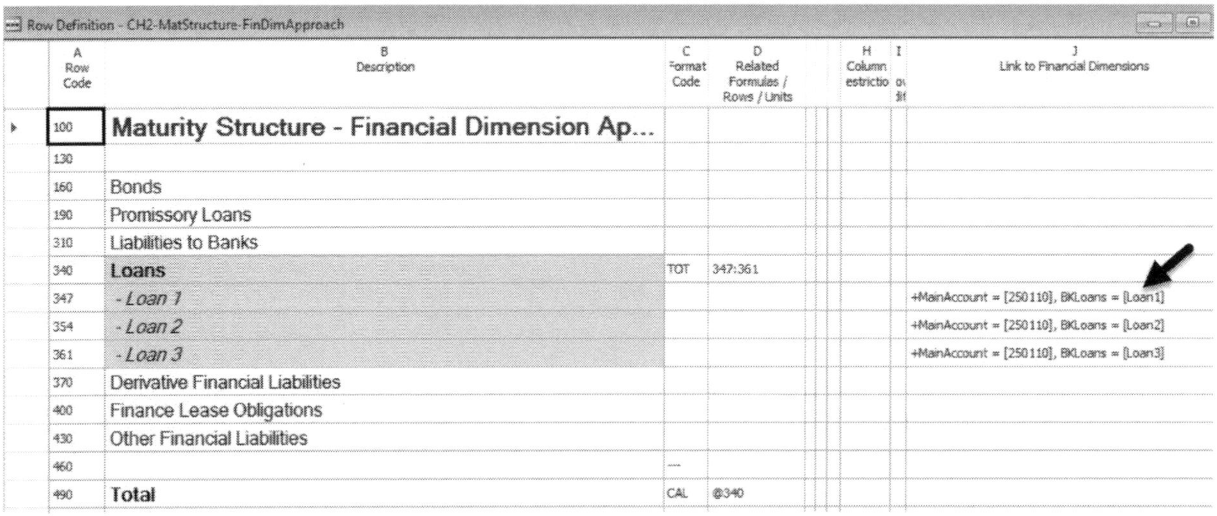

Row Definition - CH2-MatStructure-FinDimApproach

A Row Code	B Description	C Format Code	D Related Formulas / Rows / Units	H Column Restriction	I	J Link to Financial Dimensions
100	**Maturity Structure - Financial Dimension Ap...**					
130						
160	Bonds					
190	Promissory Loans					
310	Liabilities to Banks					
340	**Loans**	TOT	347:361			
347	*- Loan 1*					+MainAccount = [250110], BKLoans = [Loan1]
354	*- Loan 2*					+MainAccount = [250110], BKLoans = [Loan2]
361	*- Loan 3*					+MainAccount = [250110], BKLoans = [Loan3]
370	Derivative Financial Liabilities					
400	Finance Lease Obligations					
430	Other Financial Liabilities					
460		---				
490	**Total**	CAL	@340			

Figure 2.13 *Maturity-structure-based financial report—row structure*

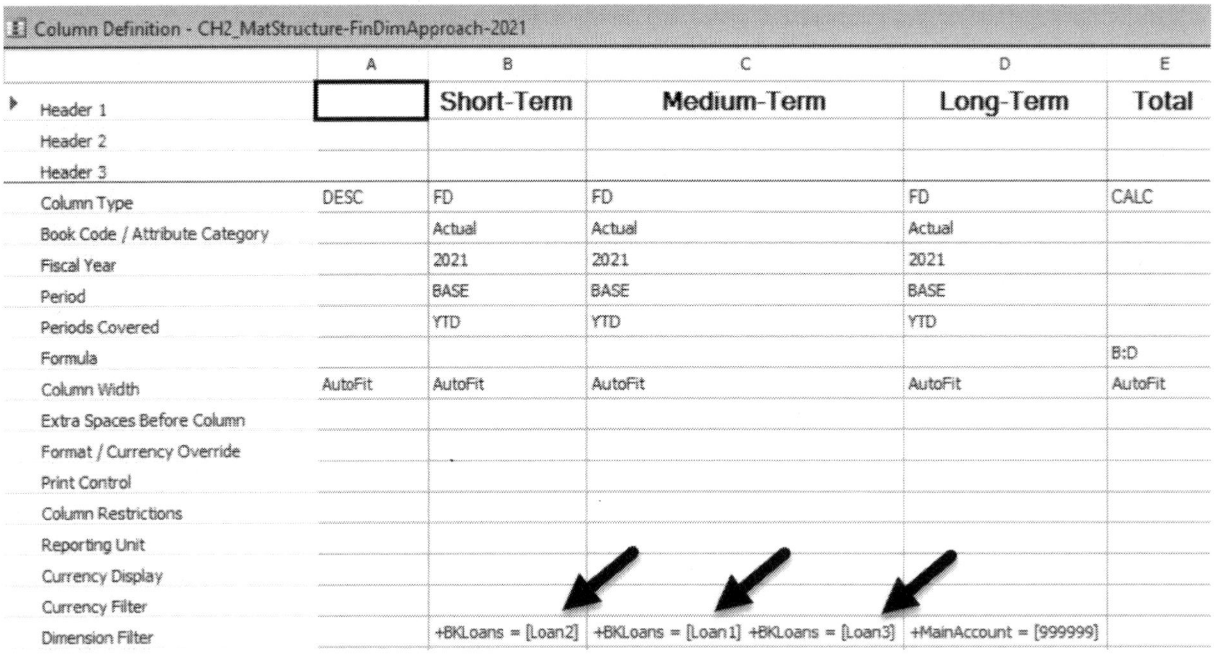

Column Definition - CH2_MatStructure-FinDimApproach-2021

	A	B	C	D	E
Header 1		**Short-Term**	**Medium-Term**	**Long-Term**	**Total**
Header 2					
Header 3					
Column Type	DESC	FD	FD	FD	CALC
Book Code / Attribute Category		Actual	Actual	Actual	
Fiscal Year		2021	2021	2021	
Period		BASE	BASE	BASE	
Periods Covered		YTD	YTD	YTD	
Formula					B:D
Column Width	AutoFit	AutoFit	AutoFit	AutoFit	AutoFit
Extra Spaces Before Column					
Format / Currency Override					
Print Control					
Column Restrictions					
Reporting Unit					
Currency Display					
Currency Filter					
Dimension Filter		+BKLoans = [Loan2]	+BKLoans = [Loan1] +BKLoans = [Loan3]	+MainAccount = [999999]	

Figure 2.14 *Maturity-structure-based financial report—column structure*

Please note that a permanent adjustment of the report-column structure is required when making use of the financial dimension approach to represent the maturity-structure of the financial instruments correctly.

The major difference in the setup of the financial report that is used when making use of the financial dimension approach versus the one that is used when making use of the ledger account approach is the incorporation of the financial dimension elements into the row- and column-structure of the report. For details, please compare the setups that are shown in figure 2.7 and figure 2.8 with those that are made in figure 2.13 and figure 2.14.

The maturity-structure-based financial report that results when making use of the financial dimension approach for the period ending in September 2018 is shown in figure 2.15.

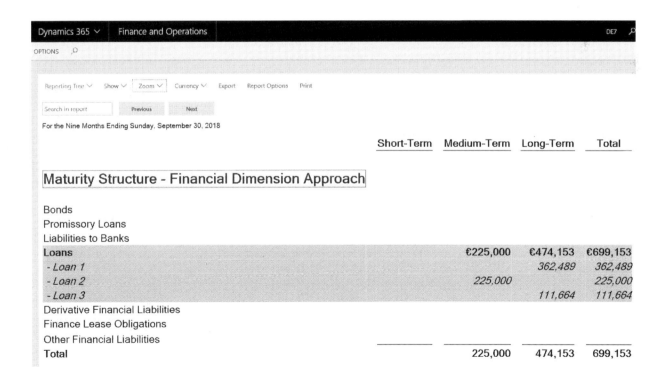

Figure 2.15 *Sample maturity-structure-based financial report for September 2018*

2.2.4. Electronic-Reporting Approach

A major disadvantage of the approaches that were presented in chapter 2.2.2. and chapter 2.2.3. is that permanent and manual adjustments to the maturity-structure-based financial reports are required.

In the following, an alternative approach—which makes use of electronic-reporting standard functionalities—is introduced, and it can create maturity-structure-based financial reports in a way that no manual report adjustments are required. To implement this alternative approach, a number of setups and data operations are necessary, which are detailed in the next four subchapters.

2.2.4.1. Step 1: Save Loan Data on SharePoint

The first setup that is required for the implementation of the alternative maturity-structure-based-reporting approach is specifying details of the financial instruments used in a cloud-based storage. Details of the bank loans that have been used in this example have consequently been recorded in a SharePoint list that is illustrated in figure 2.16.

+ New   Export to Excel   ◇◇ PowerApps ∨

Book3CH2_SPList

Title ∨	LoanType ∨	LoanVersion ∨	LoanAmount ∨	StartDate ∨	EndDate ∨	AnnualInter...
Loan1	Simple	New	$500.000,00	01.01.2016	31.12.2025	0 %
Loan2	Simple	New	$300.000,00	01.07.2017	30.06.2022	0 %
Loan3	Simple	New	$125.000,00	01.02.2018	30.04.2024	0 %

Figure 2.16 *Sample loan data in SharePoint*

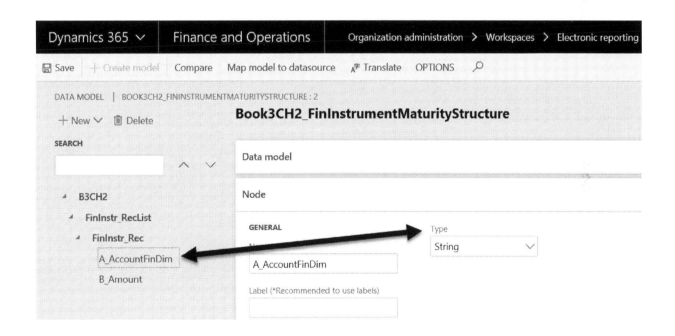 The loan details used in this example have been entered manually in the SharePoint list. Rather than entering those details manually, supporting apps can be used for data-entrance purposes. An example of such an app can be found on the following website: https://dynamicsax-fico.com/2018/07/23/bank-loans-in-msdyn365fo-with-the-help-of-flow-and-powerapps-part-1-2/.

2.2.4.2. Step 2: Create and Process Electronic-Report

Once the loan details are recorded, an electronic-report can be created in MSDyn365FO. Figure 2.17 shows the elements that make up this report.

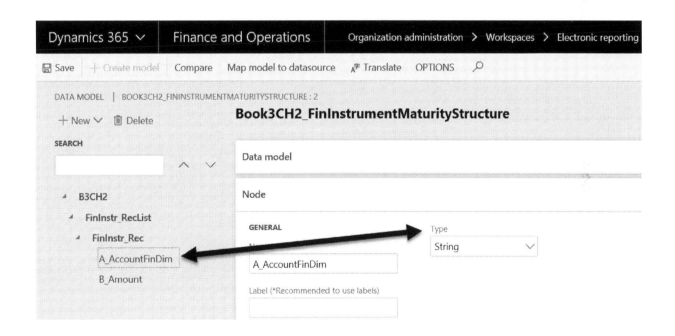

Figure 2.17 *Electronic-report model designer*

An investigation of the electronic-reporting elements shown in figure 2.17 reveals that only two elements are required: one that records the information of the ledger account and financial dimension used (*A_AccountFinDim*) and a second one (*B_Amount*) that holds the current loan balance.

Please note that the first electronic-report element (*A_AccountFinDim*) is set up with the *string* type and that the second electronic-report element (*B_Amount*) is set up with the type *real*.

After the report elements have been set up, a mapping to the data held in the MSDyn365FO accounting tables can be made. This mapping is illustrated in figure 2.18, where one can identify a two-step mapping process.

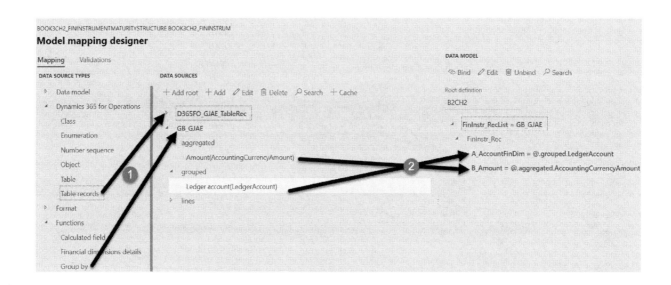

Figure 2.18 *Electronic-report model configuration*

In the first step, one needs to select the loan data transactions that are recorded in the GeneralJournalAccountEntry (GJAE) table. Once those table records are selected, the *group by* functionality can be used for a second mapping step, which summarizes the data that have been recorded for a specific bank loan. Figure 2.18 shows this by illustrating that the *group by* functionality summarizes the accounting currency amounts recorded for the ledger account and financial dimension combinations used.

Note The *group by* functionality used ensures that the various bank loan transactions recorded are summarized for the calculation of the current bank loan balance. This summary is made in the company where the bank loan transactions have been recorded on a single ledger account with the bank loans separated by financial dimensions (*financial* dimension approach). The *group by* functionality, however, can also be used if loan data are recorded on different ledger accounts, as shown in chapter 2.2.2.

The next step required is the creation of a report configuration, which is needed for the generation of the electronic-report output.

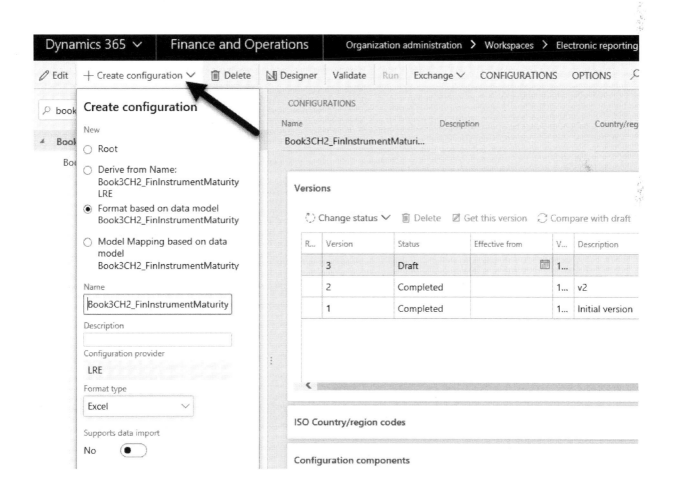

Figure 2.19 *Creating electronic-report configuration*

Figure 2.19 shows that Excel is selected as the report format type. To create this Excel-based electronic-report, one has to configure the structure of the Excel output file first. This configuration is made by defining cell names in an Excel document and binding those cells to an Excel table. Please see figure 2.20 for details.

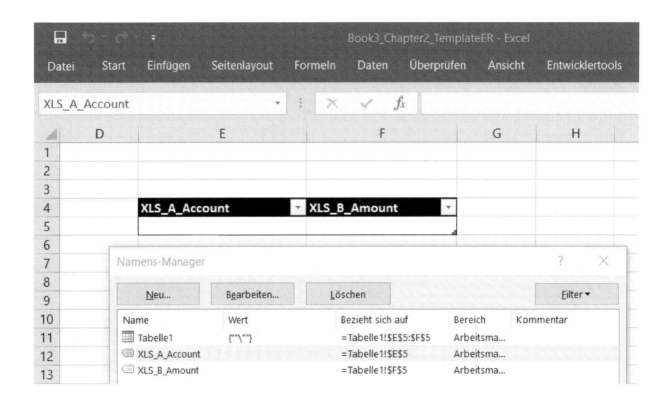

Figure 2.20 *Excel-based report-output format template*

The last setup step required before the electronic-report can be generated is the import of the Excel-based report-output format template into the configuration designer and the mapping of the Excel-based report-output elements with the elements of the electronic-reporting model that have been defined before (please see figure 2.18). The next figure illustrates this mapping.

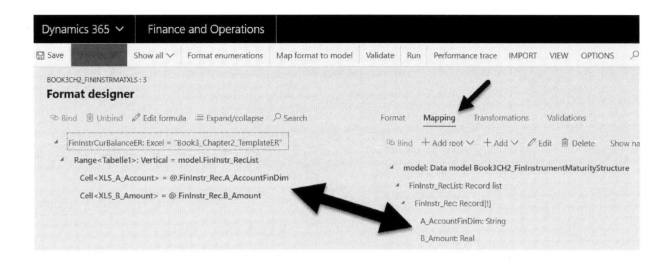

Figure 2.21 *Mapping electronic-reporting model elements with Excel-based report-output format*

With all of those setups and configurations in place, the electronic-report can be generated. Generating the electronic-report for creating a maturity-based financial report requires that

1. filters are specified for the selection of the ledger account, the fiscal-period type, and the transaction date;

2. an output destination is defined; and

3. a recurrence for the generation of the report is selected.

Figure 2.22 highlights those configurations.

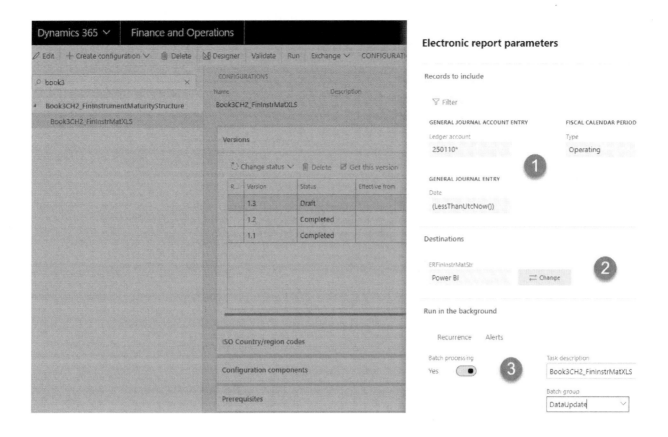

Figure 2.22 *Electronic-report processing*

The filters applied when generating the report ensure that all bank loan transactions recorded on ledger account 250110 are considered in the report generation. In addition, the operating-type filter ensures that year-end closing vouchers are excluded from the calculation of the loan balances. This exclusion is necessary to guarantee that the year-end closing transactions do not distort the calculation results. The last filter applied in the first section relates to the transaction date and ensures that only those bank loan transactions before the current system date and time (*LessThanUtcNow()*) are taken into consideration.

Note The output destination shown in figure 2.22 can be defined by creating an electronic-reporting-destination setting that is used for storing the report output. In the following, a SharePoint document library (*SP_ERMatStr*) is used for this purpose.

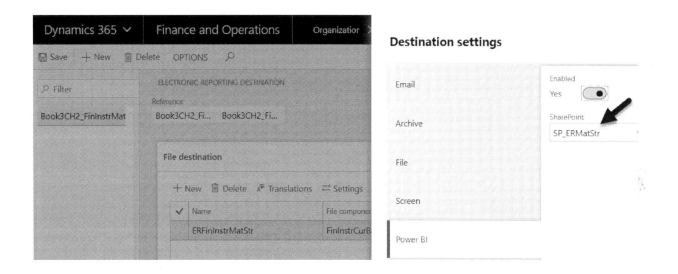

Figure 2.23 *Electronic-reporting-destination setup*

Note The last report parameter used defines the recurrence pattern of the report generation. If the maturity-structure-based financial report is, for example, an element of a company's monthly reporting package, a monthly report-generation-recurrence pattern can be defined.

Processing the sample electronic-report with the report parameters shown on the previous pages results in the following Excel output document that is stored in the SharePoint document library selected.

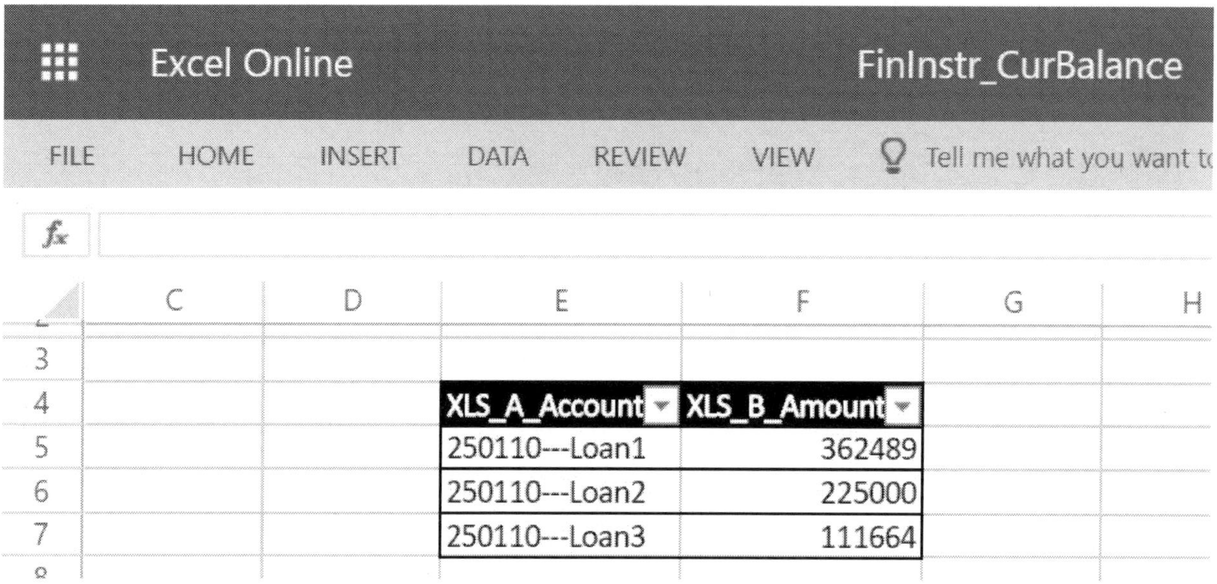

Figure 2.24 *Sample electronic-report output*

Note The loan balances shown in figure 2.24 represent the balances at the end of September 2018. This can be verified, for example, for the first bank loan that was borrowed for a total of $500,000. With thirty-three repayments of $4,167 each, a remaining loan balance of $362,489 remains at the end of September 2018. For the second loan with an original amount of $300,000, fifteen repayments of $5,000 each have been recorded by the end of September 2018, resulting in a current loan balance of $225,000. Finally, for the last loan with an original amount of $125,000, eight repayments of $1,667 each have been recorded by the end of September 2018, resulting in the illustrated loan balance of $111,664. Please also see the loan data reported in figure 2.15.

2.2.4.3.   Step 3: Use MS-Flow to Classify Loans into Maturity-Structure

After the current loan balances have been calculated and the electronic-report saved to SharePoint, MS-Flow is used for classifying the financial instruments into the short-term, medium-term, and long-term maturity-structure buckets.

The MS-Flow that is used for this purpose starts with a recurrence trigger that executes the MS-Flow on a regular basis. Please see MS-Flow step *A* in figure 2.25.

The recurrence trigger used for starting the MS-Flow needs to be aligned with the recurrence pattern that is set up for processing the electronic-report (see figure 2.22). As an example, if the electronic-report is processed on a given date in a month at 4:00 p.m., MS-Flow cannot start before this date and time. Otherwise old data would be processed, resulting in a wrong maturity-structure-based financial report.

The first MS-Flow action step (*B*) collects the data of the bank loans that have been recorded on SharePoint (see figure 2.16). Thereafter, the electronic-report loan balances are collected in step *C*, before the actual classification of the financial instruments into the maturity-structure buckets starts.

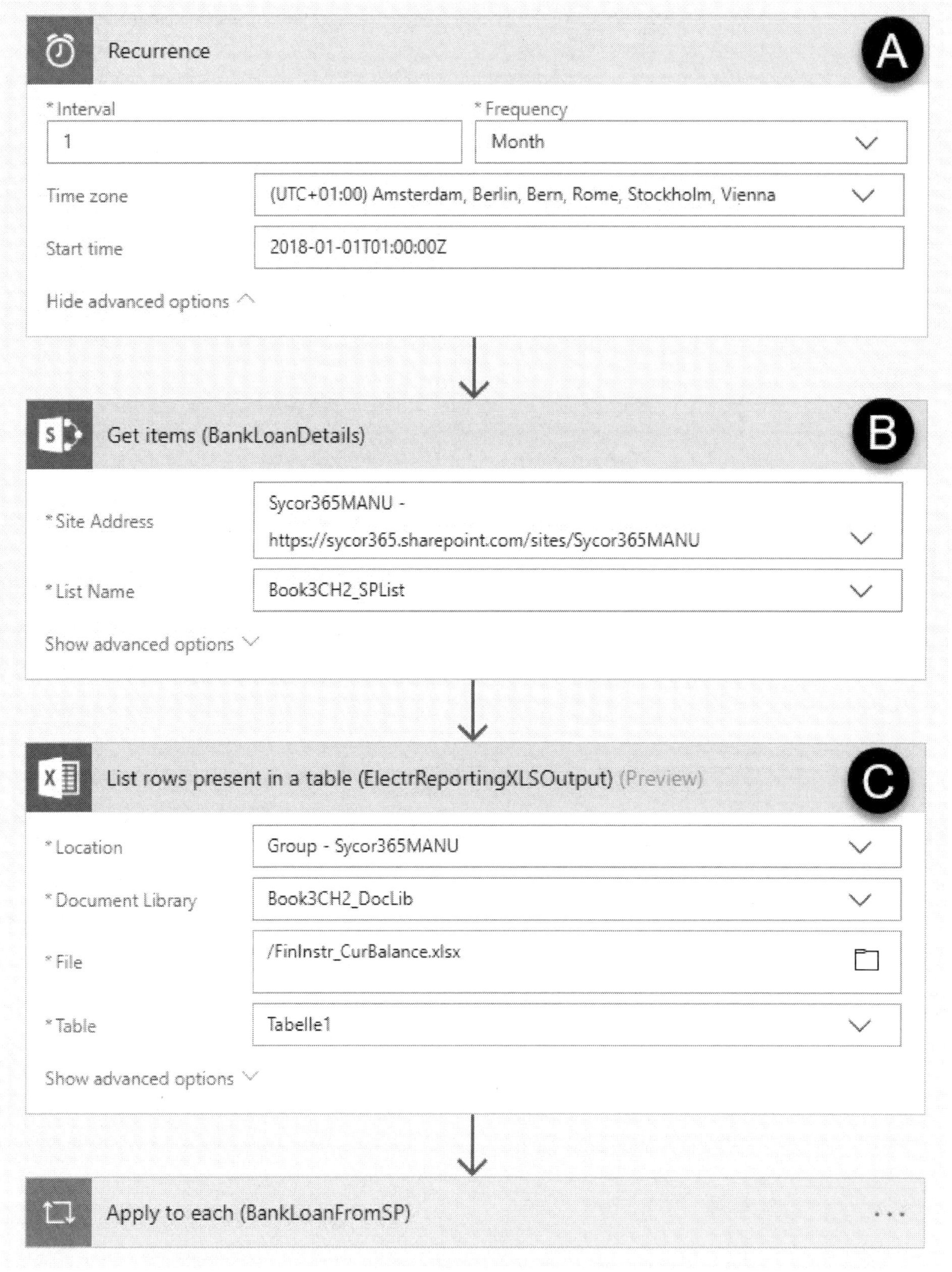

Figure 2.25 *MS-Flow for maturity-structure-based classification of financial instruments (1)*

With the bank loan base and current balance data collected, three temporary data-composition steps (*D*, *E*, and *F*) are used. Those steps—among others—are required for defining the condition that is set up in step *G* and which verifies that the loan data recorded on the SharePoint site (step *B*) matches the one listed in the Excel document (step *C*).

Figure 2.26 *MS-Flow for maturity-structure-based classification of financial instruments (2)*

The expression used in step *F* is as follows: *substring(outputs('Compose_(HoldAccount FinDimFromXLS)'),9,5)*. In step *G*, the following condition is used: *@equals(outputs('Compose_(HoldLoanID)'), outputs('Compose_(ExtractLoanIdFromXLS)'))*.

Once the matching loan pairs from the SharePoint list and the Excel document have been found, the actual classification of the financial instruments starts by checking into which maturity-structure bucket the individual bank loans fall. This classification is shown in figure 2.27.

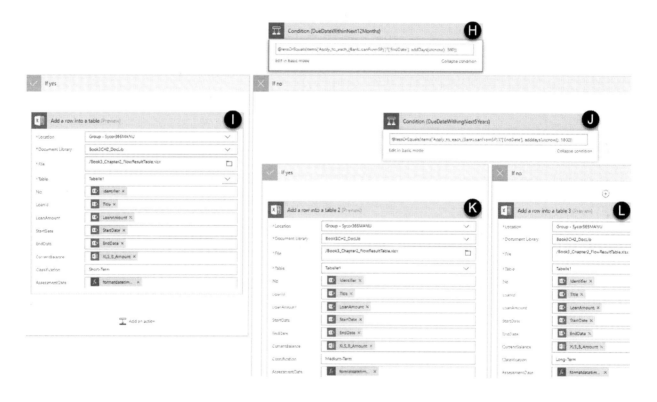

Figure 2.27 *MS-Flow for maturity-structure-based classification of financial instruments (3)*

The condition used in step *H* checks whether the due date of the loan falls within the next 360 days by making use of the following condition: *@lessOrEquals(items('Apply_to_each_ (BankLoanFromSP)')?['EndDate'], addDays(utcnow(), 360))*. If this condition is validated as true, a row with the loan details and the classification *short-term* is entered in a new Excel result document in step *I*.

If the first condition is evaluated as false, a second condition is applied in step *J* that checks whether the loans are due within the next 1,800 days. This is realized by making use of the following condition: *@lessOrEquals(items('Apply_to_each_(BankLoanFromSP)')?['EndDate'], adddays(utcnow(), 1800))*. Provided that this second condition is evaluated as true, an update to the aforementioned Excel result document is made in step *K* with the classification *medium-term*. Otherwise, an update to the Excel result document with the classification *long-term* is made in step *L*. The next figure illustrates details of the resulting Excel document.

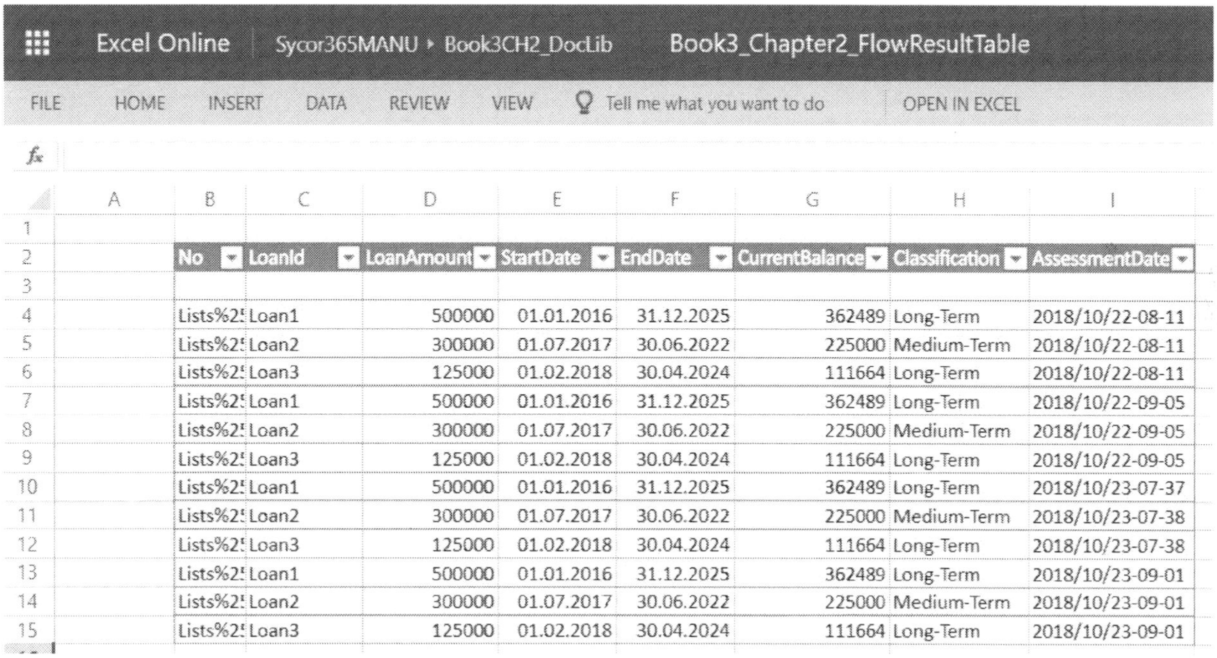

No	LoanId	LoanAmount	StartDate	EndDate	CurrentBalance	Classification	AssessmentDate
Lists%2!	Loan1	500000	01.01.2016	31.12.2025	362489	Long-Term	2018/10/22-08-11
Lists%2!	Loan2	300000	01.07.2017	30.06.2022	225000	Medium-Term	2018/10/22-08-11
Lists%2!	Loan3	125000	01.02.2018	30.04.2024	111664	Long-Term	2018/10/22-08-11
Lists%2!	Loan1	500000	01.01.2016	31.12.2025	362489	Long-Term	2018/10/22-09-05
Lists%2!	Loan2	300000	01.07.2017	30.06.2022	225000	Medium-Term	2018/10/22-09-05
Lists%2!	Loan3	125000	01.02.2018	30.04.2024	111664	Long-Term	2018/10/22-09-05
Lists%2!	Loan1	500000	01.01.2016	31.12.2025	362489	Long-Term	2018/10/23-07-37
Lists%2!	Loan2	300000	01.07.2017	30.06.2022	225000	Medium-Term	2018/10/23-07-38
Lists%2!	Loan3	125000	01.02.2018	30.04.2024	111664	Long-Term	2018/10/23-07-38
Lists%2!	Loan1	500000	01.01.2016	31.12.2025	362489	Long-Term	2018/10/23-09-01
Lists%2!	Loan2	300000	01.07.2017	30.06.2022	225000	Medium-Term	2018/10/23-09-01
Lists%2!	Loan3	125000	01.02.2018	30.04.2024	111664	Long-Term	2018/10/23-09-01

Figure 2.28 *MS-Flow for maturity-structure-based classification of financial instruments—result table*

2.2.4.4. Step 4: Report on Maturity-Structure

An important characteristic of the result table shown in figure 2.28 is that the MS-Flow results are differentiated by an assessment-date value, which is shown in the last column in the previous figure.

The MS-Flow expression used for filling this information into the Excel table is as follows:

formatdatetime (utcnow(), 'yyyy/MM/dd-HH-mm').

Being able to differentiate between the MS-Flow processing results is important for a regular reporting on the company's financial maturity-structure. That is because the illustrated solution design allows the generation of an automatically updated Excel Pivot table that can be filtered by the MS-Flow assessment date. Figure 2.29 shows the result of such a maturity-structure-based financial report for the loan data used in the example.

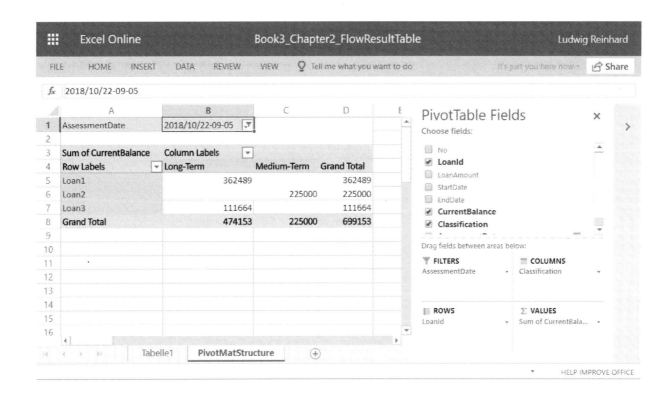

Figure 2.29 *MS-Flow for maturity-structure-based classification of financial instruments—reporting*

output table

The data shown in the reporting output table in figure 2.29 are identical to those shown in figure 2.9 and figure 2.15. Yet the major difference is that the results shown in figure 2.29 are created automatically with the help of the MSDyn365FO electronic-reporting features and MS-Flow.

2.3. Summary

Within the previous sections, different approaches to how one can report on the maturity-structure of the company's financial instruments were introduced. The first two approaches presented in section 2.2.2. and section 2.2.3. relied on a manual and regular assessment and classification of the company's financial instruments. Such a manual assessment seems feasible in situations where companies have to report on the maturity-structure of their financial instruments in irregular or distant time periods, such as once a year, for example. If a more frequent reporting on the maturity-structure of the company's financial instruments is required, the approach that makes use of the MSDyn365FO electronic-reporting features in combination with MS-Flow seems preferable.

3.   Lower-of-Cost-or-Net-Realizable-Value Inventory Valuation

In this third chapter, we will investigate in depth how companies evaluate their inventory. Evaluating a company's inventory is done multiple times: first, when the inventory is acquired, for example, through a purchase from a vendor; second, in regular time intervals—typically at the end of a month, quarter, or year; and finally, at the time the inventory leaves the company for example through a sale to a customer.

In the following, a focus is made on the second evaluation point in time that deals with regular reevaluations of a company's inventory. Before one can apply those reevaluations in MSDyn365FO, inventory accounting standards and their inventory reevaluation-related regulations need to be taken into consideration. This will be done in the following subchapter before the implementation of those regulations in MSDyn365FO is illustrated.

3.1.   Legislative Background

As mentioned above, when it comes to reevaluating a company's inventory, the regulations stipulated in the accounting standards that a company applies have to be taken into consideration. Unfortunately it is not possible or reasonable to try to explain all available inventory-related accounting standards that are used around the world. For that reason, a focus is made on the most commonly used accounting standards (IFRS and USGAAP) and their treatment of inventory reevaluations.

The accounting regulations that have to be applied when it comes to reevaluating a company's inventory are termed *lower of cost or net realizable value* or *lower of cost or market* and can be found in IAS 2 (IFRS) and ASC 330 (USGAAP).

Note   Previously the USGAAP accounting standard used the term *lower of cost or market*. This traditionally used term was, however, replaced with the last amendments made to ASC 330 and changed into *lower of cost or net realizable value*. Despite this change, the traditional abbreviation *LoCoM* is used in the following—for reasons of simplicity and recognition—to refer to the *lower-of-cost-or-net-realizable-value* valuation principle.

Irrespective of the terminological differences that existed in the past, both accounting standards include a cost-price element as the first benchmark that is needed when it comes to a company's subsequent inventory valuation. IAS 2 defines this inventory cost-price element as follows (see IAS 2 Sec. 9): "The cost of inventories shall comprise all costs of purchase, cost of conversion and other costs incurred in bringing inventories to their present location and condition."

For items that are interchangeable, IFRS and USGAAP allow the use of assumptions in regards to the flow of costs, such as first-in-first-out (FIFO), average or weighted-average costing, and so on. (For details, please see the aforementioned IFRS and USGAAP accounting standards.)

The second element that is necessary for subsequent inventory revaluations according to the LoCoM accounting standard refers to a *market* or *net-realizable* value (NRV). This second element can be defined as the selling price of an item in the ordinary course of business minus the estimated costs of completion, disposal, and transportation. The determination of the NRV can be broken down into the following three steps:

1. Determine the market value or expected selling price.

2. Find all costs associated with the completion and the sale, such as cost of production, testing, advertising, transportation, and alike.

3. Calculate the difference between the first and second element.

Note For items that are not sold on a regular basis—such as raw materials that are consumed in the production of other goods—and that do not have an expected sales price, the market value can be approximated by the replacement costs of those items.

To illustrate the calculation of the NRV, let us assume that the value of a company's inventory item—a finished product—is $15,000. However, at the end of the period, it can only be sold for $14,000 provided that an additional $2,000 is spent on packaging, sales commission, and shipping expense. As a result, the inventory item's NRV is $12,000.

When the NRV of the inventory is less than its cost, the inventory has to be written down to the NRV by recording an expense in the company's income statement (IS).

Note IAS 2 defines that inventories are usually written down on an item-by-item basis. Yet there might be circumstances when it may be appropriate to group similar or related items for reevaluation purposes; for example, if those items relate to the same product line, have a similar purpose or end use, are produced and marketed in the same geographical area, or cannot practically be evaluated separately.

The last consideration that needs to be made when it comes to reevaluating a company's inventory relates to the subsequent treatment of the inventory-value-adjustments that have been recorded. In this respect, an important difference between IFRS and USGAAP comes into play, because IFRS determines that previously recorded inventory-value-adjustments need to be reversed when the circumstances that caused the inventories to be written down below costs no longer exist. The corresponding USGAAP standard does not allow such a reversal. How this difference and the implementation of the LoCoM can be realized in MSDyn365FO will be investigated in the following subchapters.

3.2.   Implementation in MSDyn365FO

After this brief investigation of the accounting regulations that determine when and how companies have to reevaluate their inventory, let us now have a look at how those accounting standards can be implemented in MSDyn365FO.

3.2.1.   Cost Element

The first element one needs to take care of when applying the LoCoM-valuation principle is the cost-price of an item. An important question in regards to this cost-price is where to get this cost-price from. Initially one might think of the cost-price that can be found in the manage cost section in the released-product form that is shown in the next figure.

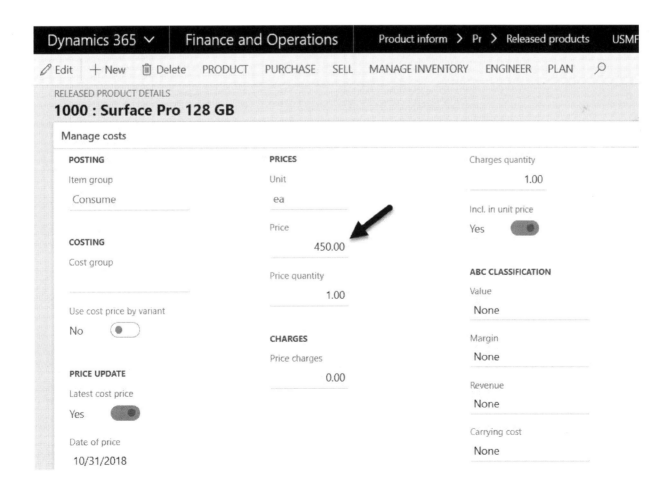

Figure 3.1 *Cost-price—released-product form*

What makes this cost-price unsuitable, however, is the fact that it does not necessarily represent the actual cost-price of an item but rather the cost-price that was recorded—for example—when the item was purchased the last time. In other words, the cost-price that can be identified in the manage-cost tab is a static value that is not permanently updated.

As there is no other single field available in MSDyn365FO that allows extracting an item's current cost-price in a straightforward manner, an item's current cost-price needs to be calculated from its inventory transactions. When making this item cost-price calculation, a related question—whether all inventory transactions for an item need to be taken into consideration—arises.

This question can be answered with *no,* because not all inventory transactions influence an item's cost-price. As an example, internal inventory transfers between warehouses that record a receipt and issue transaction typically do not affect an item's cost-price. The same holds for issue and receipt transactions that are linked to each other by making use of the MSDyn365FO marking functionality. As a result, those marked transactions can also be ignored in the item cost-price calculation.

Note Inventory transfers between different inventory locations, such as sites and warehouses, might exert an influence on an item's cost-price if—for example—the item makes use of a standard cost-price inventory valuation model. For reasons of simplicity, however, those internal inventory transfers are ignored in the following.

A subsequent question related to the calculation of an item's cost-price is whether physical and financial inventory-values or only financial inventory-values need to be taken into account in the calculation of an item's cost-price.

Note MSDyn365FO differentiates between physical and financial inventory transactions, prices, and values. In a nutshell, physical inventory transactions are those that temporarily influence a company's inventory-value based, for example, on picking list or packing-slip postings. Financial inventory transactions reverse and update those physical inventory transactions with a financial cost amount—for example, when invoices are recorded. Despite the fact that financial inventory transactions reverse and update financial inventory transactions, they cannot be considered final values. That is because financial inventory amounts are in turn updated and adjusted by the inventory closing process that takes the inventory flow assumptions of an item—for example, FIFO, LIFO, and so on—into account. For additional information, please have a look at the Microsoft documentation websites.

In the following, physical and financially updated inventory transactions are taken into consideration for the calculation of an item's cost-price. That is because it is assumed that the risk of ownership and destruction changes with the shipment of the products—in other words, the physical item transactions—necessitating the consideration of physical and financial inventory transactions.

3.2.2.   Net-Realizable Value

The second element required for the LoCoM comparison is the NRV that is approximated by the market value or the expected sales price of an item. From an ERP-system perspective, the expected sales price is the one that is regularly recorded in system tables. As a result, this sales price is the one to be used when applying the LoCoM valuation principle.

However, the products or items that a company sells are typically not sold to a single customer for a single price. Instead, one can regularly find various price ranges that define prices on a customer-by-customer basis and which are recorded in so-called trade-agreement tables or journals.

Those trade agreements pose a practical problem to the calculation of the NRV, because it is not feasible trying to go through all trade agreements that have been set up in MSDyn365FO in order to calculate a weighted-average sales price. What can be used instead as an approximation of an item's expected sales price is the so-called *base sales price* that can be found in the released products form in MSDyn365FO. The next figure illustrates this base sales price.

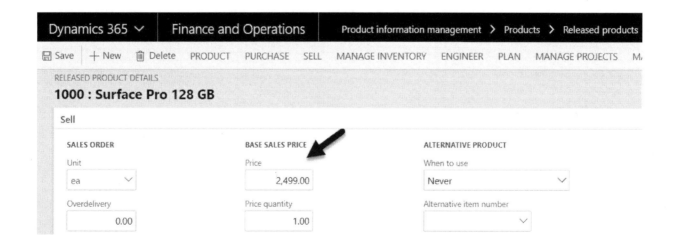

Figure 3.2 *Base sales price item*

![Note] The base sales price shown in figure 3.2 is a static value that requires regular updates.

3.2.3.   Solution Approach

Based on the previous explanations, the following solution approach is selected for the implementation of the LoCoM principle in MSDyn365FO.

Figure 3.3 *Solution approach to LoCoM in MSDyn365FO*

Figure 3.3 shows that electronic-reporting functionalities are used in a first step for the calculation of an item's cost-price and the extraction of its base sales price. Those calculated or extracted values are then put in a cloud-based storage (SharePoint) that can be accessed by MS-Flow to create the ledger journals that are required for posting the inventory-value-adjustments. The last process step shown in figure 3.3 refers to the posting of the created ledger journals in MSDyn365FO.

In line with the previously mentioned IFRS accounting standard that does not allow the retention of previously recorded value adjustments, and to avoid a double counting of value adjustments that are made in subsequent months, all value-adjustment postings are reversed at the beginning of the following month.

The next subchapters exemplify the illustrated solution approach based on sample data from the standard MS Contoso USMF demo company.

3.2.4. Implementation of Solution Approach

3.2.4.1. Step 1: Electronic-Report

3.2.4.1.1. Step 1a: Electronic-Report Model

As illustrated in figure 3.3, the first step in the solution approach presented necessitates the setup of an electronic-reporting (ER) model. The model used for the following illustrations and explanations is shown in figure 3.4.

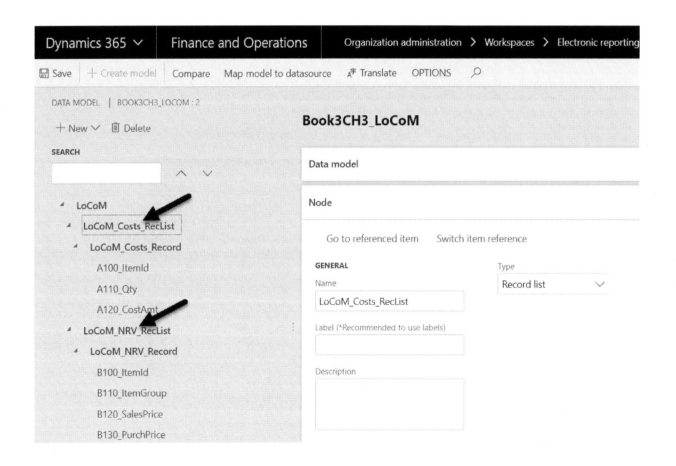

Figure 3.4 *Electronic-reporting model—LoCoM elements*

Figure 3.4 illustrates that the ER model contains two major sections: one in the upper part that refers to the item's cost and one in the lower part that refers to the item's NRV. In the upper part, one can identify three elements—starting with the letter *A* for an easier identification—that are needed for the cost-price calculation. Those elements are

- an item identifier (*A100_ItemId*);

- the current quantity of the item (*A110_Qty*); and

- the current cost amount of the item in stock (*A120_CostAmt*).

In the lower part of figure 3.4, elements that start with the letter *B* can be identified, which are required for the determination of the NRV. Those elements are

- *B100_ItemId*, for identifying the individual item and linkage to the cost elements in the upper part;

- *B110_ItemGroup*, as an optional element to allow companies a reevaluation of their inventory on an item-group basis rather than on an item-by-item basis;

- *B120_SalesPrice*, as an approximation of the market or NRV of an item; and

- *B130_PurchPrice*, as an approximation of the NRV for those items that are not sold.

Note In the following, all reevaluations are made on an item-by-item rather than an item-group basis.

Once the elements that are required for the LoCoM calculations are specified, they can be linked to their originating data-source in MSDyn365FO. In other words, one has to define where the values required for the LoCoM valuation come from. This definition is made in the ER-model designer that is shown in the next figure.

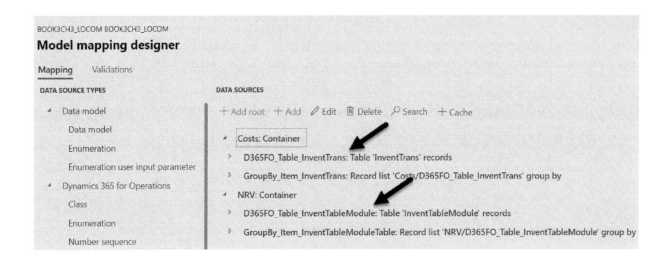

Figure 3.5 *ER-model designer—LoCoM*

The data-sources shown in figure 3.5 are separated into a cost part, which can be identified in the upper part of the data-source section, and a NRV part, which can be identified in the lower section of the figure. Both parts show a reference to MSDyn365FO tables—the InventTrans table and the InventTableModule table—which are highlighted by the arrows in figure 3.5.

As the tables might include the same item or item-related transactions multiple times, the table elements are grouped and aggregated by making use of the *GroupBy* functionality. For details, please see figure 3.6 and figure 3.7 below.

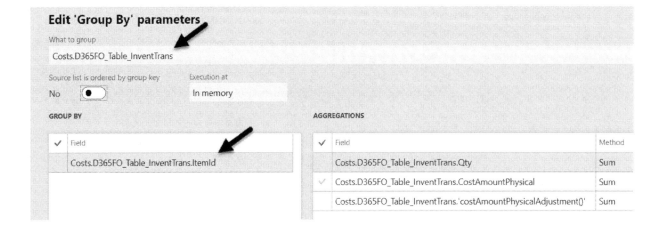

Figure 3.6 *ER-model designer—LoCoM—InventTrans GroupBy element*

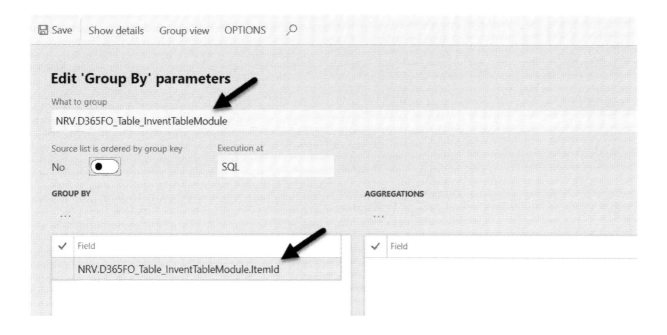

Figure 3.7 *ER-model designer—LoCoM—InventTableModule GroupBy element*

The first *GroupBy* element that is used for the InventTrans table (see figure 3.6) aggregates the quantity, physical-cost amount, and cost-adjustment amount of a specific item. The second *GroupBy* element that is used for the InventTableModule table does not require a specific aggregation and simply groups the table elements by the item identifier (ID) (please see figure 3.7).

After the data-sources have been selected and grouped, the ER-model elements can be mapped to the data-sources. This mapping is exemplified in figure 3.8.

Figure 3.8 *ER-model designer—LoCoM—mapping data-sources to model elements*

Note The *A120_CostAmt* element that is shown in figure 3.8 is mapped to the physical cost amount and the cost-amount adjustments recorded in the InventTrans table to ensure that subsequent adjustments of an item's inventory-value are taken into account. For the mapping of the NRV ER elements, it has to be noted that the item group, sales price, and purchase price elements cannot be found in the InventTableModule table directly, but can be identified by making use of the standard built-in table methods. Those methods can be identified by the opening and closing brackets on the right-hand side of figure 3.8.

The last step required before the ER model can be used for retrieving the cost and NRV data from MSDyn365FO is changing the status of the ER model to complete. This is illustrated in figure 3.9.

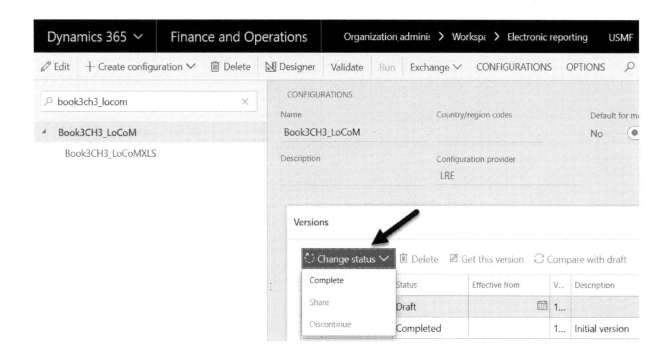

Figure 3.9 *ER-model designer—LoCoM—status*

3.2.4.1.2. Step 1b: Electronic-Report-Model Configuration

After the ER model and the various elements that are required for the calculation or determination of the item cost and NRV are defined, the ER configuration can be set up. Setting up the ER configuration necessitates the creation of an Excel workbook template in a first step if the ER output shall be stored in an Excel workbook on SharePoint. The worksheets, tables, and fields required in this Excel template are presented in the following.

In the first Excel sheet—denominated *Cost*—an Excel table is defined, which is needed for holding the cost-related data of the various items. Please note that the table holds the same three cost-related elements that have been defined in the ER model further above. For details, see figure 3.4.

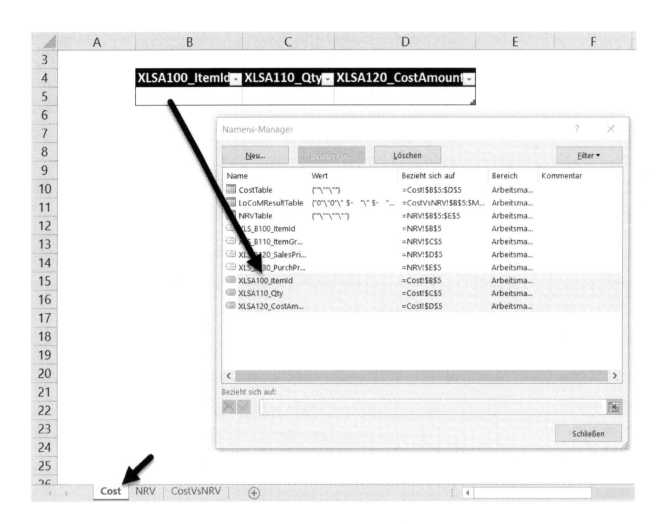

Figure 3.10 *ER-output Excel template—cost sheet*

In addition to the definition of the Excel table, cell names have to be defined for all cells in the first table row. Those names are shown in the Excel name manager that is illustrated in the middle part of figure 3.10.

For the second Excel sheet—denominated *NRV*—a similar setup of a table and cell names is required. Please see figure 3.11 for details.

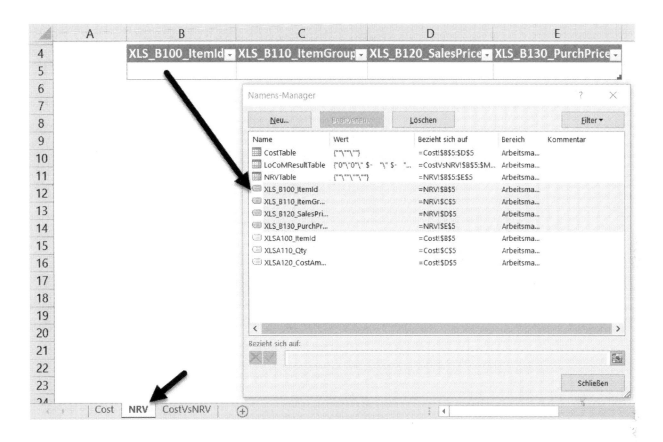

Figure 3.11 *ER-output Excel template—NRV sheet*

The last Excel worksheet—denominated CostVsNRV—is used for combining the data that are recorded in the first two tables in the other Excel sheets.

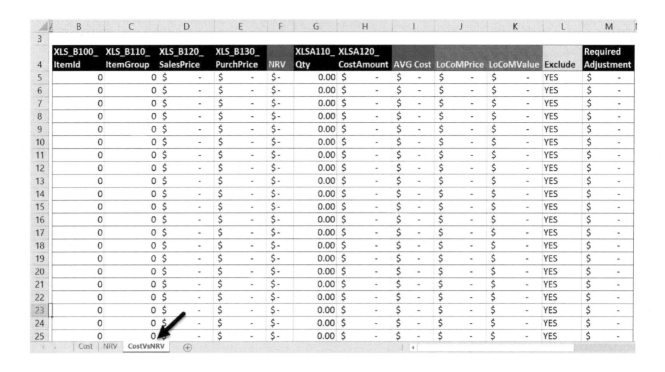

XLS_B100_ ItemId	XLS_B110_ ItemGroup	XLS_B120_ SalesPrice	XLS_B130_ PurchPrice	NRV	XLSA110_ Qty	XLSA120_ CostAmount	AVG Cost	LoCoMPrice	LoCoMValue	Exclude	Required Adjustment
0	0	$ -	$ -	$ -	0.00	$ -	$ -	$ -	$ -	YES	$ -
0	0	$ -	$ -	$ -	0.00	$ -	$ -	$ -	$ -	YES	$ -
0	0	$ -	$ -	$ -	0.00	$ -	$ -	$ -	$ -	YES	$ -
0	0	$ -	$ -	$ -	0.00	$ -	$ -	$ -	$ -	YES	$ -
0	0	$ -	$ -	$ -	0.00	$ -	$ -	$ -	$ -	YES	$ -
0	0	$ -	$ -	$ -	0.00	$ -	$ -	$ -	$ -	YES	$ -
0	0	$ -	$ -	$ -	0.00	$ -	$ -	$ -	$ -	YES	$ -
0	0	$ -	$ -	$ -	0.00	$ -	$ -	$ -	$ -	YES	$ -
0	0	$ -	$ -	$ -	0.00	$ -	$ -	$ -	$ -	YES	$ -
0	0	$ -	$ -	$ -	0.00	$ -	$ -	$ -	$ -	YES	$ -
0	0	$ -	$ -	$ -	0.00	$ -	$ -	$ -	$ -	YES	$ -
0	0	$ -	$ -	$ -	0.00	$ -	$ -	$ -	$ -	YES	$ -
0	0	$ -	$ -	$ -	0.00	$ -	$ -	$ -	$ -	YES	$ -
0	0	$ -	$ -	$ -	0.00	$ -	$ -	$ -	$ -	YES	$ -
0	0	$ -	$ -	$ -	0.00	$ -	$ -	$ -	$ -	YES	$ -
0	0	$ -	$ -	$ -	0.00	$ -	$ -	$ -	$ -	YES	$ -
0	0	$ -	$ -	$ -	0.00	$ -	$ -	$ -	$ -	YES	$ -
0	0	$ -	$ -	$ -	0.00	$ -	$ -	$ -	$ -	YES	$ -
0	0	$ -	$ -	$ -	0.00	$ -	$ -	$ -	$ -	YES	$ -
0	0	$ -	$ -	$ -	0.00	$ -	$ -	$ -	$ -	YES	$ -
0	0	$ -	$ -	$ -	0.00	$ -	$ -	$ -	$ -	YES	$ -

Cost | NRV | CostVsNRV

Figure 3.12 *ER-output Excel template—CostVsNRV sheet*

Most columns shown in the CostVsNRV worksheet in figure 3.12 use simple lookup formulas for copying the values listed in the cost and NRV tables. Yet different from the cost and NRV tables, the table used in the last Excel worksheet in figure 3.12 does not only list records that have been extracted by the ER but also calculates values.

The first calculated value is the NRV that can be found in column *F* in figure 3.12. The calculation of this value is summarized in a graphical mode in figure 3.13.

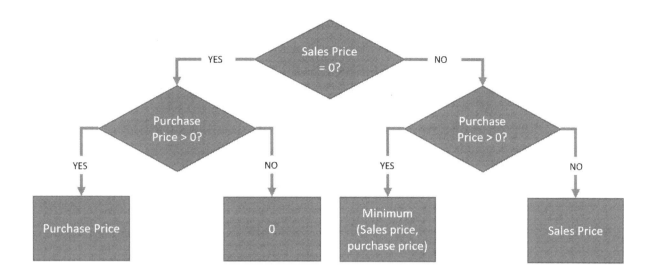

Figure 3.13 *Calculation of NRV*

Figure 3.13 shows that a check for whether or not a sales price other than $0 exists is made for each item. In addition to this first sales price check, a secondary check for the existence of a purchase price is made. Depending on the existence of a sales or purchase price, a decision—which value to use as the proxy for the NRV—is made. The different decision options are shown in the squared boxes that can be identified at the bottom of figure 3.13.

The reason for the dual check of an existing sales and purchase price shown in figure 3.13 is based on the fact that items might be purchased and sold at the same time and consequently have both prices set up. If this is the case—if an item has a purchase and sales price configured—a question arises: Which of those prices should be used as the proxy for the NRV? This question is answered here in the way that the minimum of those two prices serves as a proxy for the NRV. For additional details, please see the different calculation branches in figure 3.13.

The next calculation that is made in the last Excel worksheet relates to the cost amount in column *I* in figure 3.12. This cost amount is calculated as the quotient of the summarized cost amount and the summarized quantity of an item.

Note Dividing the summarized costs by the summarized quantity of an item results in an average cost-price (*AVG Cost*) that is used as a proxy for an item's cost-price. To avoid allowing outliers to influence and distort the calculation of this cost-price, an additional check that excludes negative calculation results is put in place.

With the NRV and the cost value specified, the LoCoM price is calculated in column *J* in figure 3.12, based on the calculation principle shown in figure 3.14.

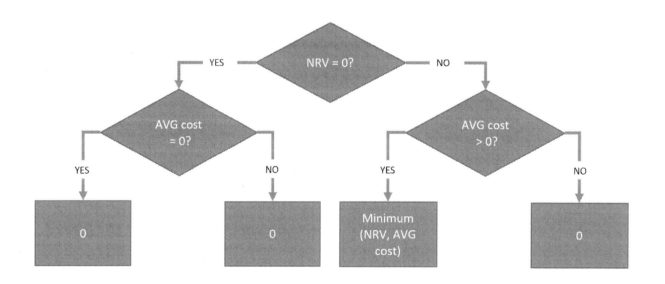

Figure 3.14 *Calculation of LoCoM price*

The LoCoM calculation principle shown in figure 3.14 illustrates that a LoCoM price is calculated only if an NRV and an AVG cost amount exist. If one of those values does not exist, an NRV of $0 is used.

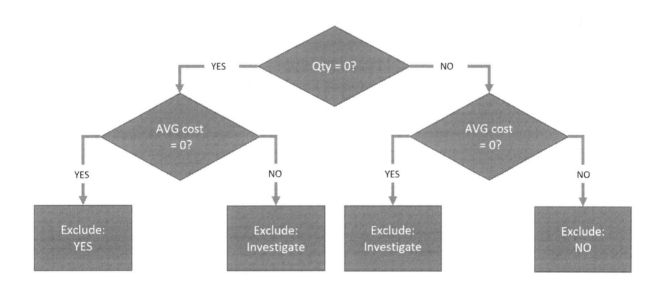

The LoCoM value that is shown in column *K* in figure 3.12 is calculated by multiplying the LoCoM price with the quantity of the item that is shown in column *G*.

The Excel table column denominated *Exclude* is included in the table shown in figure 3.12 to identify outliers and to make inventory managers aware of those outliers. Please see figure 3.15. The identifiers used for the outliers are

- *YES*, if an item does not have an inventory quantity and cost amount;

- *Investigate,* if an item has no inventory quantity but an inventory cost amount or vice versa; and

- *No,* in all other cases.

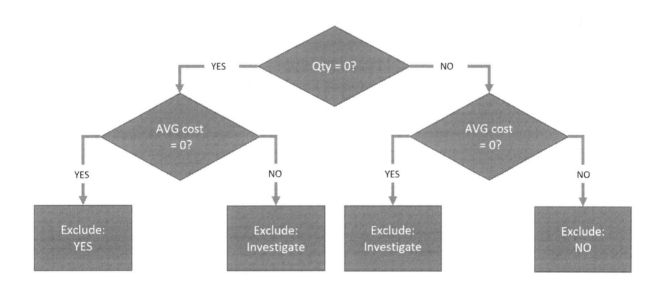

Figure 3.15 *Identification of outliers—LoCoM*

Finally, the last column in figure 3.12 calculates the required adjustment amount as the difference between the cost amount in column *H* and the LoCoM value in column *K*. This adjustment amount needs to be recorded in MSDyn365FO.

With the Excel template defined, the ER configuration can be created. The creation of this configuration is exemplified in figure 3.16 and shows that a reference to the Excel output format type—the data-model version and the data-model definition that have been set up before—is made.

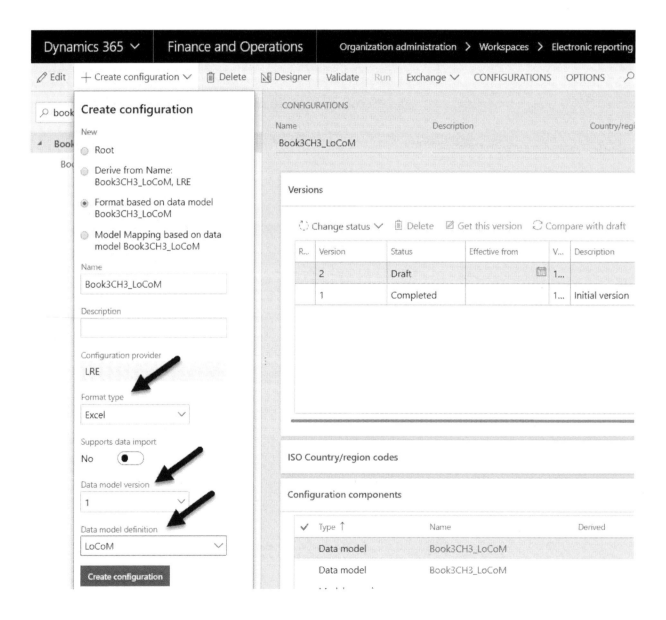

Figure 3.16 *ER LoCoM configuration*

The next step after the creation of the ER configuration is the import of the previously configured Excel template via the following import functionality (see figure 3.17), which can be found in the ER-configuration designer.

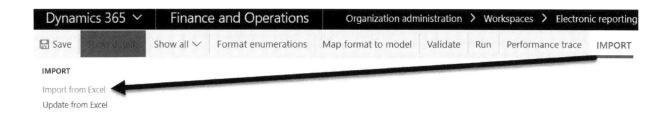

Figure 3.17 *ER configuration—import functionality*

After the Excel template is imported, one has to ensure that the data types in the ER configuration match those of the ER model, which has been set up previously (please see chapter 3.2.4.1.1. above for details). Figure 3.18 illustrates how one can ensure that the data types used in the Excel template match those of the ER model.

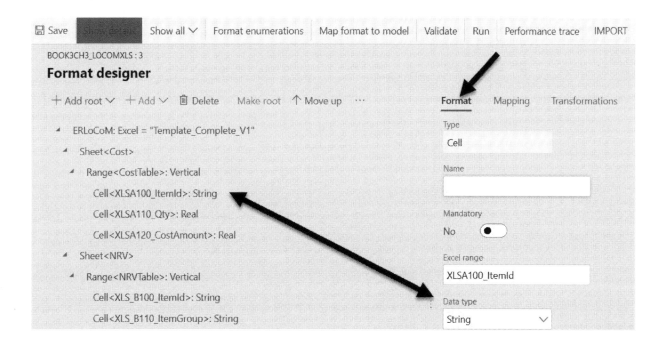

Figure 3.18 *ER configuration—data-type specification*

The last setup required in the ER-configuration-designer form is the mapping of the ER-model elements with the cells specified in the imported Excel template. This mapping is shown in figure 3.19.

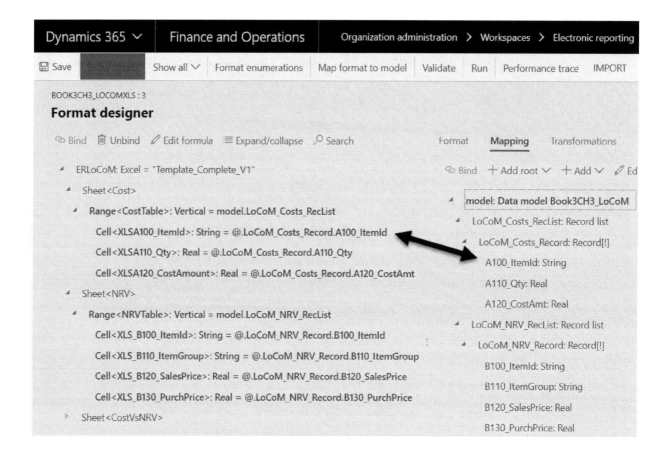

Figure 3.19 *ER configuration—mapping ER-model elements with Excel template cells*

Finally, the ER configuration status also needs to be changed to a completed stage before the ER can be used and processed.

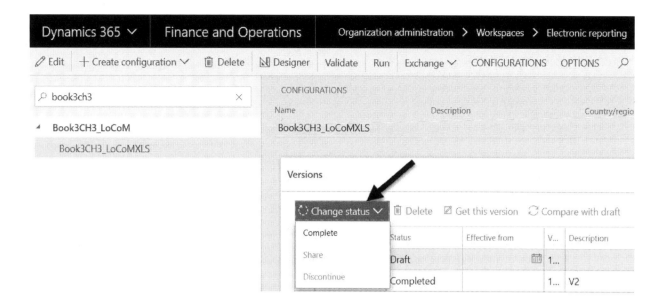

Figure 3.20 *ER configuration—status change*

After the ER model and ER configurations are completed, the ER can finally be processed by selecting the *Run* button that is available in the action pane of the ER configuration window. Please see figure 3.20 above.

When selecting the *Run* button, one can set up various filters that are applied when running the ER. In the example used, issue and receipt status filters are used to ensure that only inventory transactions that have an influence on the inventory-value are taken into consideration.

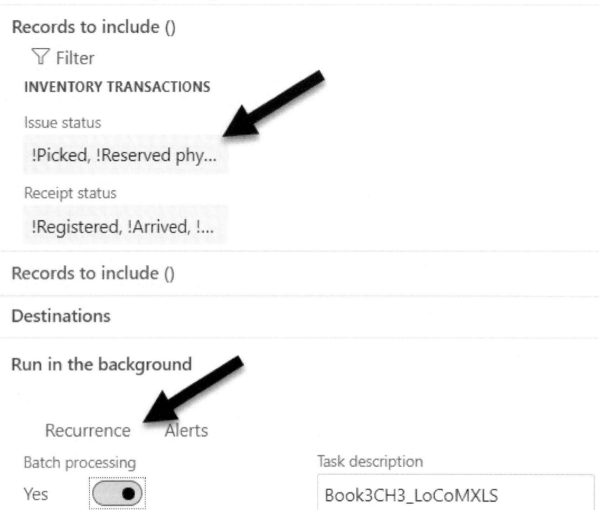

Electronic report parameters

Records to include ()

▽ Filter

INVENTORY TRANSACTIONS

Issue status

!Picked, !Reserved phy...

Receipt status

!Registered, !Arrived, !...

Records to include ()

Destinations

Run in the background

Recurrence   Alerts

Batch processing

Yes   ⬤

Task description

Book3CH3_LoCoMXLS

Figure 3.21 *Processing of ER with filters*

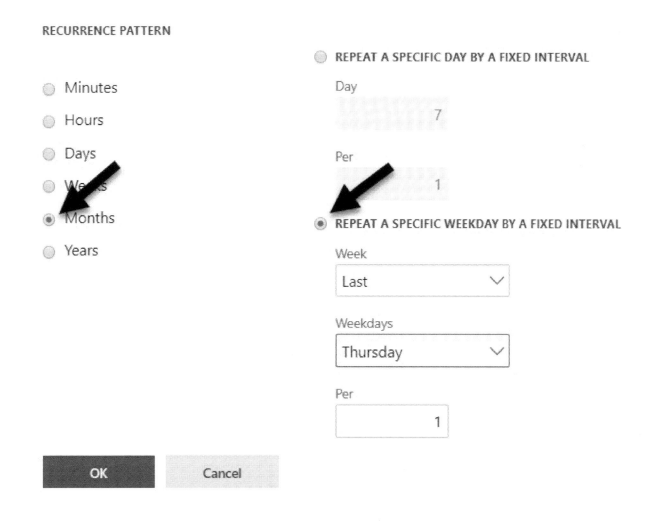

The filters applied are:

- Issue status: *!Picked, !Reserved physical, !Reserved ordered, !On order, !Quotation issue*

- Receipt status: *!Registered, !Arrived, !Ordered, !Quotation receipt*

In addition to ER filters, one can define the recurrence pattern for the generation of the ER. That is, users do not have to manually start the report by selecting the *Run* button but can have the report generated automatically in regular time intervals. Figure 3.22 below provides an example how such a time interval—which runs the report on the last Thursday of each month—can be set up.

RECURRENCE PATTERN

Minutes

Hours

Days

Weeks

Months

Years

REPEAT A SPECIFIC DAY BY A FIXED INTERVAL

Day

7

Per

1

REPEAT A SPECIFIC WEEKDAY BY A FIXED INTERVAL

Week

Last

Weekdays

Thursday

Per

1

OK   Cancel

Figure 3.22 *ER recurrence pattern for report generation*

3.2.4.2.   Step 2: SharePoint

Running the ER with the specifications shown in the previous chapter generates an Excel document that can be downloaded directly from the internet browser. To get the report automatically created in a cloud-based storage such as SharePoint, a number of additional setups are required.

The first additional setup required is a document type that establishes a link to the SharePoint document library used. Please see figure 3.23 for an example.

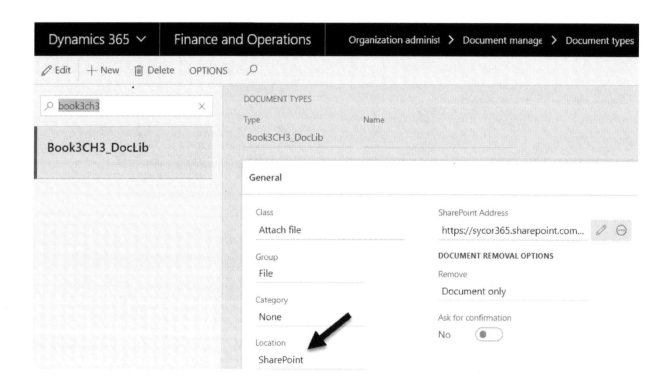

Figure 3.23 *Setup of SharePoint-related document type*

The next additional setup required relates to the electronic-reporting destination form, where one has to establish a link between the ER and the (SharePoint) document type. Figures 3.24 and 3.25 illustrate this setup.

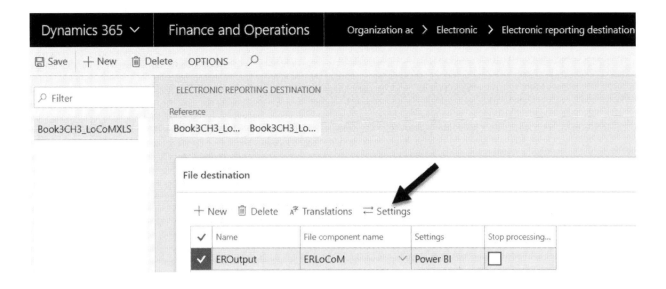

Figure 3.24 *Linkage of ER configuration to document type (1)*

Destination settings

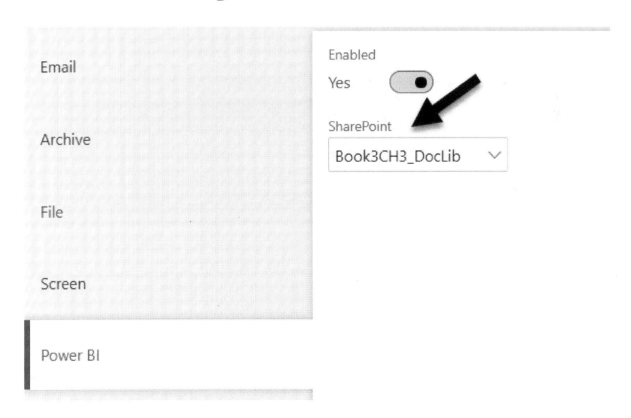

Figure 3.25 *Linkage of ER configuration to document type (2)*

With those two additional setups in place, the defined output destination defaults when the ER is generated (see figure 3.26), and the report output can finally be identified in the selected SharePoint location (see figure 3.27) after the report has been processed.

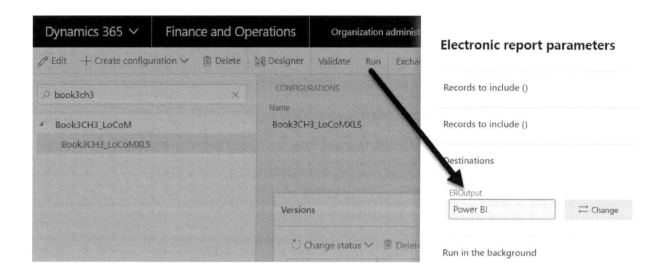

Figure 3.26 *ER with defaulting SharePoint-output location*

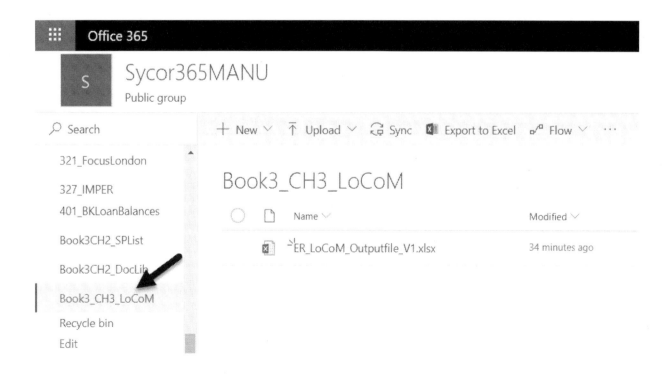

Figure 3.27 *ER Excel output file stored on SharePoint*

124

3.2.4.3.   Step 3: MS-Flow

After the ER Excel output file has been generated or updated on SharePoint, the data recorded in this file can be accessed and processed further by MS-Flow. In the following, a simplified MS-Flow process is used that consists of the following MS-Flow steps *A* to *K*.

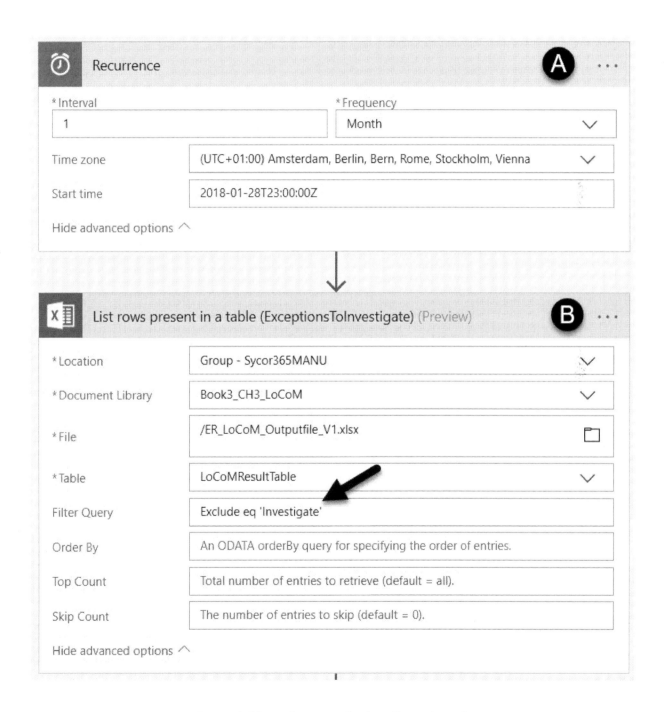

Figure 3.28 *LoCoM—MS-Flow Steps* A *and* B

Figure 3.28 shows that the MS-Flow starts with a recurrence trigger in step *A*. This recurrence trigger ensures that the different MS-Flow steps are processed in a regular, recurring time interval.

Note Please note that the recurrence pattern for the generation of the ER that is shown in figure 3.22 needs to be aligned with the MS-Flow recurrence trigger that is displayed in figure 3.28 to ensure that the most current data are processed.

The second MS-Flow step, step *B*, filters those ER data from the ER Excel output file that need a detailed investigation by the inventory manager because the items either have no inventory quantity but have an inventory cost value specified, or vice versa. The filter that is applied in figure 3.28 can be identified by the arrow and shows that only those records that have *Investigate* specified in the *Exclude* column of the ER Excel output file are extracted in this step.

The next MS-Flow step, step *C*, converts the filtered data into an HTML file, which is subsequently attached to an email that is sent to the inventory manager in step *D*.

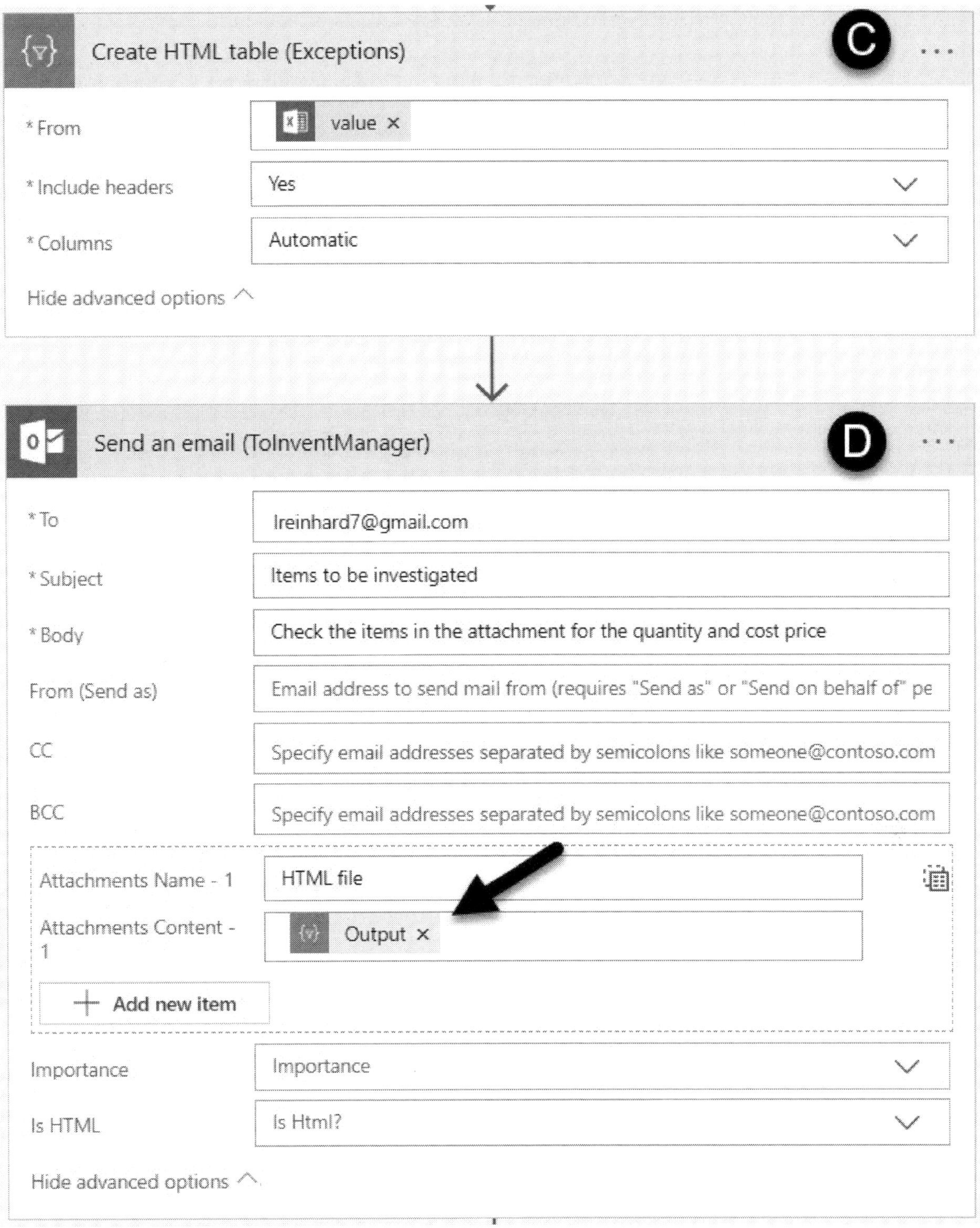

Figure 3.29 *LoCoM—MS-Flow Steps* C *and* D

After the inventory manager is informed about the items that need a detailed investigation, the item's actual reevaluation MS-Flow process starts in step *E* by filtering the records that are classified as nonexceptional. Once those records are filtered, a general ledger (GL) journal is created in step *F* by referring to the *LedgerJournalHeaders* data entity.

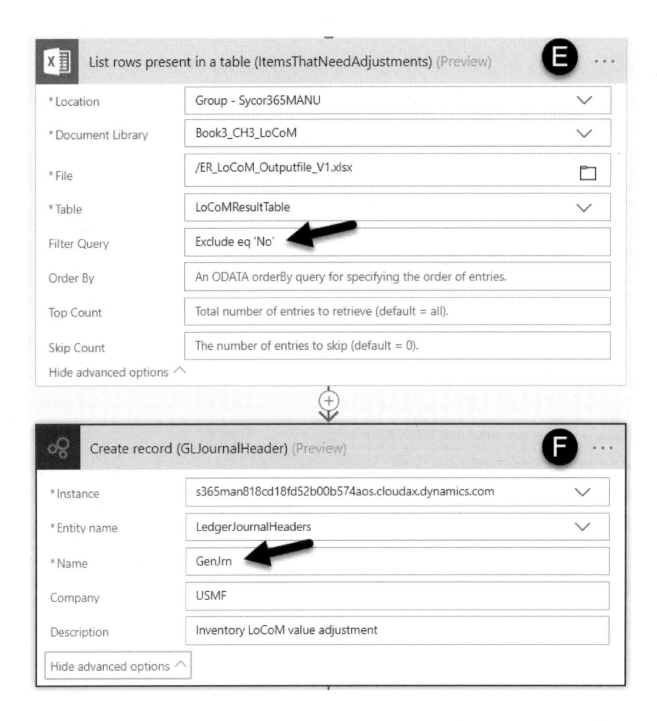

Figure 3.30 *LoCoM—MS-Flow Steps* E *and* F

Once the journal header is created, the journal lines need to be created. Creating the journal lines is realized by making use of an *ApplyToEach* MS-Flow action in step *G* that starts with the composition of the adjustment amount from the ER Excel output file (see step *H*).

Note
The composition step *H* is needed because the Excel data—which are transferred to MS-Flow with the help of the Excel data action in step *E*—are recorded as text or so-called string values that cannot directly be used in conditions and other MS-Flow actions without further modification.

The aforementioned condition and data modification can be identified in step *I*, where the inventory-adjustment amount from step *H* is converted into a floating number with the help of a MS-Flow expression. The converted adjustment amount is then compared to an absolute amount of -$10, which has been specified by the author. For details, please see the following figure.

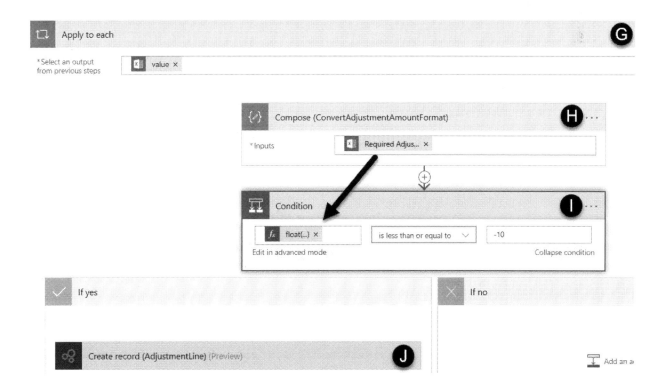

Figure 3.31 *LoCoM—MS-Flow Steps G to J*

Note The reason for implementing the conditional step in the MS-Flow is to avoid the need to post small inventory-adjustment amounts (i.e., those that are smaller than $10).

Once all small inventory-adjustment amounts have been excluded by the condition used in step *1*, the inventory-journal adjustment lines can be created with the help of the *LedgerJournalLines* data entity. The following two figures detail how those journal lines are created.

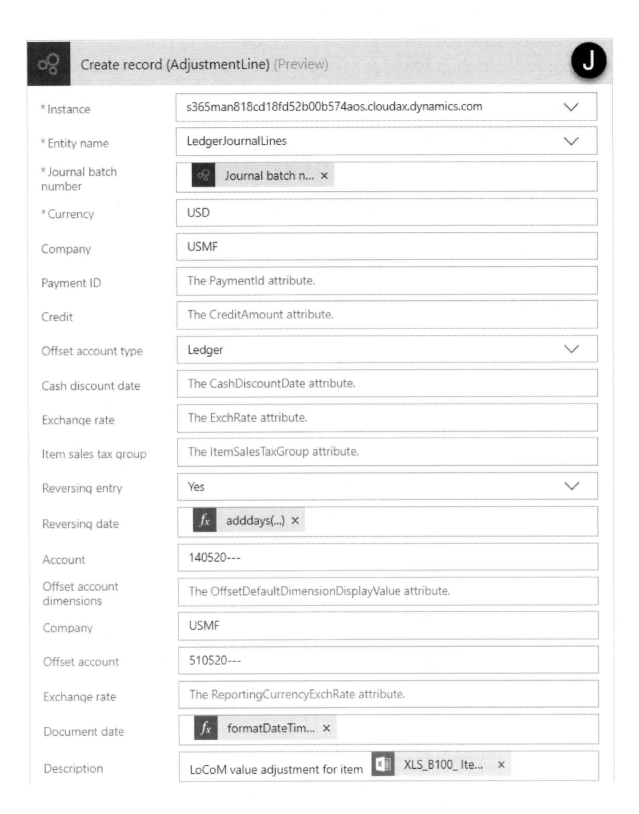

Figure 3.32 *LoCoM—MS-Flow Step* J *(1)*

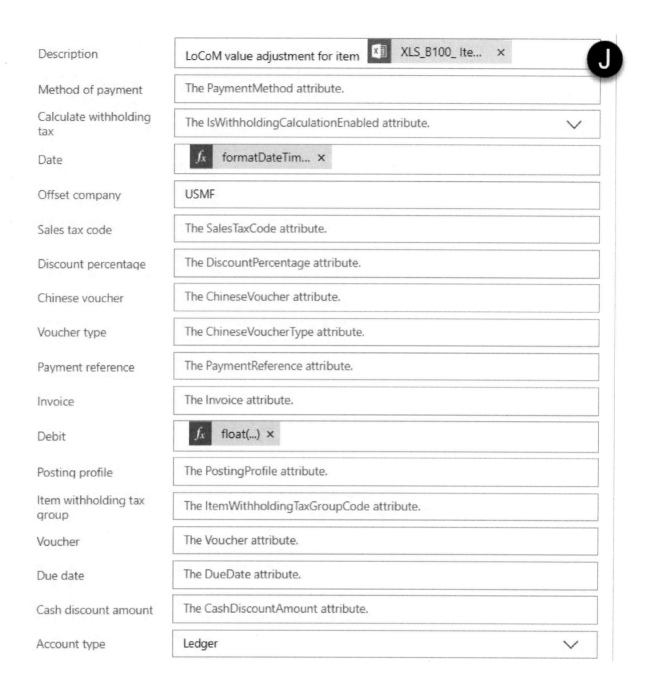

Description	LoCoM value adjustment for item [×] XLS_B100_ Ite... ×	J
Method of payment	The PaymentMethod attribute.	
Calculate withholding tax	The IsWithholdingCalculationEnabled attribute. ⌄	
Date	[fx] formatDateTim... ×	
Offset company	USMF	
Sales tax code	The SalesTaxCode attribute.	
Discount percentage	The DiscountPercentage attribute.	
Chinese voucher	The ChineseVoucher attribute.	
Voucher type	The ChineseVoucherType attribute.	
Payment reference	The PaymentReference attribute.	
Invoice	The Invoice attribute.	
Debit	[fx] float(...) ×	
Posting profile	The PostingProfile attribute.	
Item withholding tax group	The ItemWithholdingTaxGroupCode attribute.	
Voucher	The Voucher attribute.	
Due date	The DueDate attribute.	
Cash discount amount	The CashDiscountAmount attribute.	
Account type	Ledger ⌄	

Figure 3.33 *LoCoM—MS-Flow Step* J *(2)*

Please note that the journal lines are created with the help of an expression—*formatDateTime (utcnow(), 'yyyy-MM-dd')*—that refers to the current system date. In other words, the posting date (*Date*) of the different journal lines is determined by the date MS-Flow is run. In the example used, this is the twenty-eighth day of a month, as specified by the start time and recurrence pattern defined in the MS-Flow trigger. (Please see step *A* in figure 3.28 further above.)

In line with the IFRS accounting regulations, all inventory adjustments recorded are reversed in the following month. This reversal is realized by setting the *reversing entry* parameter to *yes* and by specifying a reversing-date value.

Note The reversing-date value shown in figure 3.32 is created by making use of the expression *adddays(utcnow(),8,'yyyy-MM-dd')*. This expression reverses the inventory adjustment posting eight days after it is created. The eight-days date difference was selected by the author because different months in a year have different numbers of days.

Next, one can identify the inventory-adjustment account 140520 and the related profit-and-loss account 510520—which records the corresponding expense—from figure 3.32. Those accounts are used for posting the inventory adjustments and reversals and can be identified and analyzed in all standard MSDyn365FO reports and inquiry forms.

Finally, to ensure that the posting of the inventory-value-adjustment journals is not interrupted by rounding issues related to the adjustment amount, the adjustment amount—which is recorded in the debit field in figure 3.33—is rounded to whole dollars by making use of the following expression: *float(first(split(string(float(outputs('Compose_(ConvertAdjustmentAmount Format)'))),'.'))).*

Note The expression used for rounding the adjustment amount converts the Excel record first into a floating number and then into a string, because the string value can subsequently be split by the decimal separator. Once the adjustment amount is split, its first part is converted back into a floating number and used for creating the journal lines.

The last MS-Flow step, step *K*, is shown in figure 3.34 and copies the used ER Excel output file to an archive folder to allow internal and external auditors a reproduction of the inventory-value-adjustment amounts posted.

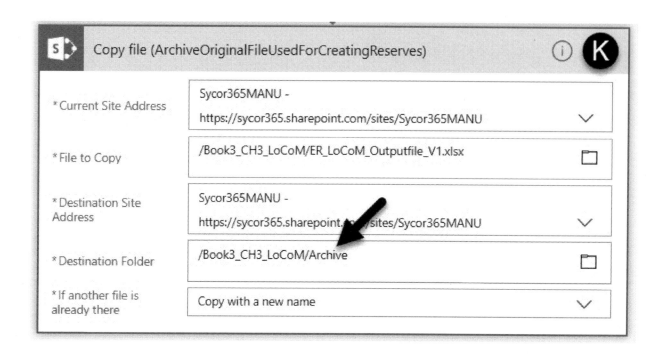

Figure 3.34 *LoCoM—MS-Flow Step* K

3.2.4.4.   Step 4: MSDyn365FO

Processing the MS-Flow results in the creation of a general ledger journal similar to the one illustrated in figure 3.35 that can be validated and posted either manually or by making use of the batch-posting functionality.

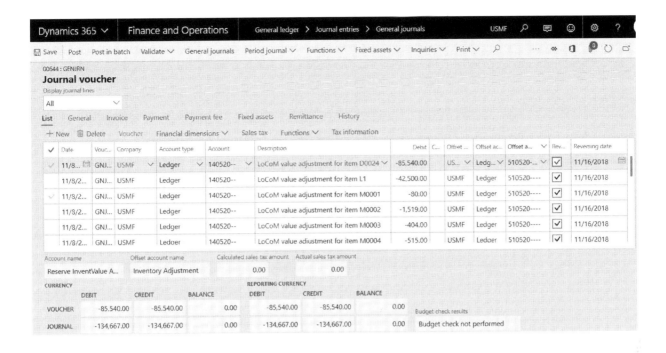

Figure 3.35 *Resulting inventory-value-adjustment journal*

The inventory-value-adjustment journal in figure 3.35 shows posting and reversal dates, which are different from what one would expect based on the previously illustrated setup steps. Those differences can be explained by the fact that the MS-Flow was triggered manually for demonstration purposes rather than by the automatic recurrence trigger.

3.3.   Summary

This chapter illustrated how the LoCoM inventory-valuation principle can be incorporated into MSDyn365FO with the help of ER, SharePoint, and MS-Flow. Before moving on to the next topic in chapter four, it has to be noted that the example illustrated in this chapter represents a simplified example that can be enriched, for example, by additional ER-report information extracted or MS-Flow steps. Irrespective of the illustrated opportunities that can be used for improving the process, the major takeaway of this chapter is that no system modifications or specialized ISV solution are needed to incorporate the LoCoM valuation principle in MSDyn365FO.

4. Journal Imports

This chapter will focus on and compare the different functionalities that are available in MSDyn365FO for journal imports. Due to the large number of journals that are available in MSDyn365FO, and because of space limitations, a focus on general ledger (GL) journal imports is made in the following.

4.1. Journal Templates

4.1.1. Required Setup

A first option for journal imports is the use of standard journal templates that are available for most journals used in MSDyn365FO. Before GL journals can be imported, default and ledger-dimension integration setups have to be made. Those setups relate to main accounts and financial dimensions that can be imported with the help of journal templates. Figures 4.1 and 4.2 show the respective integration setup forms.

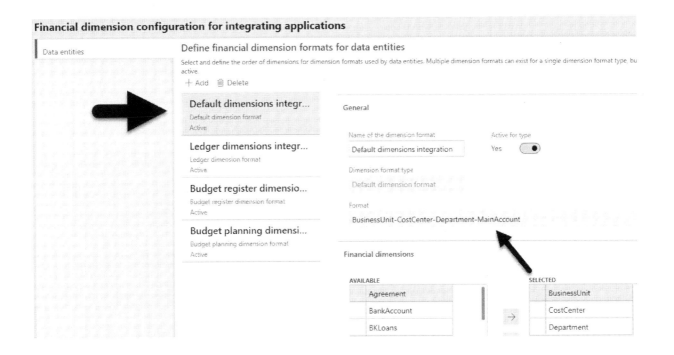

Figure 4.1 *Default-dimension integration setup*

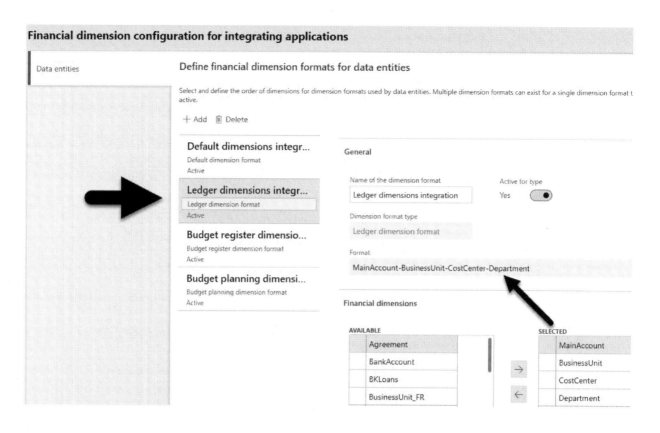

Figure 4.2 *Ledger-dimension integration setup*

Note The default-dimension integration setup is required for importing default dimension values that are related to a customer or vendor account, for example. Financial dimension values cannot directly be entered in combination with the customer or vendor account field. Ledger-dimension integration setups are needed for importing financial dimension values that are directly related to ledger accounts.

Note The financial dimension integration setups shown in figure 4.1 and figure 4.2 are not company-specific but global, meaning that these settings apply to all journal imports irrespective of the company account where those imports are executed.

4.1.2.   Process Demonstration

4.1.2.1.   General Import Process

With those two setups in place, GL journals can be imported by (*a*) creating a new journal and (*b*)

opening the journal lines in Excel with the *general-journal-line-entry* template. Those steps are

illustrated in figure 4.3.

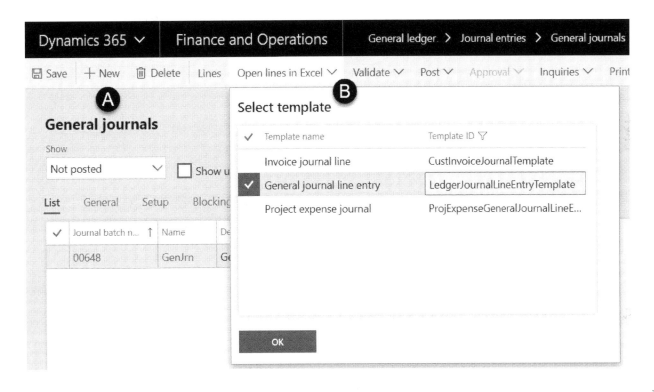

Figure 4.3 *GL journal import (1)*

Once the template selection has been confirmed with *OK*, an Excel import template opens and

requires the user to log in to MSDyn365FO.

The logged-in user can be identified in the upper-right-hand corner of the Excel import template

and is highlighted by an arrow in figure 4.4.

139

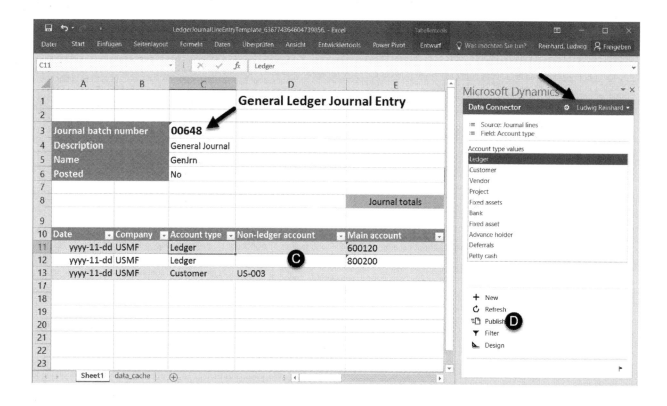

Figure 4.4 *GL journal import (2)*

After the user has logged in to MSDyn365FO via the Excel data connector, the journal lines can

be entered (*C*) and published (*D*). Publishing the journal lines recorded in the Excel template updates

the MSDyn365FO journal lines, which can be identified in the next figure.

Figure 4.5 *GL journal import (3)*

140

4.1.2.2.   Importing Financial Dimension Values

The illustrated GL journal import has a number of limitations. The first limitation is that only a number of account types are supported for the journal import. Those account types are as follows: ledger, customer, vendor, and bank. Project and fixed asset related transactions cannot be imported with the help of the *general-journal-line-entry* template but require other journal-template types to be used.

A second limitation of the default *GL journal-line-entry* import template is that the financial dimensions, such as the cost center or department information, cannot be recorded directly in the main account field that is shown in figure 4.4. This second limitation can be overcome by modifying the design of the GL journal import template, which is exemplified in figure 4.6.

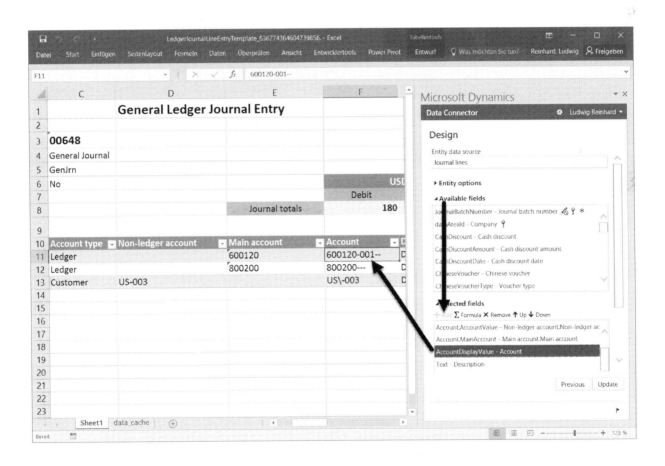

Figure 4.6 *Modification of the GL journal import template*

141

Please note that the template modification shown above adds an account field to the Excel template line section that allows entering main account and financial dimension information—separated by a dash—in a single field. Publishing the information recorded in the modified Excel template updates the financial dimensions in the corresponding GL journal in MSDyn365FO. Figure 4.7 exemplifies this.

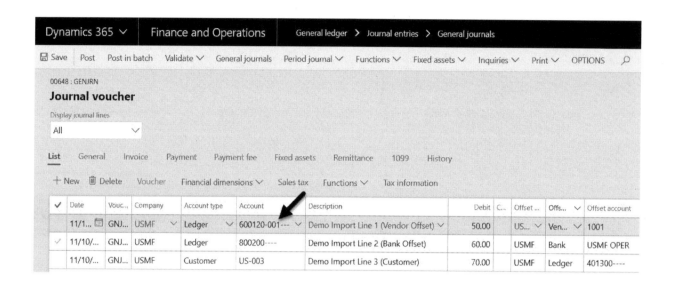

Figure 4.7 *GL journal import (4)*

Entering main accounts and financial dimensions in a single field necessitates knowledge of the order and sequence of the main account and financial dimension combinations, because no supporting lookup functionality is available for the account field that has been added to the Excel template. Stated differently, users have to know the configured ledger-dimension integration setup (see figure 4.2) by heart.

Note An alternative to entering main accounts and financial dimensions in a single account field is adding additional financial dimension columns into the Excel template. Adding those columns requires a system modification and cannot be achieved by a simple design change similar to the one that is illustrated in figure 4.6 above. Details of the required system modification can be found on the following website: https://docs.microsoft.com/en-us/dynamics365/unified-operations/dev-itpro/financial/dimensions-overview.

4.1.2.3. Creating New Journals

The previously illustrated GL journal import process not only allows creating and uploading journal lines in already existing journals but also supports the creation of new journals. Creating new journals can be realized by moving the cursor to the journal-template header section and by selecting the new button, as exemplified in section *E* of figure 4.8.

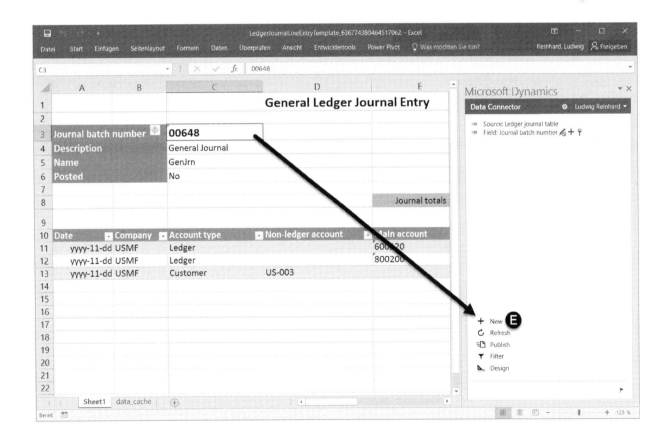

Figure 4.8 *Create new GL journals from template (1)*

Selecting the new button in section *E* of figure 4.8 removes the information in the journal-template header section and allows users to enter the data required for creating a new GL journal. This can be seen in template section *F*, which is shown in figure 4.9.

Once all necessary data that are required for generating a new GL journal have been recorded in section *F*, the journal-header data can be published to MSDyn365FO by selecting the *publish* button in section *G* of the template. As a result, a new GL journal is created in MSDyn365FO. The newly created GL journal can be identified in figure 4.10 below.

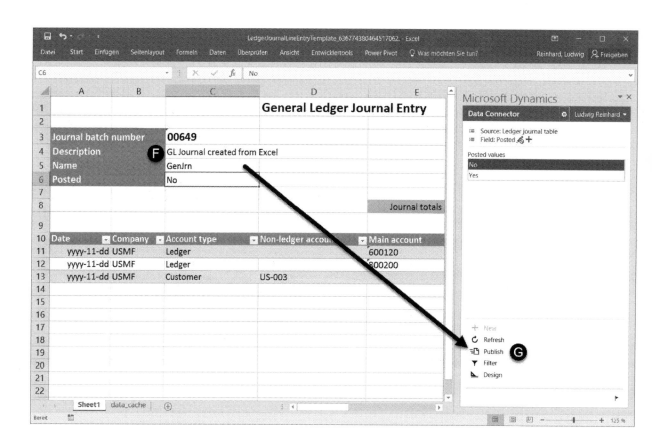

Figure 4.9 *Create new GL journals from template (2)*

144

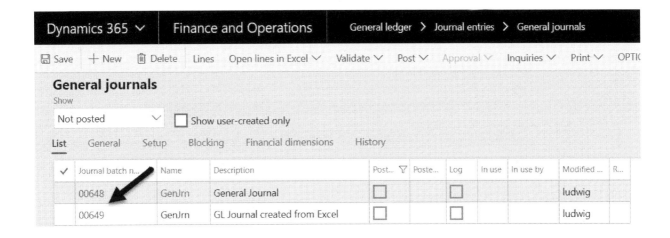

Figure 4.10 *Create new GL journals from template (3)*

Before one can enter lines in the newly created journal, the journal-line filter—which still references the old journal batch number—has to be changed and updated. Please see section *H* in figure 4.11 for details.

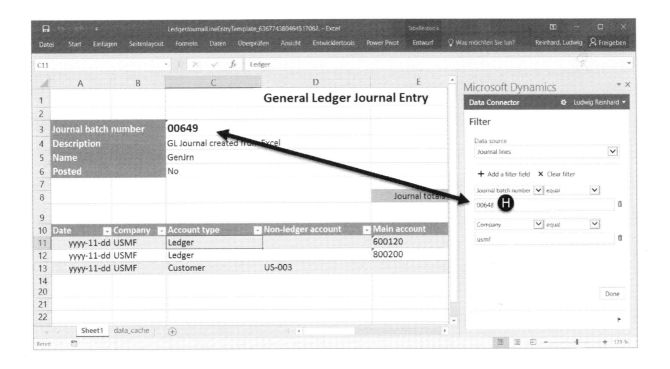

Figure 4.11 *Create new GL journals from template (4)*

Once this update has also been made, new journal lines can be created (seen in section *I*) and published in the same way as shown further above.

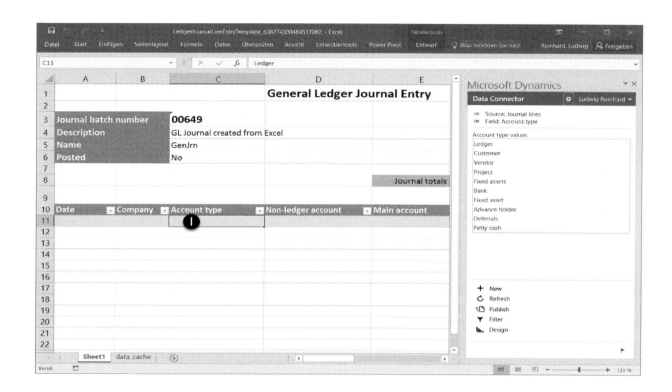

Figure 4.12 *Create new GL journals from template (5)*

4.1.2.4. Lost Personalizations

A final limitation of the general-journal-line-entry template introduced in this subchapter is that all personalizations that are made to the Excel template are lost once it is closed. To retain all necessary design changes, a new template has to be created—or, alternatively, the existing default template has to be changed and replaced. In the following, the creation of a new general-journal-line-entry template is illustrated.

Creating a new general-journal-line-entry template can be achieved by downloading the existing (default) template from the document-templates section in MSDyn365FO. This is illustrated in figure 4.13.

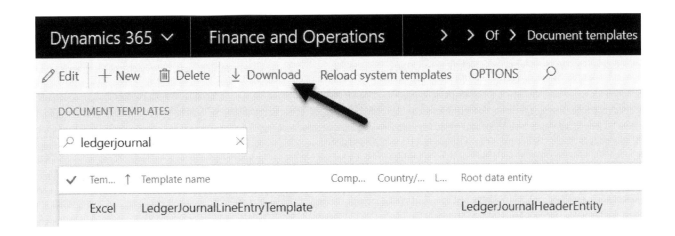

Figure 4.13 *Download default general-journal-line-entry template*

Once this is downloaded, the user needs to log in to MSDyn365FO via the Excel data connector before design changes can be made. In the following, two simple design changes are realized: first, a change to the name of the template; and second, the addition of the account field in the journal-lines section. Please see figure 4.14 for details.

Note For an easier identification of the changes made, arrows and the initials of the author (LRE) have been added into figure 4.14.

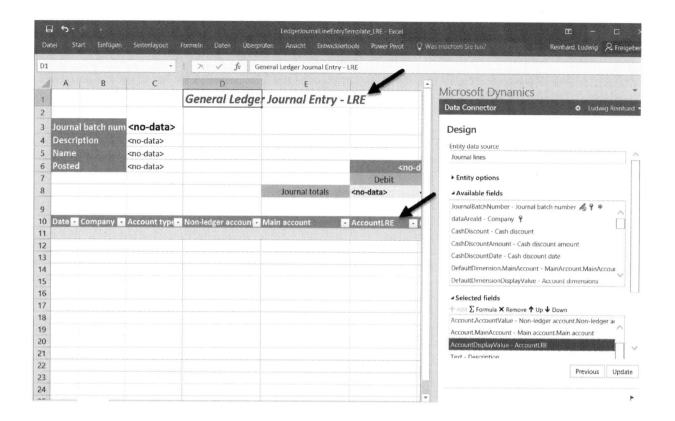

Figure 4.14 *Design changes—general-journal-line-entry template*

After all required changes are completed, the modified general-journal-line-entry template needs to be saved before it can be made available for usage in MSDyn365FO through an upload in the document-template section.

The upload process of the newly designed or modified template is exemplified in figure 4.15 and requires the utmost care when it comes to the selection of the template name that automatically defaults from the selected file name. What needs to be taken care of specifically is that the template name matches the previously downloaded template name exactly. This exact matching requirement necessitates that all ending numbers, letters, symbols, and so on that default from the file name are removed. Without the removal of those suffixes, the upload and provision of the newly created template does not work.

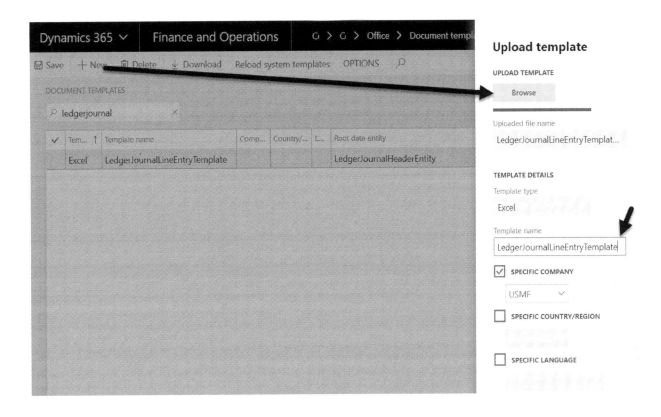

Figure 4.15 *Upload newly created general-journal-line-entry template*

Note Please note that the modified Excel template is uploaded with a restriction to a specific company (USMF). In other words, the design changes made to the general-journal-line-entry template are available in this company only. This restriction has been made because the upload cannot be realized without having a specific company, country, region, or language selected, unless the original Excel template is deleted.

Figure 4.14 shows the newly uploaded Excel template, for which the display name *LRE Template* has been entered.

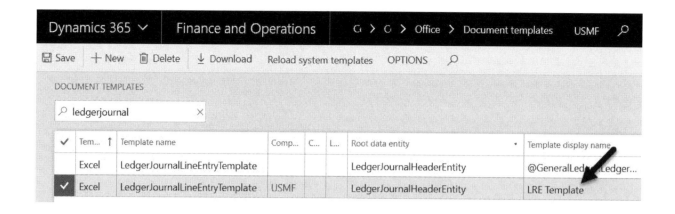

Figure 4.16 *New general-journal-line-entry template*

With the upload, the new template becomes available for selection in the general ledger journal template section. This is exemplified in the next two figures.

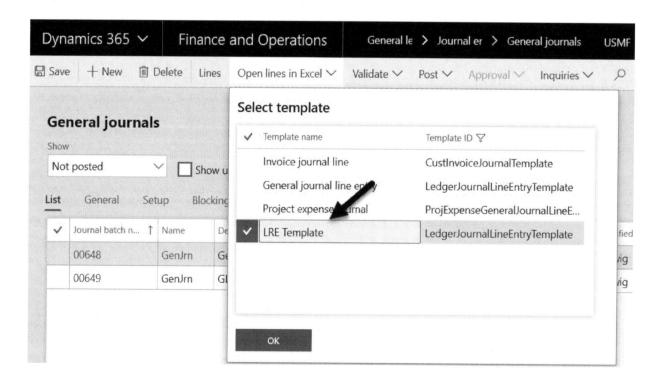

Figure 4.17 *Selection of new general-journal-line-entry template*

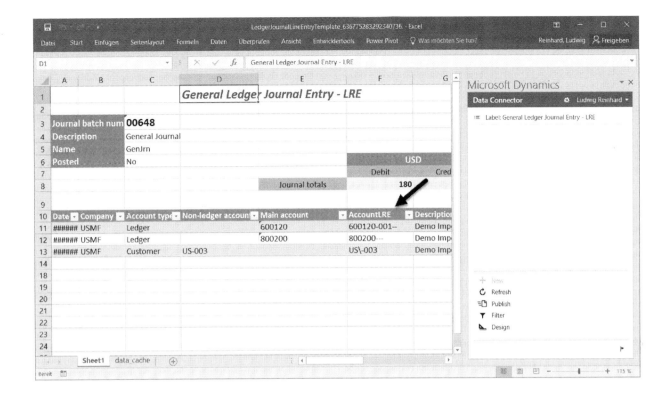

Figure 4.18 *Data entry in new general-journal-line-entry template*

151

4.2. PowerApps and MS-Flow

4.2.1. General Concept

An alternative to using journal templates for preparing and uploading accounting information into MSDyn365FO journals is the combined use of PowerApps and MS-Flow for the journal-import process. Figure 4.19 provides a high-level overview of this import process, which is described in detail in the following subchapters.

Figure 4.19 *High-level overview of the PowerApps and MS-Flow journal-import process*

Figure 4.19 illustrates that the import process starts with the preparation of the journal lines in Excel that shall be imported into a MSDyn365FO journal. The Excel document is then saved in a cloud-based SharePoint document library. Next, a PowerApp that is embedded in MSDyn365FO is used for triggering an MS-Flow, which creates the journal and the journal lines in MSDyn365FO. The last process step consists of posting the created journal.

In the following chapter, chapter 4.2.2., the setups required for the illustrated import process are described in detail, and then a process demonstration is provided in chapter 4.2.3.

4.2.2.   Required Setup

4.2.2.1.   Set Up Excel Journal Template

As shown in figure 4.19 above, the alternative journal-import process starts with the preparation of the

journal lines that need to be imported into MSDyn365FO. This preparation requires—at a

minimum—the specification of all fields that are required for posting general ledger journal transactions

in MSDyn365FO. Figure 4.20 and figure 4.21 exemplify the information used for the following process

demonstration.

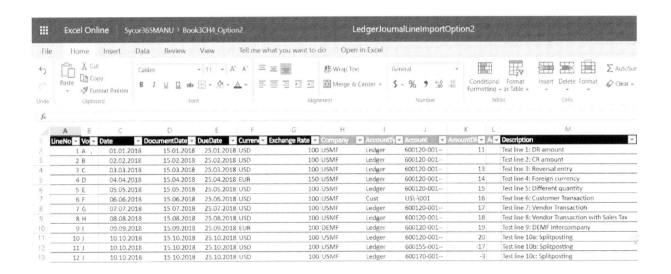

Figure 4.20 *Journal import template (1)*

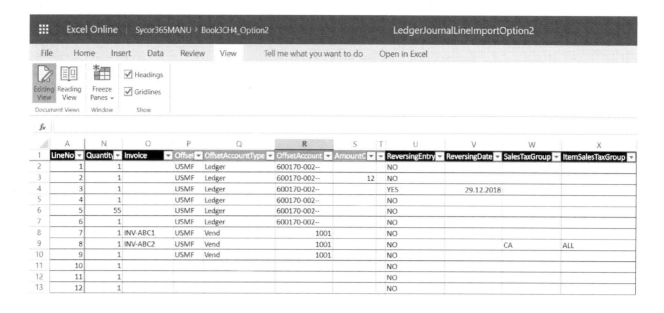

Figure 4.21 *Journal import template (2)*

Note Not all of the columns and data shown the previous two figures are required for creating and posting general ledger journals in MSDyn365FO. As an example, the sales-tax-group and item-sales-tax-group information shown in the last two columns in figure 4.21 are optional fields that are included for demonstration purposes only.

Note The data prepared in the Excel journal-import template shown in figure 4.20 and figure 4.21 need to be embedded into an Excel table to allow the subsequent processes to extract the prepared data.

4.2.2.2. Create MS-Flow for Data-Import Processing

The second setup step required relates to the setup of the MS-Flow process steps, which are shown in the following figures.

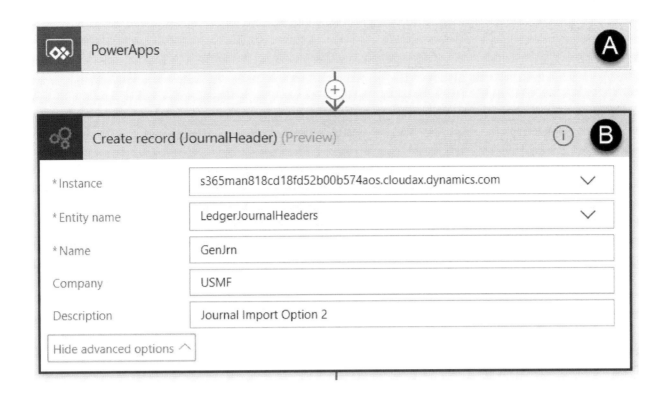

Figure 4.22 *MS-Flow journal import (1)*

Figure 4.22 shows that the MS-Flow process is initialized by a PowerApp in step *A*, which is described in detail further below. Once that MS-Flow is started, a general journal header is created in step *B*.

Note Please note that the creation of this journal is made with the help of the *LedgerJournalHeaders* entity and by selecting the journal name *GenJrn*.

The third process, step *C*, makes use of an Excel action step, which extracts all lines from the journal-import template that has been prepared.

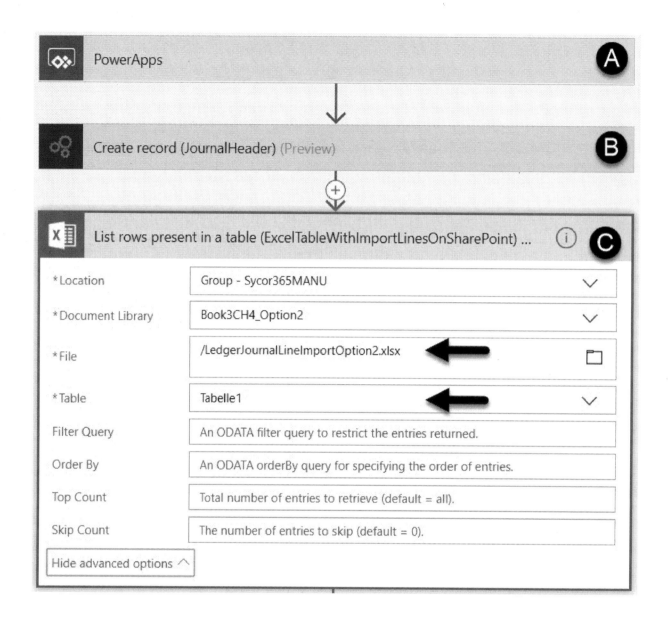

Figure 4.23 *MS-Flow journal import (2)*

The following MS-Flow steps (*D* to *L*) are required because the data extracted in step *C* have a text-value format, which cannot directly be used for the creation of the journal lines in step *M*. Please note that each of the composition steps (*D* to *L*) simply hold the respective Excel value that for demonstration purposes is included in the composition-step name. Those values are later on converted with the help of MS-Flow expressions and are used for the creation of the journal lines in step *M*.

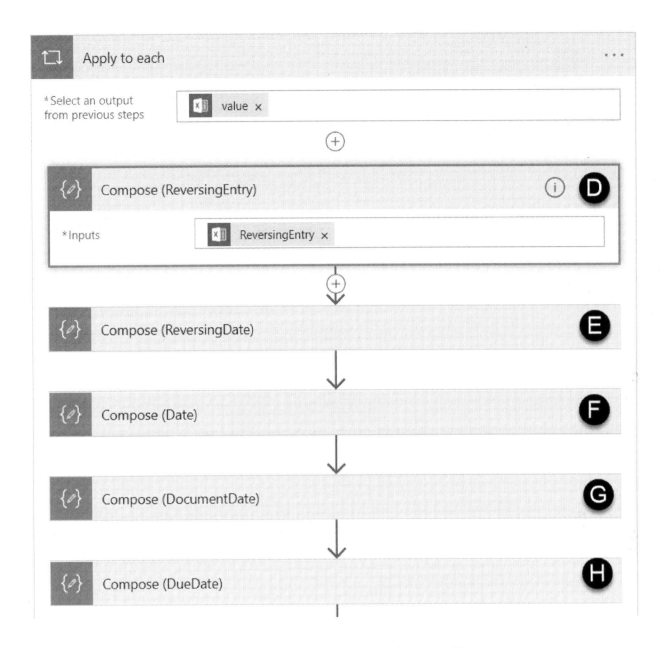

Figure 4.24 *MS-Flow journal import (3)*

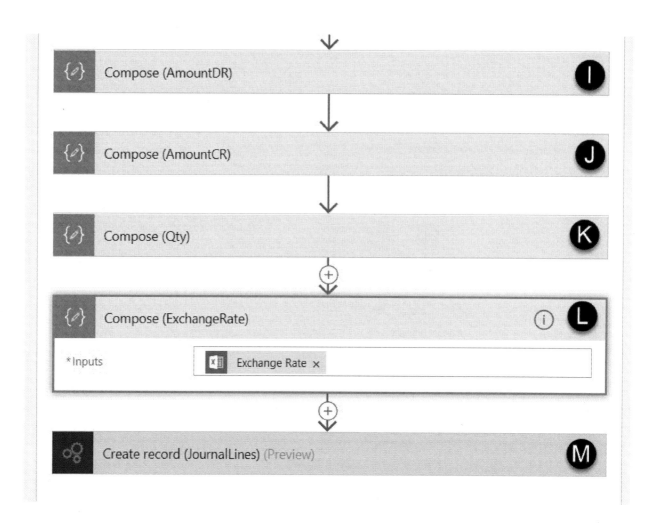

Figure 4.25 *MS-Flow journal import (4)*

The last MS-Flow step, step *M*, creates the journal lines with the help of the *LedgerJournalLines* entity. Many of the text-value fields that were extracted in step *C* can directly be entered in the *create record (JournalLines)* MS-Flow action step. Those fields can be identified by the Excel icon shown in front of the different elements in figure 4.26, figure 4.27, and figure 4.28.

In addition to the fields that can directly be entered in the *create record* MS-Flow action step, a number of fields—which can be identified by the starting *fx* icon in the next figures—need a prior format conversion before they can be used in the import process.

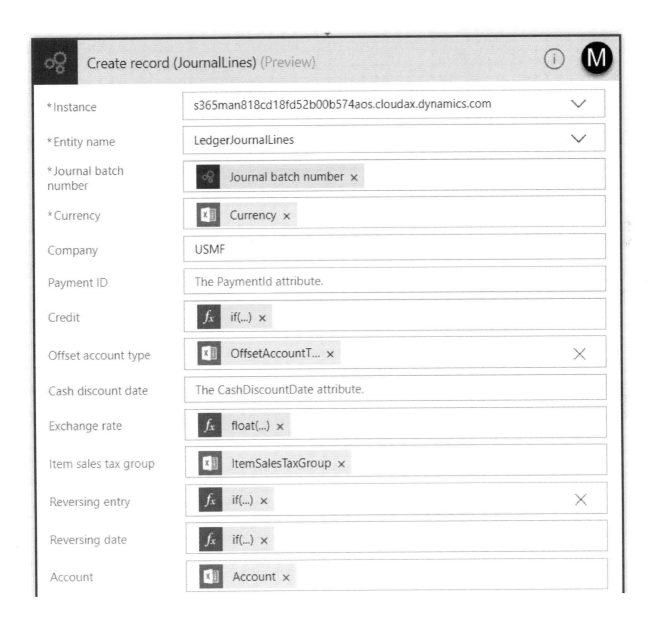

The MS-Flow expressions that are used for the required format conversions are shown right below the following figures where the expressions are used.

Figure 4.26 *MS-Flow journal import (5)*

Expressions used for format conversion:

- Credit:

  if(equals(outputs('Compose_(AmountCR)'),''),0,float(outputs('Compose_(AmountCR)')))

- Exchange rate:

  float(outputs('Compose_(ExchangeRate)'))

- Reversing entry:

  if(equals(outputs('Compose_(ReversingEntry)'),'NO'),0,1)

- Reversing date:

  if(equals(outputs('Compose_(ReversingDate)'),''),'1900-01-01T12:00:00Z',

  formatdatetime(addDays('1899-12-30',int(outputs('Compose_(ReversingDate)'))),'yyyy-MM-

  dd'))

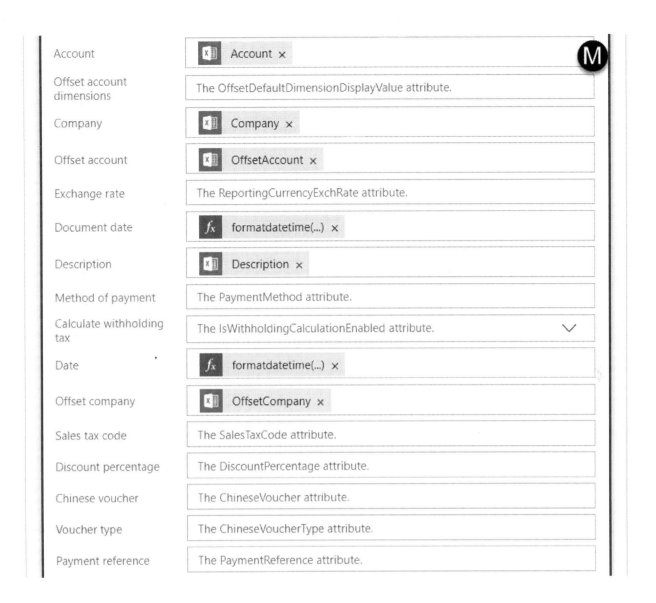

Account	Account ×
Offset account dimensions	The OffsetDefaultDimensionDisplayValue attribute.
Company	Company ×
Offset account	OffsetAccount ×
Exchange rate	The ReportingCurrencyExchRate attribute.
Document date	formatdatetime(...) ×
Description	Description ×
Method of payment	The PaymentMethod attribute.
Calculate withholding tax	The IsWithholdingCalculationEnabled attribute.
Date	formatdatetime(...) ×
Offset company	OffsetCompany ×
Sales tax code	The SalesTaxCode attribute.
Discount percentage	The DiscountPercentage attribute.
Chinese voucher	The ChineseVoucher attribute.
Voucher type	The ChineseVoucherType attribute.
Payment reference	The PaymentReference attribute.

Figure 4.27 *MS-Flow journal import (6)*

Expressions used for format conversion:

- Document date:

  formatdatetime(addDays('1899-12-30',int(outputs('Compose_(DocumentDate)'))), 'yyyy-MM-dd')

- Date:

  formatdatetime(addDays('1899-12-30',int(outputs('Compose_(Date)'))), 'yyyy-MM-dd')

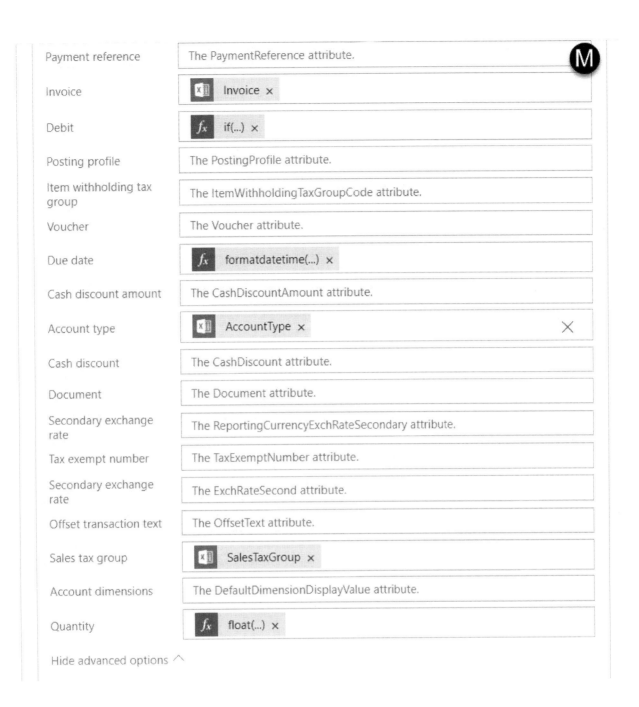

Payment reference	The PaymentReference attribute.	
Invoice	Invoice ×	
Debit	if(...) ×	
Posting profile	The PostingProfile attribute.	
Item withholding tax group	The ItemWithholdingTaxGroupCode attribute.	
Voucher	The Voucher attribute.	
Due date	formatdatetime(...) ×	
Cash discount amount	The CashDiscountAmount attribute.	
Account type	AccountType ×	×
Cash discount	The CashDiscount attribute.	
Document	The Document attribute.	
Secondary exchange rate	The ReportingCurrencyExchRateSecondary attribute.	
Tax exempt number	The TaxExemptNumber attribute.	
Secondary exchange rate	The ExchRateSecond attribute.	
Offset transaction text	The OffsetText attribute.	
Sales tax group	SalesTaxGroup ×	
Account dimensions	The DefaultDimensionDisplayValue attribute.	
Quantity	float(...) ×	

Hide advanced options ∧

Figure 4.28 *MS-Flow journal import (7)*

Expressions used for format conversion:

- Debit:

  if(equals(outputs('Compose_(AmountDR)'), ' '),0,float(outputs('Compose_(AmountDR)')))

- Due Date:

  formatdatetime(addDays('1899-12-30',int(outputs('Compose_(DueDate)'))), 'yyyy-MM-dd')

- Quantity:

  float(outputs('Compose_(Qty)'))

4.2.2.3.   Create PowerApp for Starting the MS-Flow

The aforementioned PowerApp that is used for triggering the previously demonstrated MS-Flow process is illustrated in figure 4.29. As one can identify from this figure, the PowerApp consists of a single button only (*Import Journal Lines*) that executes the MS-Flow *run* command when selected.

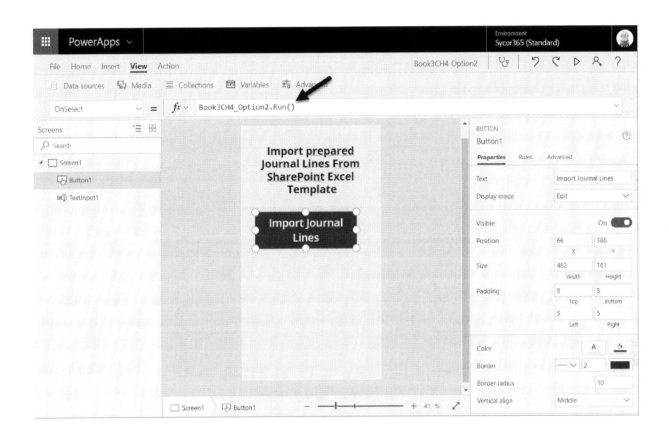

Figure 4.29 *PowerApp for starting journal import—MS-Flow*

After completing the PowerApp design, it gets embedded into MSDyn365FO by referring to the PowerApp ID. The identification of the PowerApp ID and the embedment in MSDyn365FO are illustrated in the figures 4.30 and 4.31.

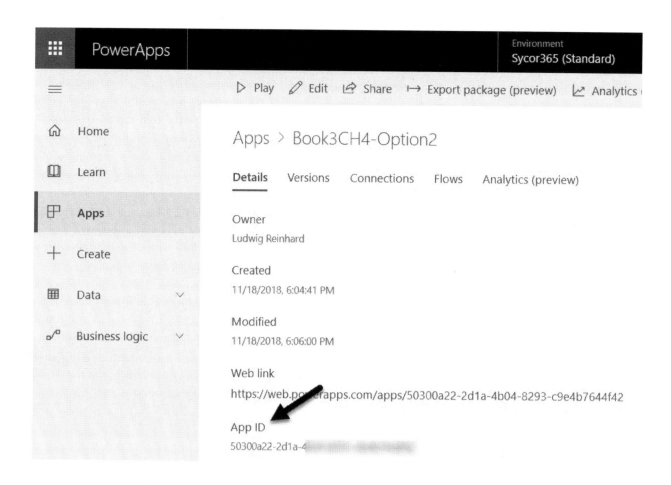

Figure 4.30 *PowerApp ID*

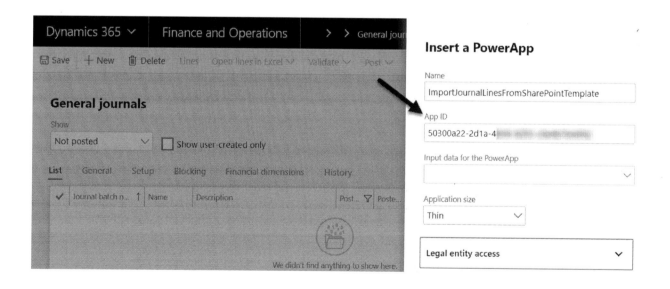

Figure 4.31 *Embedding PowerApp in MSDyn365FO*

Once the PowerApp has been embedded in MSDyn365FO, it can be selected and used for starting the MS-Flow journal import. This is illustrated in the next two figures.

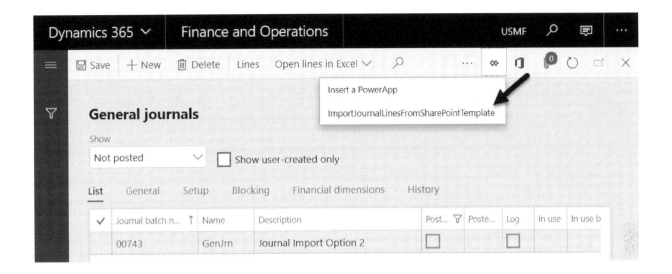

Figure 4.32 *Starting PowerApp for journal import—MS-Flow (1)*

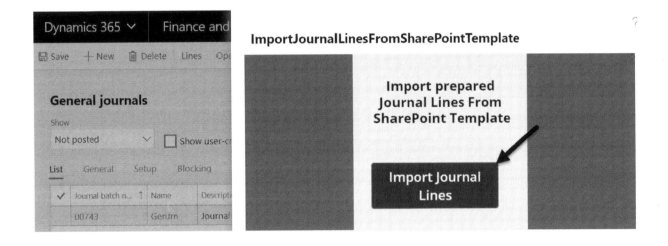

Figure 4.33 *Starting PowerApp for journal import—MS-Flow (2)*

4.2.3.   Process Demonstration

The next subchapters provide a demonstration of the steps required for the GL journal import with the help of PowerApps and MS-Flow.

4.2.3.1.   Step 1: Fill Excel Journal Template

The first step in the import process consists of preparing the journal lines that need to be imported in MSDyn365FO. The next two figures provide a number of examples that

- make use of debit (DR) and credit (CR) amounts (line 1 and line 2),

- make use of reversal entries (line 3),

- make use of foreign-currency value imports (line 4),

- record different quantities (line 5),

- record customer (line 6) and vendor transactions without (line 7) and with (line 8) sales taxes,

- record intercompany journal transactions (line 9), and

- record split postings (lines 10 to 12).

Note The different examples chosen aim to illustrate the wide variety and flexibility of the transactions that can be imported in MSDyn365FO with the help of PowerApps and MS-Flow.

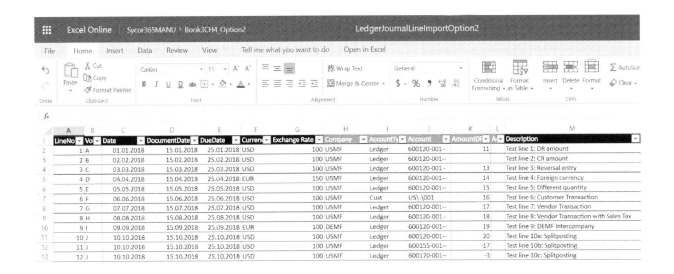

Figure 4.34 *Sample import transactions (1)*

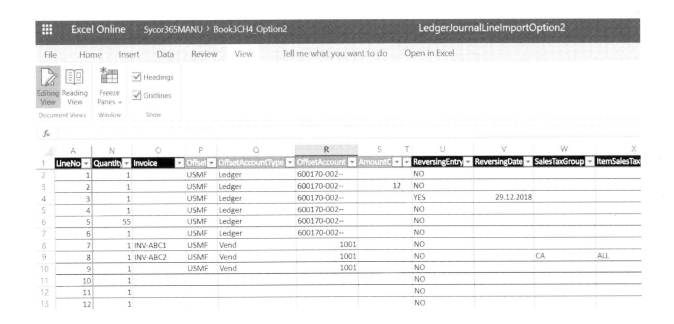

Figure 4.35 *Sample import transactions (2)*

4.2.3.2. Step 2: Start MS-Flow through Embedded PowerApp

After the import Excel template has been filled, the import process can be started by opening the PowerApp and selecting the *import journal lines* button. This is exemplified in figure 4.36.

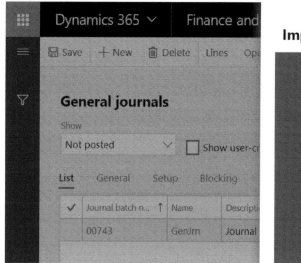
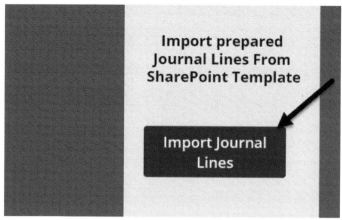

ImportJournalLinesFromSharePointTemplate

Import prepared
Journal Lines From
SharePoint Template

Import Journal
Lines

Figure 4.36 *Start journal import*

4.2.3.3. Step 3: Post Journal

The last process steps consist of validating and posting the created journal. Those final process steps are exemplified in figure 4.37 and figure 4.38.

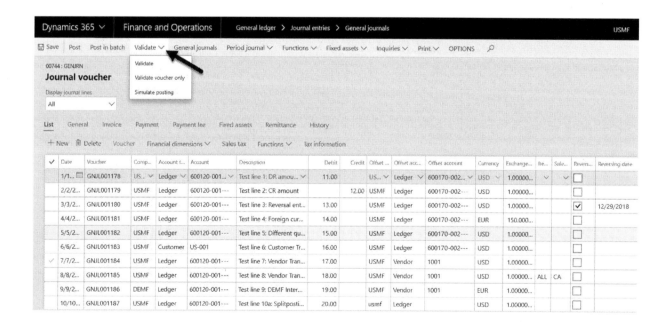

Figure 4.37 *Validate journal*

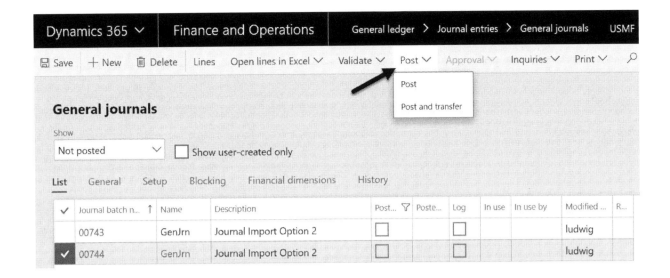

Figure 4.38 *Post created*

4.3. Data-Management

The third option for importing GL journals is the use of the data-management framework, which can be accessed from the system administration module. In the following, the general import process, which can be realized with the help of this framework, is described first, before an import with a customized import template is demonstrated.

4.3.1. General Import Process

4.3.1.1. Required Setup

Before GL journals can be imported with the help of the data-management framework, the default- and ledger-dimension integration setups, which have been described in chapter 4.1.1. above, need to be configured. In addition to those configurations, one has to decide whether the set-based processing parameter in the *general-journal* target entity shall be activated. This parameter—which is active by default—is illustrated in figure 4.39, which has been made from data-management workspace.

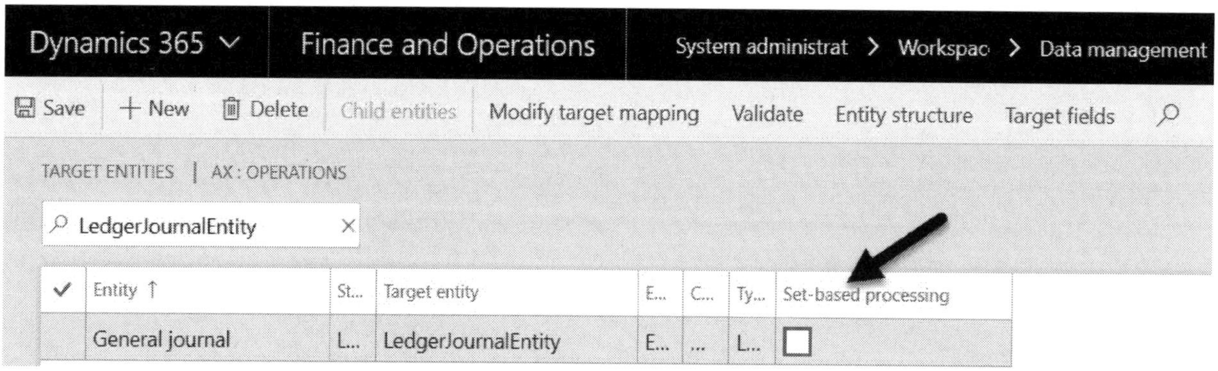

Figure 4.39 *Target entity—set-based processing parameter*

Note Deactivating the set-based processing parameter ensures that the voucher-number for the imported journal lines is created automatically from the voucher series that is linked to the journal. Activating this parameter necessitates that the voucher-numbers are specified in the import document.

4.3.1.2. Process Demonstration

Probably the easiest way to make use of the data-management for GL journal imports is creating an import template based on previously recorded GL journal transactions. Once this template has been generated, journal lines can be created and imported with the help of the data-management framework. Those process steps are illustrated and described in the following.

Creating an import template based on previously created GL journal transactions starts in the data-management workspace with the selection of the export section that is highlighted in the next figure.

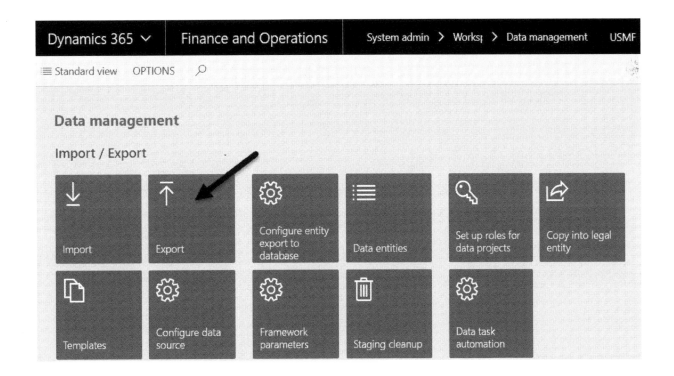

Figure 4.40 *Data-management workspace—export section*

In the opened export form, one has to define a name of the export job (*Book3-EXP*), the target output format (*Excel*), and the entity name (*general journal*) first. Those steps can be identified by the letters *A* to *C* in figure 4.41.

Once those selections have been made, the data entity needs to be added to the export section (*D*) before the export can be started with step *E*.

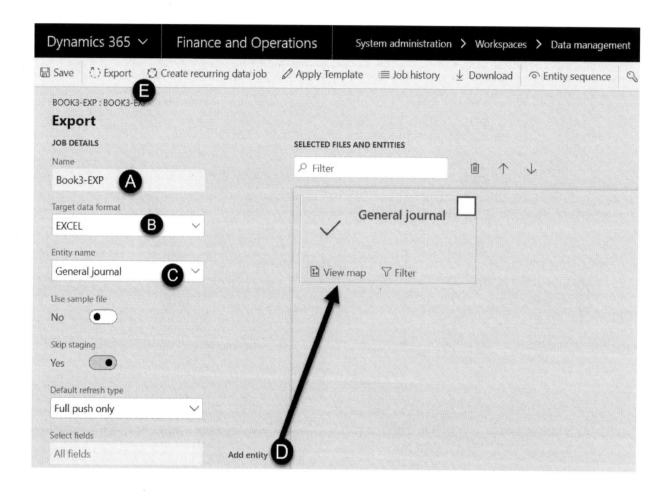

Figure 4.41 *Data-management workspace—configuration of export job*

Users are informed about the completion of the export process by a check mark. After the check mark can be identified, the generated Excel document can be downloaded via the download-package button that is shown in step *F* in figure 4.42.

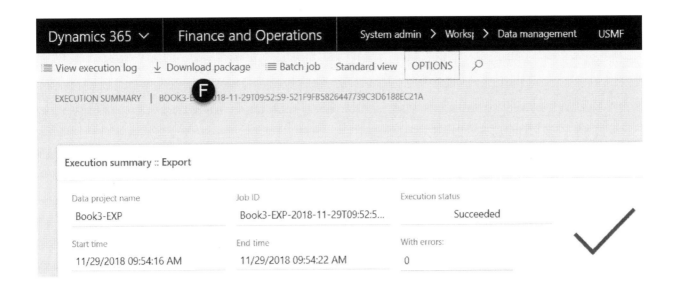

Figure 4.42 *Data-management workspace—data export*

Figure 4.43 and figure 4.44 illustrate the downloaded package folder that includes the Excel document with the exported general ledger transactions.

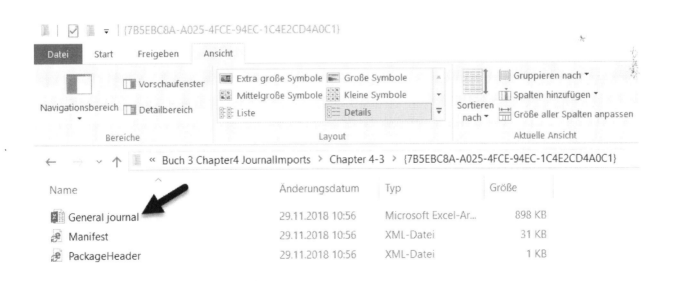

Figure 4.43 *Data-management export—output (1)*

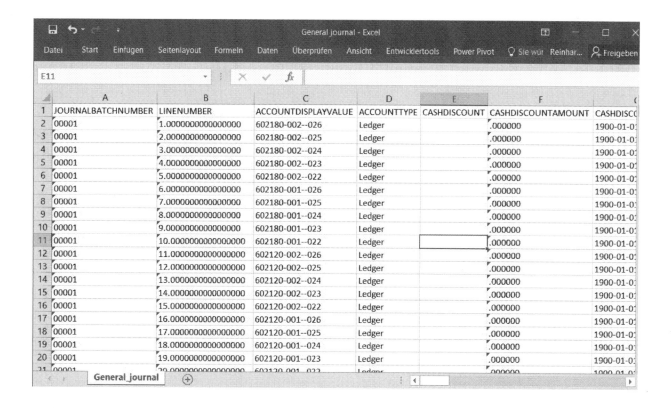

Figure 4.44 *Data-management export—output (2)*

The next process step consists of modifying the exported ledger transactions and preparing the journal lines that need to be imported to MSDyn365FO. This is exemplified in figure 4.45.

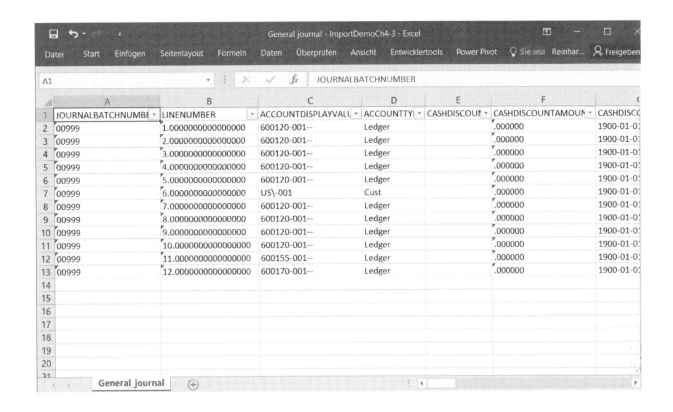

Figure 4.45 *Data-management—preparation of journal-import lines*

Note The journal lines shown in figure 4.45 have been created by copying the lines from a previously posted journal and entering a new journal batch number.

After all journal lines have been prepared, the data-management-workspace import section needs to be opened for the configuration of the import job.

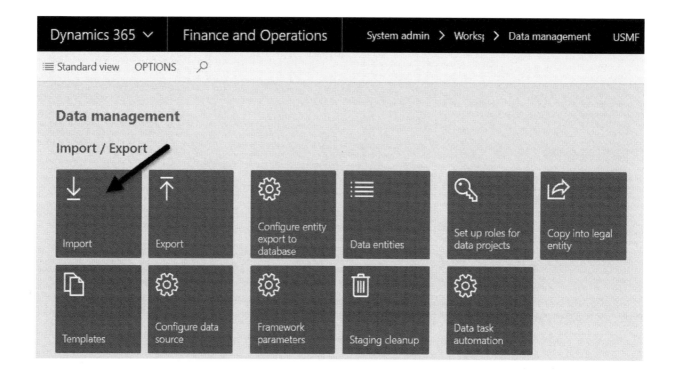

Figure 4.46 *Data-management import section*

The configuration of the import job follows the same principles that have been applied to the configuration of the export job shown before. That is, after specifying a name (*G*), the source-data format (*H*), and the entity name (*I*), the prepared import lines can be selected (*J*) and uploaded to MSDyn365FO (*K*). The corresponding process steps and letters are highlighted in figure 4.47.

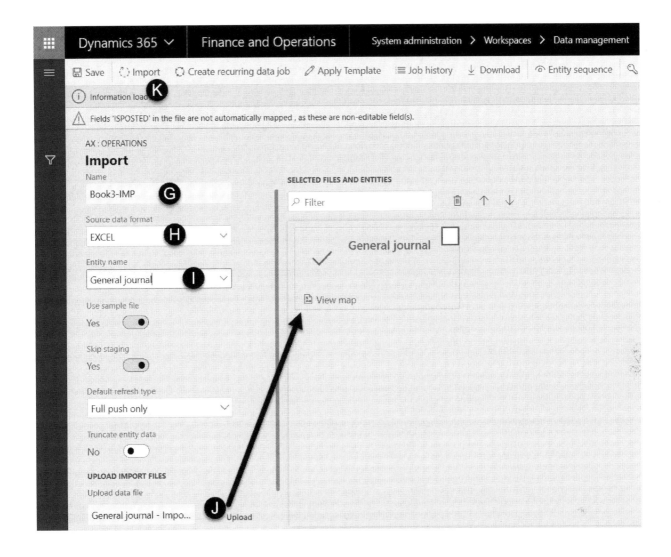

Figure 4.47 *Data-management workspace—configuration of import job*

As for the export job, users are informed about the completion of the import job by a check mark, which is illustrated in the next figure.

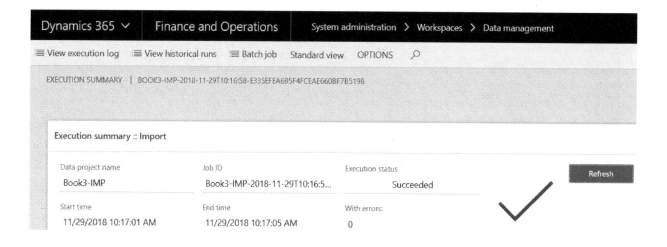

Figure 4.48 *Data-management workspace—data import*

Once the completion check mark can be identified, the created journal and the imported journal lines can be investigated, validated, and posted in MSDyn365FO. The next two figures demonstrate the imported journal and the corresponding journal lines.

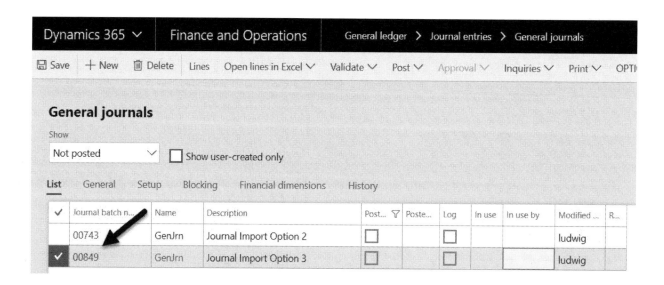

Figure 4.49 *Imported GL journal*

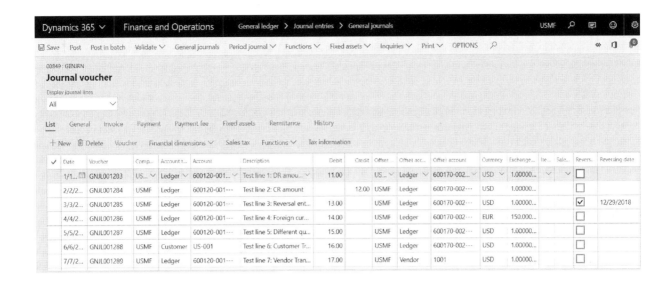

Figure 4.50 *Imported GL journal lines*

Please note that the import routine automatically changed the specified journal batch and voucher-numbers because of the previously mentioned set-based-processing-parameter configuration.

4.3.2.   Import with Customized Import Template

A major disadvantage of the journal-import approach illustrated in chapter 4.3.1. is that the import template includes many columns that might not be needed for a specific import process. As the large number of Excel template columns might confuse system users in the preparation of their journal-import lines, errors are likely to occur.

To reduce the number of errors users can potentially make when preparing the import templates, customized Excel import templates can be created that include the mandatory fields and those that are needed for creating the ledger postings only. Those mandatory, respectively necessary fields can be identified from the target-mapping form, which can be opened as shown in figure 4.51.

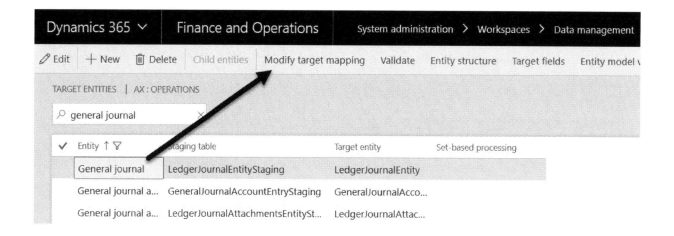

Figure 4.51 *Investigate mandatory or necessary import-template fields*

In the opened target-mapping form, a visual mapping of the import and target fields can be found. This visual mapping of the fields highlights the mandatory fields using an asterisk symbol, which is identified in figure 4.52.

Figure 4.52 *Visual mapping of import and target fields*

Once the mandatory fields have been identified, the customized Excel import template can be set up with the columns needed for making the journal postings. An important consideration in the setup of this template is that the column headers must be created with the same names as the target fields shown on the right-hand side in figure 4.52. Otherwise, a complete new mapping of the import and target fields is required. The next figure shows an example of such a customized Excel import template.

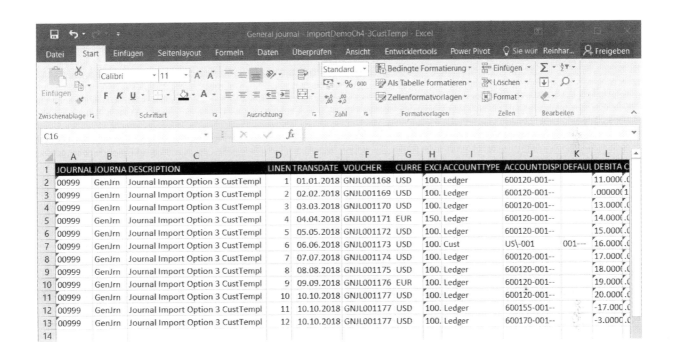

Figure 4.53 *Setup of customized Excel import template*

The last step in processing (i.e., importing the prepared journal lines) is selecting and uploading the file and running the import process as before.

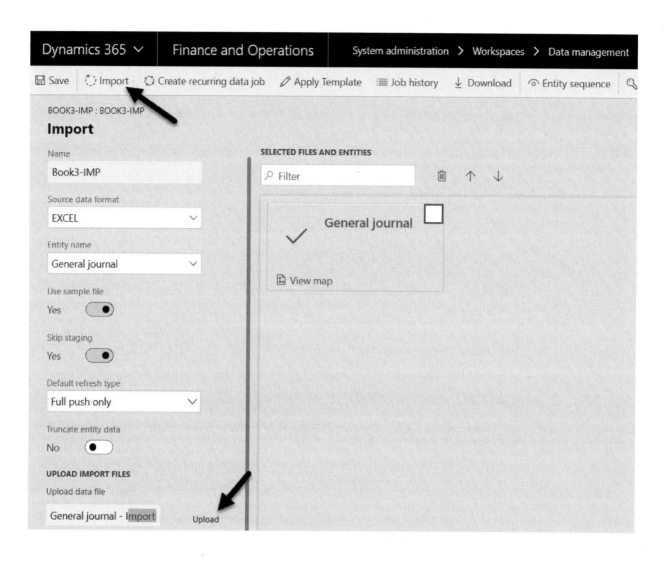

Figure 4.54 *Data-management workspace—configuration of import job*

Note   The customized Excel import template is imported with the same import job (*Book3-IMP*) that was created before. In other words, the previously used import job can be reused for journal imports that make use of other templates as long as all mandatory fields are filled.

The resulting journal and journal lines are once again illustrated in figures 4.55 and 4.56.

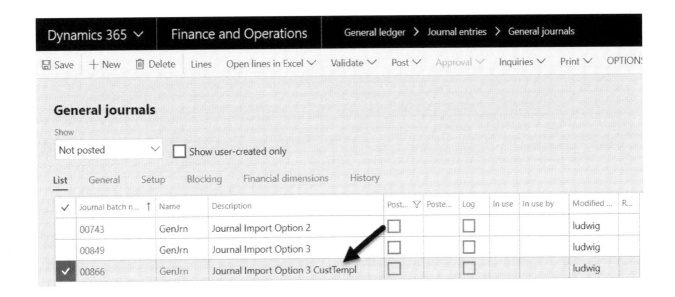

Figure 4.55 *Imported GL journal with customized Excel import journal (1)*

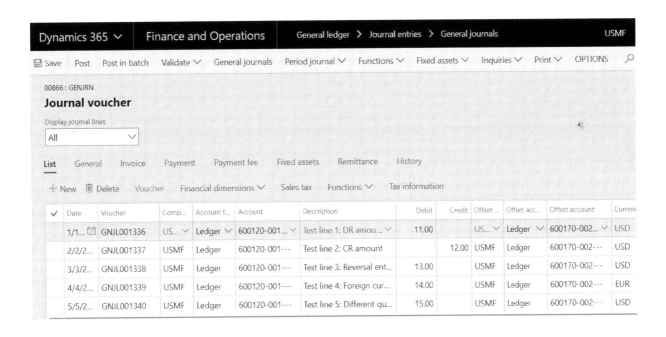

Figure 4.56 *Imported GL journal with customized Excel import journal (2)*

Note Different from the previous journal-import functionalities that have been described in chapter 4.1. and chapter 4.2., data-management-related journal imports support the import of multiple journals at a time.

4.4. Electronic-Reporting

The electronic-reporting (ER) framework that has previously been used for exporting data from MSDyn365FO is not used for data exports only but also for data imports. In the following, the use of the ER framework for GL journal imports is introduced as a fourth possible option for GL journal imports.

4.4.1. Required Setup

Importing transactions into MSDyn365FO GL journals necessitates a journal into which the transactions can be imported. This prerequisite is not different from the other journal-import methods that have been presented before. However, when making use of the ER framework for journal imports, the *new-voucher-number* assignment parameter needs to be set to *manual* (please see figure 4.57 for details). In addition to this parameter setting, one has to ensure that the voucher series (*GenJrn4*) is set up in a way that noncontinuous voucher-numbers are supported. That is because the voucher-number generation is controlled by the ER model, which is explained next.

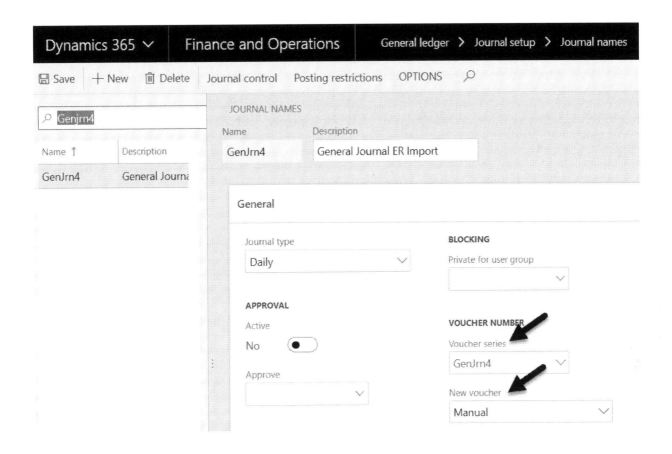

Figure 4.57 *GL import journal*

4.4.1.1. Electronic-Reporting-Model Setup

The ER model that is presented in the following consists of a header section (A) and a lines section (B). Both sections include various elements—see figure 4.58—that are required for importing data into the previously illustrated journal.

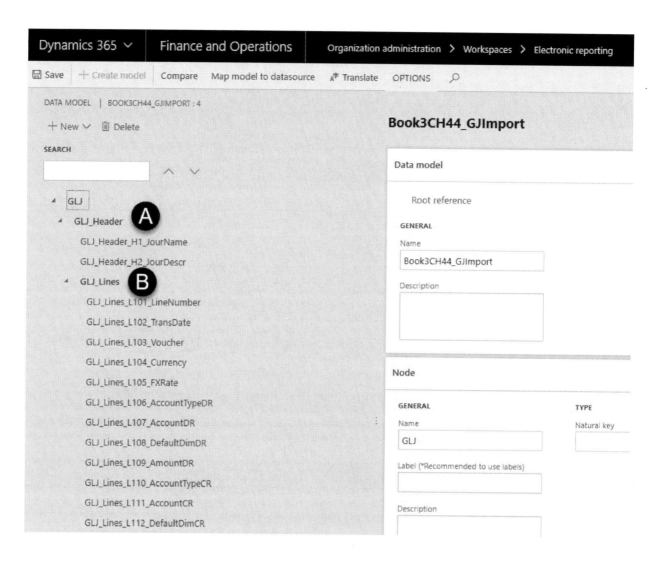

Figure 4.58 *ER model—GL import*

Note

The header section in figure 4.58 includes the journal name and journal description. Users need to provide this information in the import file before they can upload journal transactions. In the lines section shown in figure 4.58, one can identify a number of fields that are not necessarily required for journal imports. As an example, the text field is an optional field and could be left out. This and other optional fields have been included here for demonstration purposes to illustrate the variety of transactions that can be uploaded into GL journals with the help of the ER framework.

Once the model elements have been defined, the *map-model-to-data-source* form needs to be opened by selecting the respective button in order to define the destination of the ER. That is, one has to define whether data is either exported from MSDyn365FO or imported into MSDyn365FO. As data shall be imported into GL journals, the selection *to destination* is made in figure 4.59.

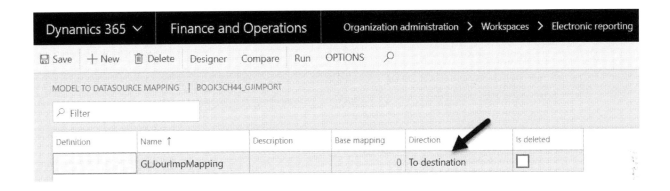

Figure 4.59 *Map-model-to-data-source form*

After the ER destination is specified, the model-mapping designer needs to be opened by selecting the *designer* button from the action pane shown in figure 4.59.

In the opened designer form, four different elements need to be selected in the data-sources section, which can be identified in the middle part of figure 4.60. The first element that needs to be selected is the journal-batch-number sequence that is needed for creating new journals. The arrows shown in figure 4.60 demonstrate how this selection can be made.

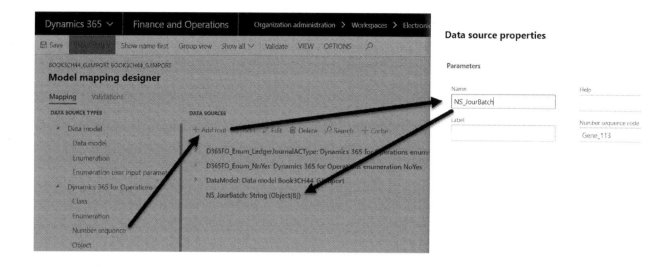

Figure 4.60 *ER-model-designer form (1)*

Note The number sequence used for creating the GL journals (*Gene_113*) is the same that is set up in the GL parameter number sequence form and is shown in figure 4.61.

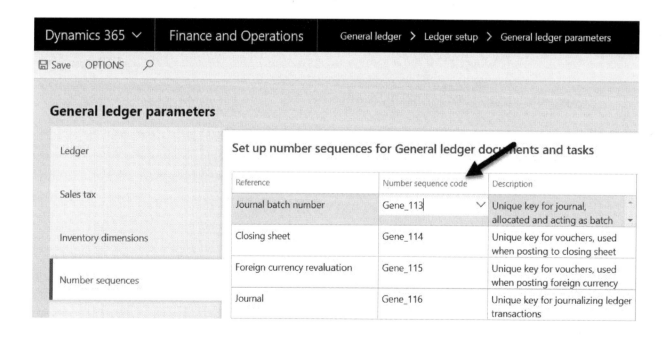

Figure 4.61 *GL parameters form*

The next two elements are so-called enums, which are needed for the correct identification and selection of the account type (*D365FO_Enum_LedgerJournalACType*) and the identification of whether or not an uploaded transaction needs to be reversed automatically at a later date (*D365FO_Enum_NoYes*). Figure 4.62 shows how the first one of those elements—the enum for the account type—can be selected.

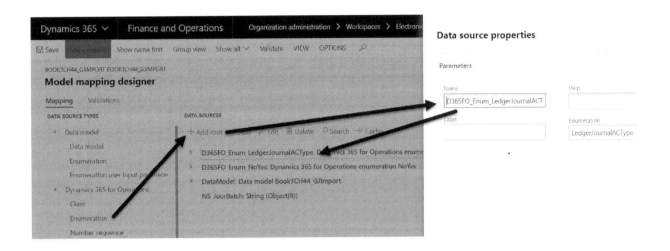

Figure 4.62 *ER-model-designer form (2)*

The selection of the second enum follows the same selection principles that are illustrated in figure 4.62. For that reason, and to conserve space, no separate figure has been included here.

The fourth and last element that needs to be selected in the data-sources section is the model and its elements, which have been set up before. Also, this selection is straightforward and exemplified in figure 4.63.

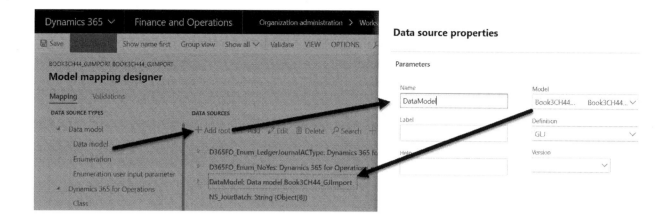

Figure 4.63 *ER-model-designer form (3)*

After the four data-source elements are configured, three fields need to be added to the lines section of the data-source model. The first two elements are the journal name (*CF_GLH1_JourName*) and journal description (*CF_GLH2_JourDescr*), which can be added by making use of the calculated-field functionality that is shown in figure 4.64.

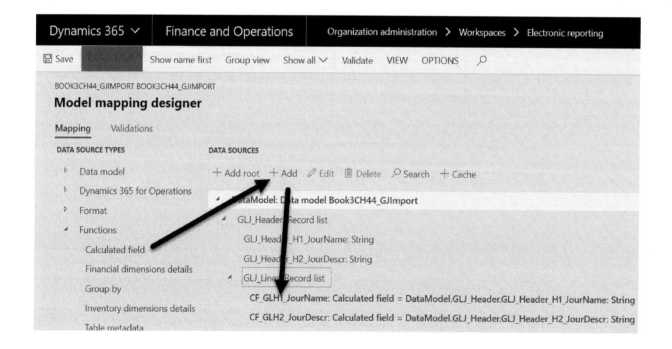

Figure 4.64 *ER-model-designer form (4)*

192

Note Adding a calculated field in the data-sources section is realized with the formula designer that can be opened when creating the calculated field. Figure 4.65 shows this formula designer, which references the journal name from the ER header section in the formula field. The same principle is applied for adding the journal description to the lines section (not shown here for reasons of brevity).

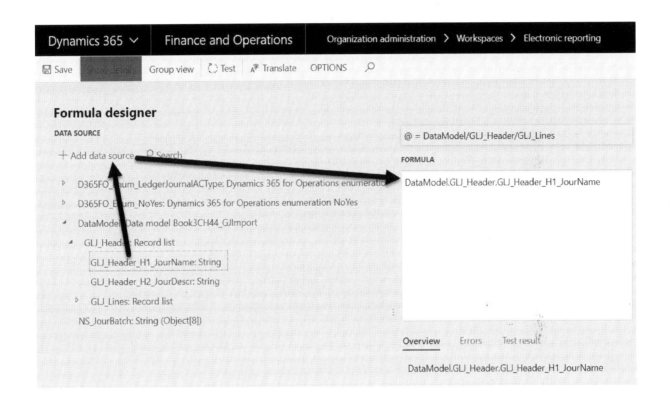

Figure 4.65 *Formula designer*

Note The journal-name and journal-description fields need to be added to the lines section of the ER data-source because the upload demonstrated here is realized from a single Excel table that does not differentiate between a header and a line section.

The last element that needs to be added to the lines section of the data-source model is the voucher-number, which is added by making use of the number-sequence function that has been used before. Please see and compare figure 4.60 with the following, figure 4.66.

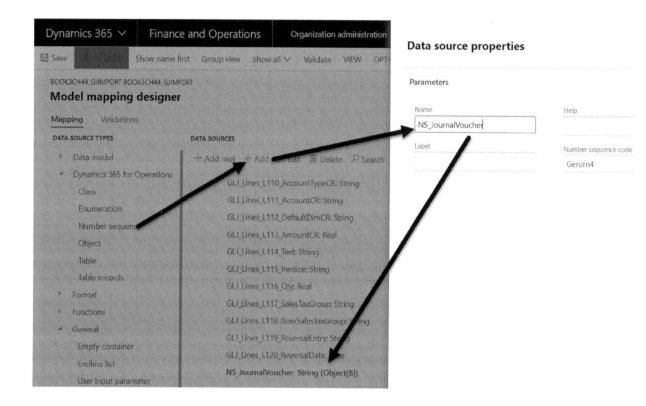

Figure 4.66 *ER-model-designer form (5)*

Adding the journal-voucher-number sequence completes the setup of the data-source model configuration.

What needs to be set up next is the ER destination (i.e., the data entity that will be filled with the transactional data from the Excel import document). Adding the ER destination is realized by choosing the *add destination* button and selecting the data entity (*LedgerJournalEntry*) required for the data import. Please see figure 4.67 and figure 4.68 for details.

Figure 4.67 *Data-model-destination entity (1)*

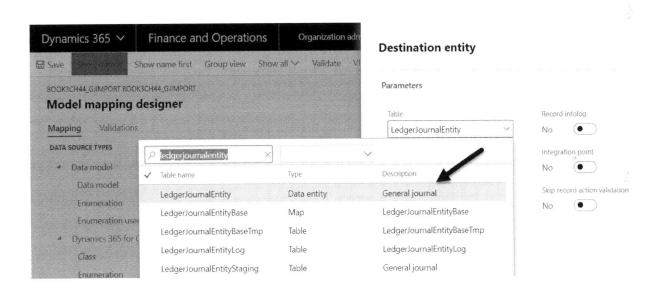

Figure 4.68 *Data-model-destination entity (2)*

Note The *LedgerJournalEntity* data entity is the same that has been used for the journal imports that have been realized with the help of the data-management framework in chapter 4.3.

Once the data entity has been selected, the fields specified in the line section of the data-model need to mapped to the fields in the data entity. Making this mapping is straightforward and can be realized by selecting the data-source element, the corresponding data-model element, and the *bind* button, as exemplified in figure 4.69.

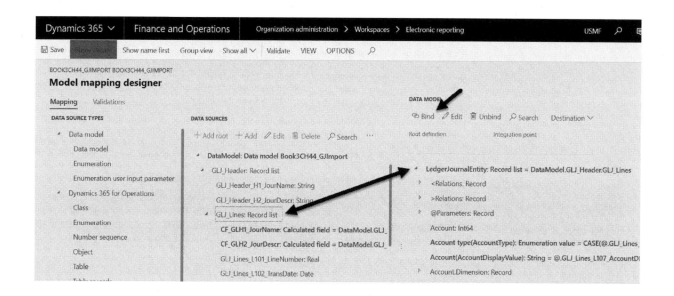

Figure 4.69 *Mapping data-source—data entity*

An exception to the aforementioned mapping process relates to the account-type and reversal-enum fields. Those fields cannot simply be mapped and bound as all the other fields but need rather to be incorporated into a case formula. Figure 4.70 illustrates the formula that is used for the mapping of the account-type field.

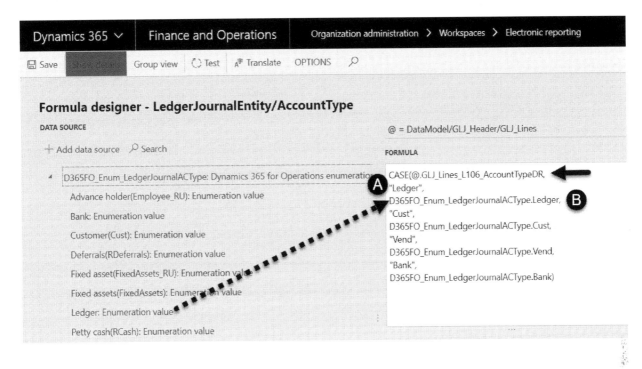

Figure 4.70 *Mapping data-source—data entity*

The case formula shown in figure 4.70 maps the import value (*ledger, cust, vend*, or *bank*) from Excel to the respective ledger account-type enum in MSDyn365FO. This is indicated by the letters *A* (for the Excel import value) and *B* (for the MSDyn365FO enum value). For the offset account-type and reversal-entry enum fields, the following formulas are used:

- Offset account-type formulas:

CASE(@.GLJ_Lines_L110_AccountTypeCR, "Ledger",

D365FO_Enum_LedgerJournalACType.Ledger, "Cust",

D365FO_Enum_LedgerJournalACType.Cust, "Vend",

D365FO_Enum_LedgerJournalACType.Vend, "Bank",

D365FO_Enum_LedgerJournalACType.Bank)

- Reversal-entry-enum formulas:

CASE(@.GLJ_Lines_L119_ReversalEntry, "NO", D365FO_Enum_NoYes.No, "YES", D365FO_Enum_NoYes.Yes)

The last setup that needs to be made relates to the status of the ER model, which has to be changed from *draft* to *complete* (see figure 4.71) before the ER configuration can be made.

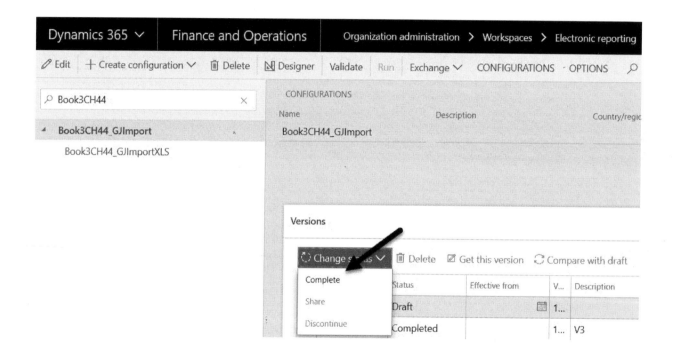

Figure 4.71 *Change ER-model status*

4.4.1.2.   Electronic-Reporting-Configuration Setup

Before digging into details of the ER-configuration setup, let us first have a look at the conceptual overview shown in figure 4.72 that has been prepared to illustrate the setup and GL journal-import process realized with the ER framework.

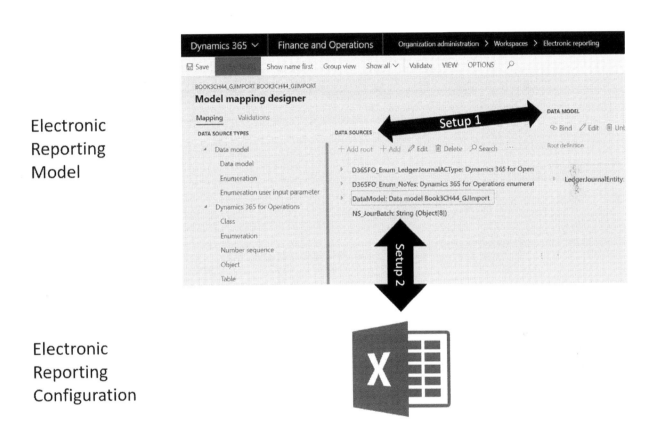

Figure 4.72 *Conceptual overview of GL journal import through ER*

Figure 4.72 highlights the three elements involved in the import process. Starting in the upper right-hand side of the figure, one can identify the data-model that holds the *LedgerJournalEntity* data entity, which is used for the data import into MSDyn365FO.

To ensure that the data entity can be filled with the data from the Excel import document, the data-model configuration—which has been explained in the previous chapter and is shown in the middle part of figure 4.72—is needed.

The last element required for the GL journal import is the Excel import document—shown in the lower part of figure 4.72—which needs to be configured and mapped with the data-model. This configuration and mapping is investigated next.

The ER-configuration setup starts with the creation of an ER-model configuration, which is shown in figure 4.73.

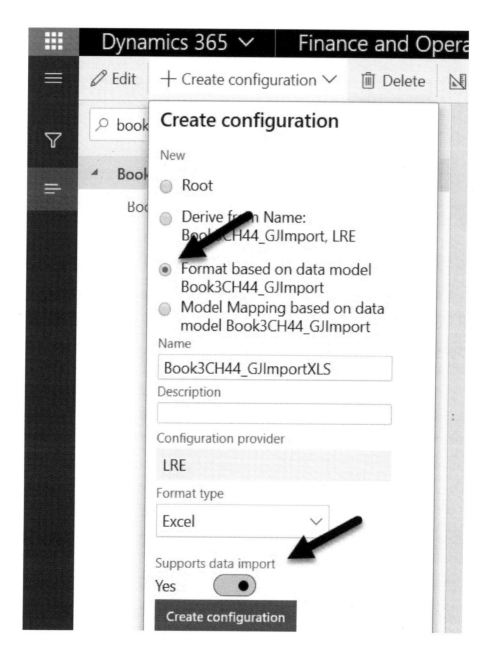

Figure 4.73 *Create ER-model configuration*

Note When creating this configuration, one has to ensure that the *supports-data-import parameter* is set to *yes*.

The next setup required relates to the preparation of the Excel GL journal-import template. This template needs to include separate columns for all fields that need to be uploaded into MSDyn365FO. An important consideration in the setup of this template relates to the field-name specification, which has to be made in a way that each field has a unique name assigned. Figure 4.74 demonstrates how this field-name specification can be made.

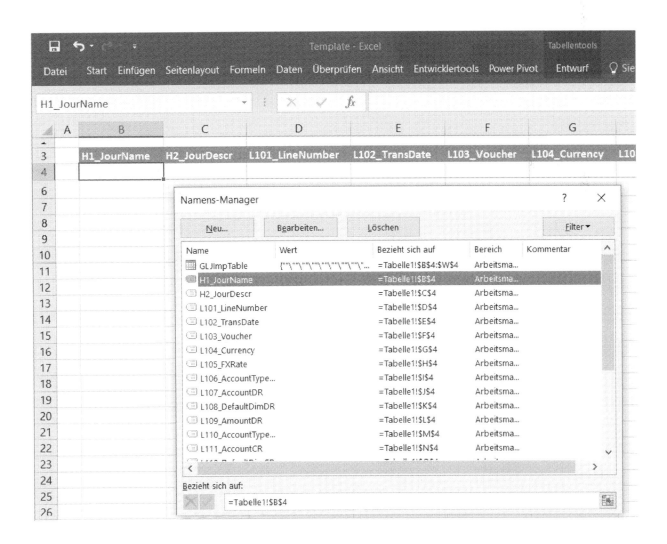

Figure 4.74 *Excel GL journal-import template*

Please note that the aforementioned field-name specification is necessary but not sufficient for the setup of the Excel GL journal-import template. What is needed in addition is to embed those fields in an Excel table. This embedment can also be identified from the first line shown in the names manager in figure 4.74.

Once the Excel GL journal-import template has been set up, it needs to be imported into MSDyn365FO. This import is self-explanatory and is illustrated in the next three figures.

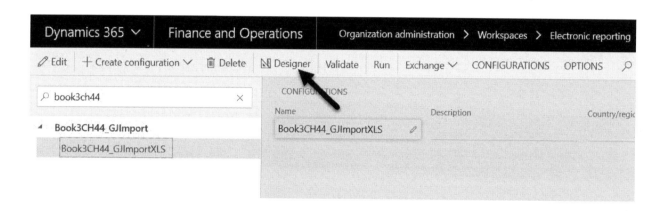

Figure 4.75 *Import of Excel GL journal-import template (1)*

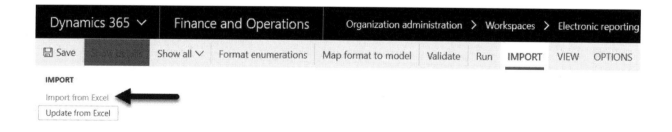

Figure 4.76 *Import of Excel GL journal-import template (2)*

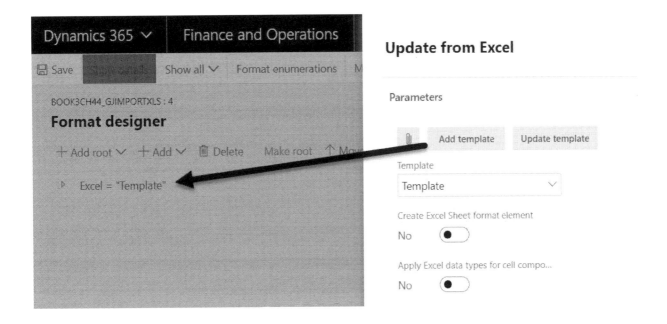

Figure 4.77 *Import of Excel GL journal-import template (3)*

After the template has been imported, one has to ensure that the data types of the imported fields match those in MSDyn365FO. This can be ensured by reviewing and adjusting the data-type fields and is illustrated in figure 4.78.

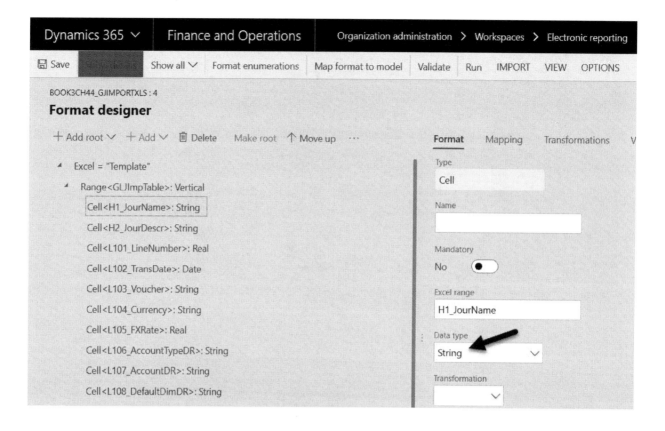

Figure 4.78 *Data-type specification of imported Excel template fields*

If the fields types have also been specified, the mapping of the Excel template fields with the ER-model fields can be started by opening the map format to model button, selecting the model definition (GLJ), and opening the designer form. Figure 4.79 and figure 4.80 illustrate those setup steps.

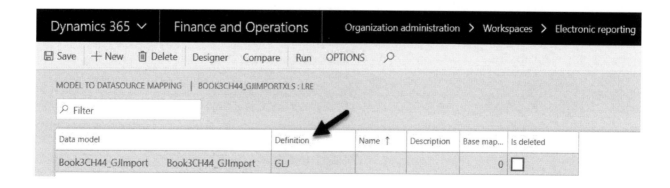

Figure 4.79 *Model-to-data-source mapping (1)*

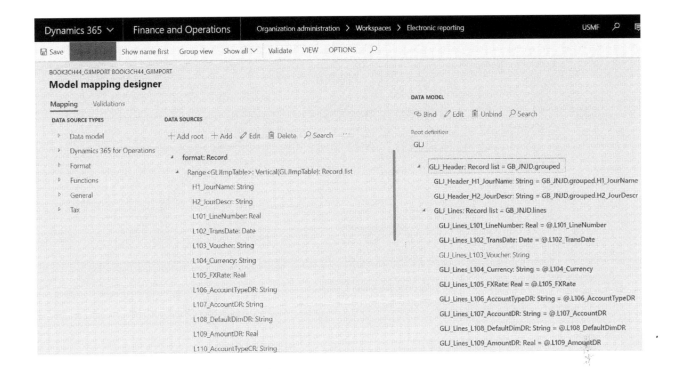

Figure 4.80 *Model-to-data-source mapping (2)*

An important consideration when making the mapping of the Excel template fields with the ER-model fields is that those fields cannot directly be mapped. Otherwise, a new journal would be created for each line included in the Excel import document.

Instead, what is needed is a summary of the different lines into a single journal. This required summary of the Excel lines can be realized by grouping the Excel template lines by the journal name and the journal description, which is exemplified in the next figures.

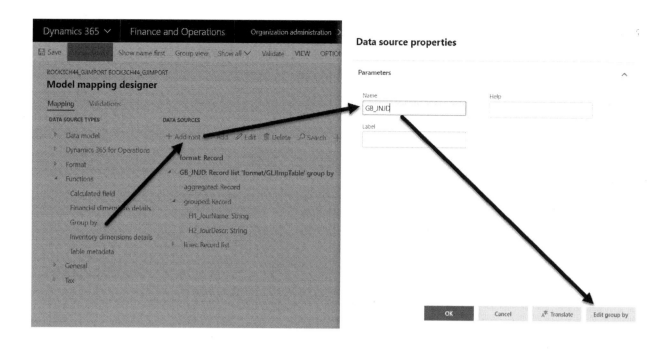

Figure 4.81 *Grouping of Excel template lines (1)*

Figure 4.82 *Grouping of Excel template lines (2)*

Once those Excel import lines are grouped, the grouped Excel template line elements can be mapped to the ER-model elements. Also this mapping process is self-explanatory and is illustrated in figures 4.83 and 4.84.

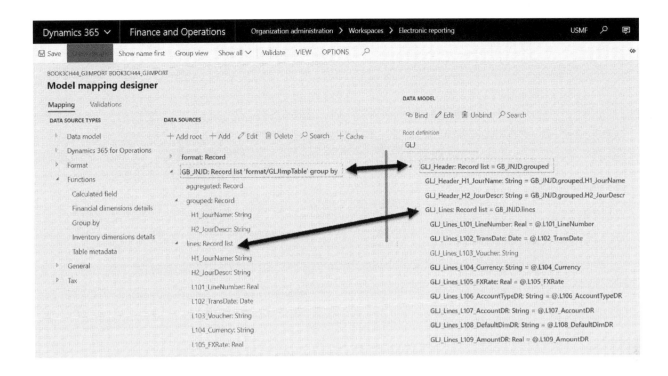

Figure 4.83 *Mapping of grouped Excel template fields with ER-model fields (1)*

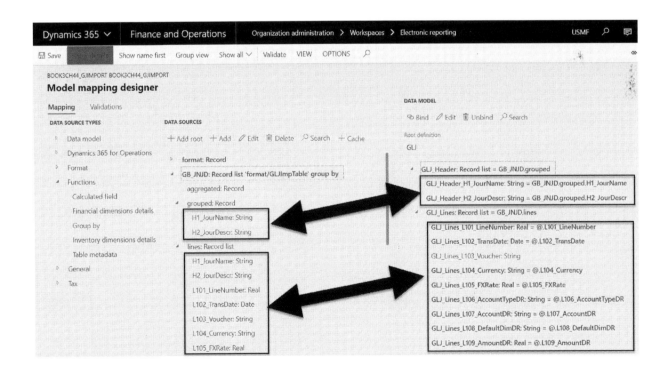

Figure 4.84 *Mapping of grouped Excel template fields with ER-model fields (2)*

The last step required before journal imports can be realized is changing the status of the ER configuration from *draft* to *complete*, which is illustrated in figure 4.85.

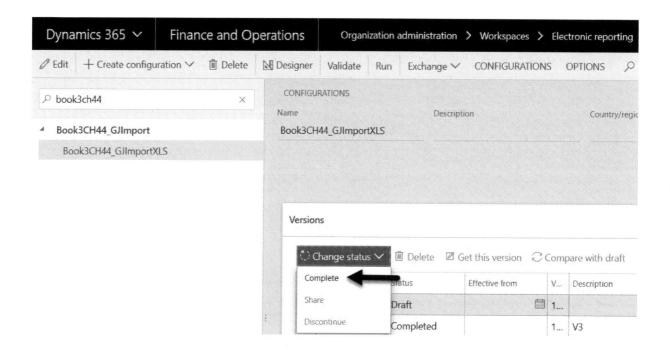

Figure 4.85 *Change electronic-reporting-version status*

4.4.2.   Process Demonstration

With the previously made ER setups, users can upload their prepared GL journal-import file by selecting the model-mapping element in the ER model (see figure 4.86).

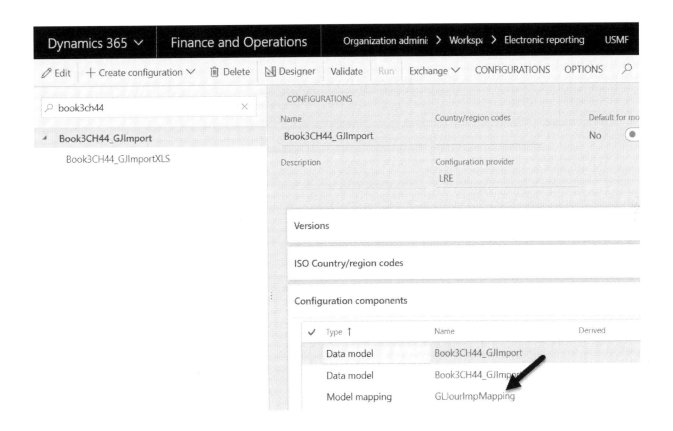

Figure 4.86 *Import of GL Excel template (1)*

Selecting the model-mapping parameter shown in the previous figure opens the form shown in figure 4.87, which allows selecting the import file (see figure 4.88) and running the import.

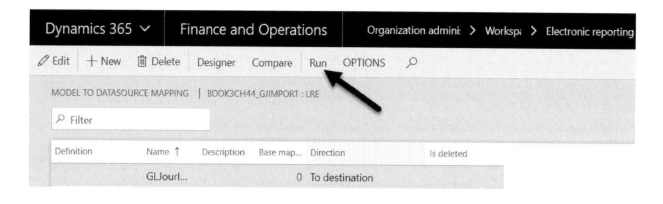

Figure 4.87 *Import of GL Excel template (2)*

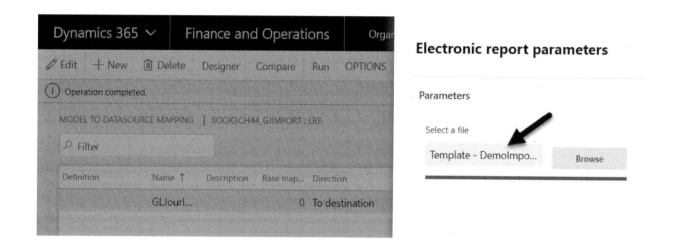

Figure 4.88 *Import of GL Excel template (3)*

Once the import process is completed, the created GL journal and the journal lines can be identified in the GL module. Figure 4.89 and figure 4.90 illustrate the imported journal and journal lines.

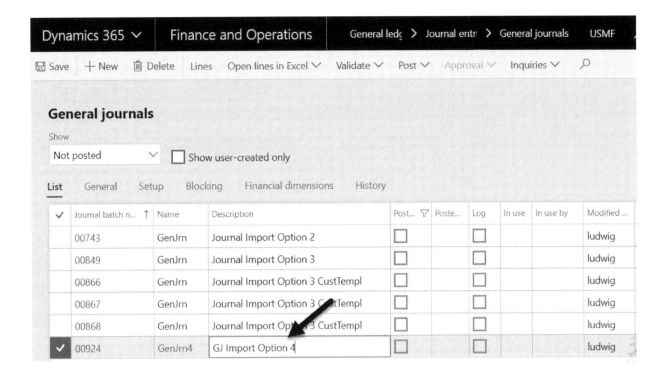

Figure 4.89 *Imported GL journal*

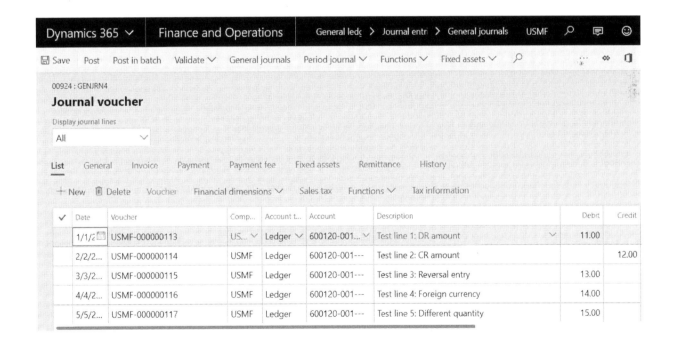

Figure 4.90 *Imported GL journal lines*

4.5.　　Summary

After introducing the different GL journal-import options, a question arises: Which import option would one use best? Answering this question is not easy, as every journal-import option presented has different characteristics. The next table summarizes those characteristics and can serve as a guideline for which option to choose in a specific company environment.

Import Option	Option 1 (Journal Templates)	Option 2 (PowerApps and MS-Flow)	Option 3 (Data-Management)	Option 4 (Electronic-Reporting)
Supported account types	Only ledger, customer, vendor and bank account transactions can be imported. [1]			
Financial dimensions in separate Excel columns	Requires system modification.	Can be realized via Excel template design. [2]	Can be realized via Excel template design. [2]	Can be realized via Excel template design. [2]
Number of journals that can be created with a single upload	Single	Single	Multiple	Single
Complexity of the required setup	Easy	Medium	Medium to complex	Complex
Security considerations	None, as controlled by MSDyn365FO credentials.	Specific admin user account might be needed for PowerApps and MS-Flow configuration.	Access to the data-management should tightly be restricted.[3]	System modification might be necessary to allow users starting the import e.g. from the GL module.
Usability	Easy	Very easy	Complex	Medium
Import speed index [4]	100	500	110	20

Figure 4.91 *Comparison of journal-import options*

Notes for figure 4.91:

1. Other account types can be imported with the help of other templates or other data entities than the ones used in this chapter.

2. Financial dimensions can be recorded in separate Excel template columns. Those separate columns can be combined with the ledger accounts used by making use of Excel cell-calculation functionalities.

3. The access to the data-management framework should be tightly restricted, as the data-management framework allows importing numerous data into MSDyn365FO and thus has the potential of disrupting operations.

4. The import-speed index was calculated for the import of one thousand journal lines. Thereby, the time required for the journal-template-import option was set to an index value of 100. The time required for the other import options was calculated relative to the journal-template-import index. As an example, the PowerApps and MS-Flow import index of 500 means that this import option took five times longer than the journal-template-import option.

5. Case Management

5.1. What Is Case Management?

Case management (CM) is a generic instrument that can be used for creating, planning, tracking, and analyzing issues in MSDyn365FO. Unlike workflows, which are usually process driven, CM can be as simple as generating a request for a customer who has difficulties with the use of a product. CM is not, however, limited to customer-related issues. It can also be used for multiple other purposes, such as recording issues related to employees, purchases, projects, and so on.

Cases can thereby be classified in various ways, they can be assigned to specific users, and issues can be tracked in detail using the available case-log functionality. From a finance perspective, the ability to establish a link to a billing project and a service-level agreement (SLA) are important functionalities related to cases, as they are a prerequisite for a comprehensive financial case analysis.

Note: Additional information on the MSDyn365FO CM functionality can be found on the Microsoft docs' sites. See https://docs.microsoft.com/en-us/dynamics365/unified-operations/fin-and-ops/organ ization-administration/cases.

5.2. Finance-Related Issues with Case Management

5.2.1. Integration of Time Recording

Notwithstanding the numerous functionalities that are associated with the MSDyn365FO CM, it has a couple of weaknesses. A first weakness of the CM functionality is that there is no automatic time recording available. That is, despite the fact that one can associate a billing project and an SLA to a case (see figure 5.1), the time spent on a case is only tracked at the case level and does not automatically create a corresponding transaction in the project module where employees regularly record their time.

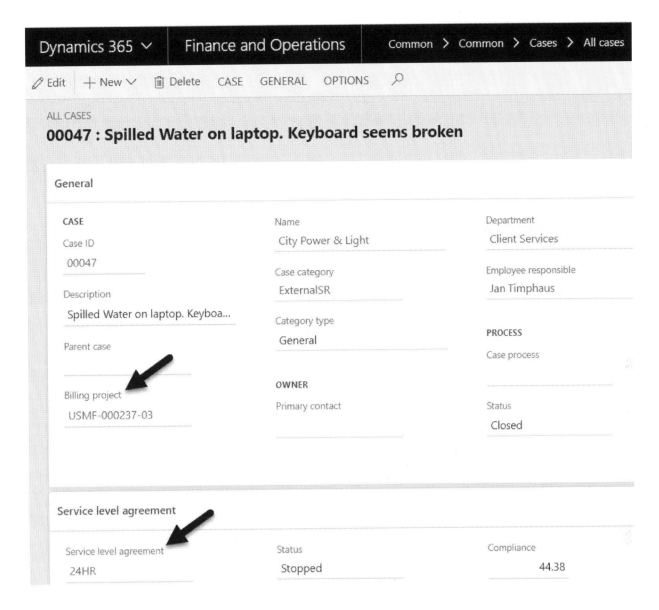

Figure 5.1 *Case association with billing project and SLA*

5.2.2. Follow Up with Open Cases

A second weakness of the standard CM functionality is that it does not ship with a comprehensive instrument that allows following up long-running cases, i.e. cases that are open for a long time. The available user-specific tracking forms allow identifying and following up cases that are open and running for a long time. (For details, please see figure 5.2.) Those forms, however, are user specific and do not allow a user independent and comprehensive tracking of open cases in MSDyn365FO.

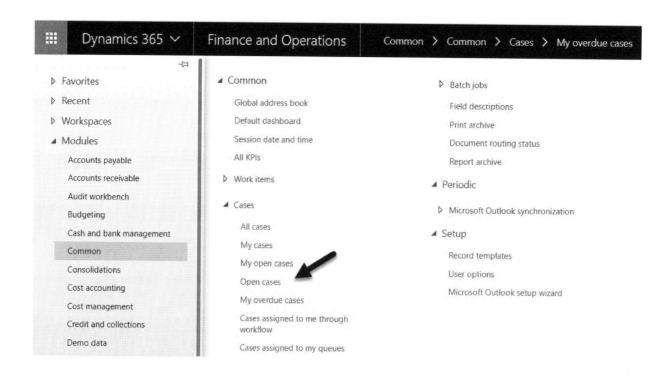

Figure 5.2 *User-specific case-tracking forms*

5.2.3.   Cost Analysis

A third and last weakness of the CM functionality is that it does not ship with a functionality that allows tracking the costs of cases from a financial perspective. Closing this gap is very important, especially in a world that is characterized by an increase in the relative portion of indirect service-related costs. This increase in indirect costs requires powerful cost-analysis tools that can assign costs and revenues to the different service-related processes of a company. Being able to make this cost assignment is a prerequisite for the management to assess and decide on procedural changes that might be required as a result of changing market conditions.

5.3. Implementation in MSDyn365FO

5.3.1. Process Overview

Before digging into details of the individual elements and setups that are necessary for overcoming the CM-related weaknesses described, let us have a look at the complete CM process in figure 5.3.

Figure 5.3 *Case management process*

The process starts with the recording and processing of an issue through the MSDyn365FO case-management tool. Thereafter, an electronic-report extracts case details in regular intervals and stores the report in a cloud-based storage, such as SharePoint. Once the report is available in this cloud-based storage, MS-Flow is used for preparing the data in a way that they can be processed and analyzed in the MSDyn365FO project-management module.

Details of the five case-management-process elements and related setups are illustrated in the following subchapters before the complete process is demonstrated based on sample data that are recorded in a standard MSDyn365FO demo environment.

5.3.2. Case Management

To make use of the CM functionality, a number of setups are required. As most of those setups are optional, a focus on the mandatory setups that are necessary for a financial analysis of cases is made in the following.

5.3.2.1. Employee Setup

The first required setup for a financial analysis of cases is related to the employee that gets the case assigned. In regards to this setup, it is important that the employee record is set up with financial dimension values that represent the department or cost center the employee is assigned to and that are used for recording the salary expense of the employee. Figure 5.4 exemplifies this setup.

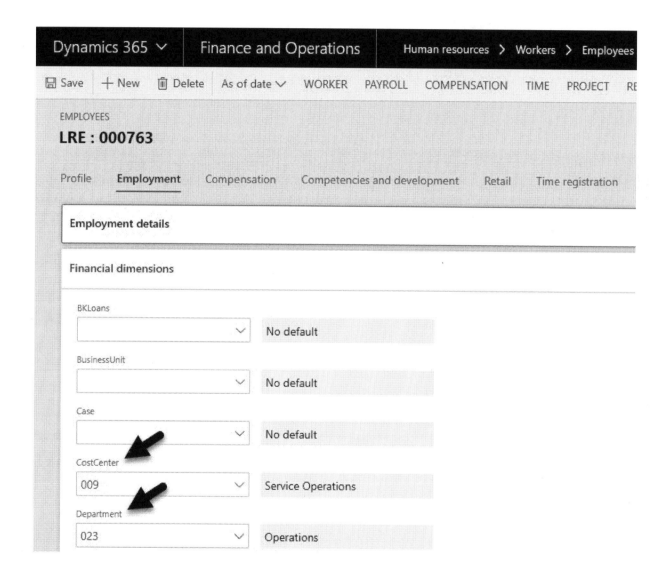

Figure 5.4 *Employee setup*

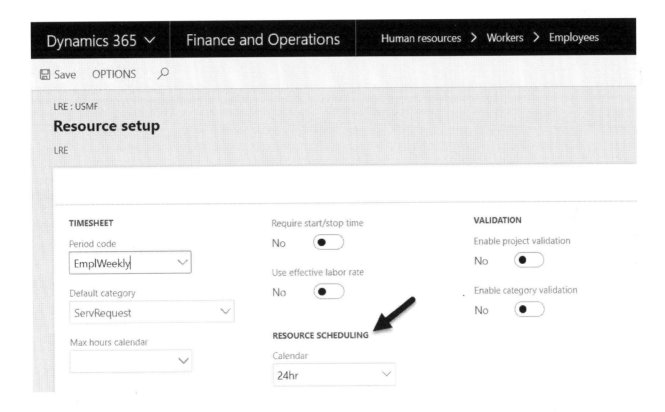

From a financial cost-analysis perspective, an employee record is ideally set up with an employee-specific financial dimension value. Such a setup is not always allowed, however, as it might be in conflict with existing labor- and data-protection laws.

A second mandatory employee-related setup is the assignment of a resource-scheduling calendar in the project-resource form that is shown in figure 5.5. This setup is necessary because only employees with a resource-scheduling specification can record times on projects.

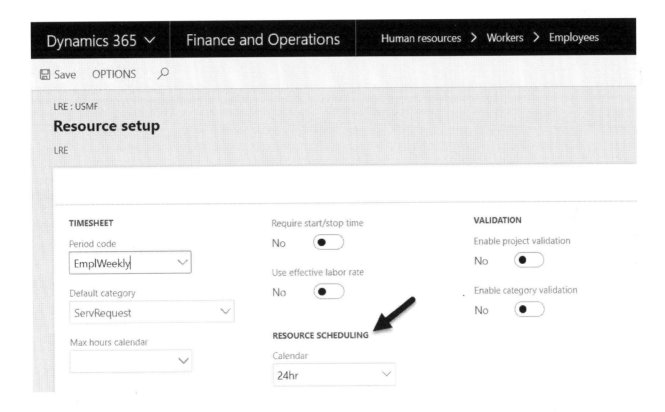

Figure 5.5 *Employee project-resource setup form*

5.3.2.2.   Project and Service-Module Setup

The next setups for the financial analysis of cases must be made in the project and service modules. In those modules, one has to set up projects, hour journals, and service-level agreements.

Projects need to be set up for time-recording purposes. When setting up those projects, it is important that a financial dimension other than the one that is used at the employee level is configured. Figure 5.6 exemplifies this configuration for a project where a project-default financial dimension value has been selected.

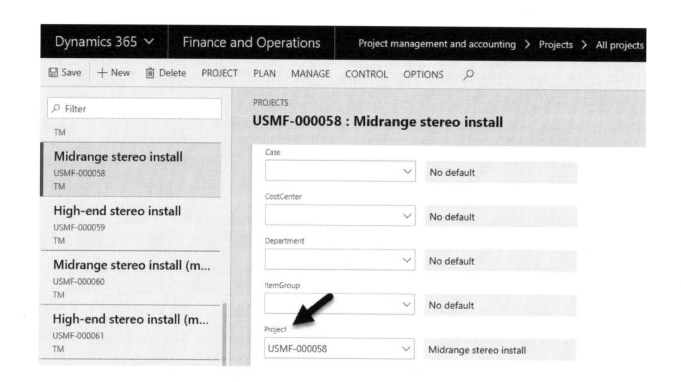

Figure 5.6 *Project financial dimension setup*

To record case-related working times on projects, the set up of a separate hour journal is recommended, as it allows assigning a separate voucher series to the transactions posted. Making use of a separate voucher series for case-related work-time transactions is beneficial because it allows an easier identification and financial analysis of the related costs. Figure 5.7 below shows the setup of the project hour journal that is used in the following.

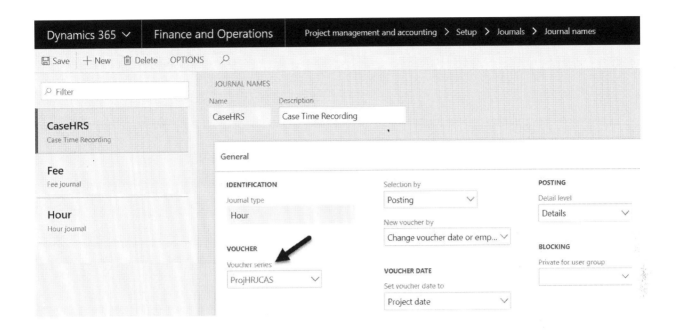

Figure 5.7 *Project hour-journal setup*

The third and last setup that needs to be made in the service module is the setup of a service-level agreement (SLA) that ensures an integrated and continuous time recording of the cases tracked in MSDyn365FO. Figure 5.8 provides some examples of how SLAs can be configured.

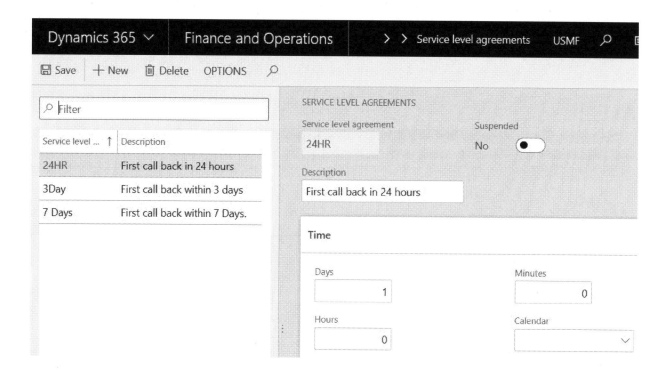

Figure 5.8 *Service-level agreement (SLA) setup*

5.3.2.3.   Case Management-Element Setup

Despite the numerous functionalities that are related to the MSDyn365FO CM tool, the only

mandatory setup that is required for a financial analysis of cases is the configuration of a case-category

hierarchy. The configuration of such a hierarchy necessitates the identification and classification of case

categories and is exemplified in figure 5.9.

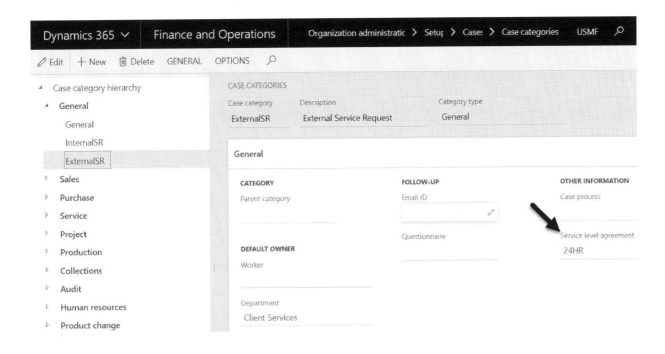

Figure 5.9 *Case-category setup*

Probably the most important setup that is related to the configuration of case categories is the linkage of the previously set up SLA. That is because the time recording for cases does not automatically start if this linkage is not provided.

Note Employees can still record time on cases even if an SLA has not been set up at the case-category level. In this case, however, the linkage to the SLA must be made manually. The same holds for the initiation of the case-related time recording.

5.3.3. Electronic-Reporting and SharePoint

The second element shown in the CM process chart in figure 5.3 refers to the electronic-reporting (ER) functionality that has already been used in the previous chapters. In regards to the financial analysis of cases, the ER function will be used for extracting case-related data from MSDyn365FO and storing those data for further processing in cloud-based storage, such as SharePoint. To realize the storage of those data, the following setups are necessary.

5.3.3.1. Electronic-Reporting Model

The first necessary setup is the ER model that holds all elements that are needed for the following financial case analysis. Figure 5.10 shows the different elements—identified by the numbers *C100–C190*—that are used in the following.

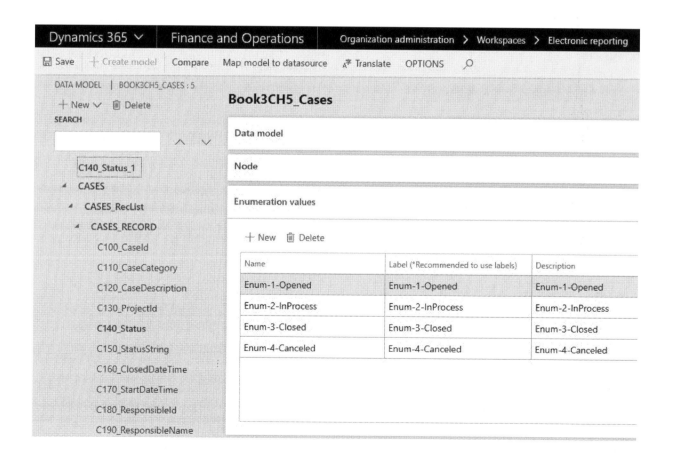

Figure 5.10 *Electronic-reporting (ER) model*

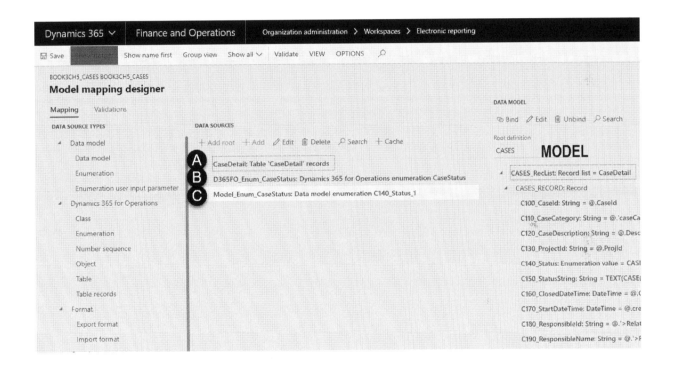

Note All ER elements shown in figure 5.10 are set up with the type *string* except the date- and time-related elements (*C160* and *C170*) and the status element *C140*, which is set up as a so-called enum. The four enum elements used can be identified on the right-hand side of figure 5.10 and are needed for filtering cases in MS-Flow. For details, please see below.

Once all ER-model elements have been defined, a mapping of the ER-model elements with the tables and enums from MSDyn365FO—identified by the letters *A* to *C* in figure 5.11—needs to be made.

Figure 5.11 *ER model mapping*

Making this mapping is straightforward and follows the same principles that have already been explained and used in the previous chapters. For that reason, please refer to what has been explained in chapter 3.

5.3.3.2.   Electronic-Reporting-Model Configuration

After the ER model has been configured and its status changed to *completed*, the ER-model configuration can be made. A prerequisite for making this configuration is the setup of an Excel template with all the ER-model elements. These elements need to be set up with an Excel cell name and bound into an Excel table. This is exemplified in figure 5.12.

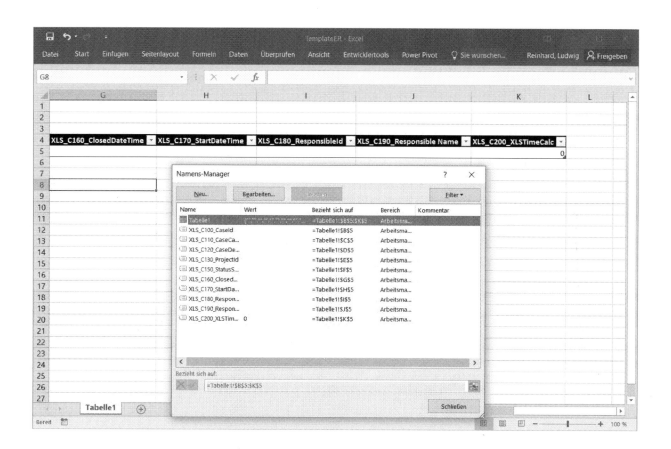

Figure 5.12 *ER-model configuration—Excel template*

The last Excel table column denominated *XLS_C200_XLSTimeCalc* is not included in the ER model but rather is used in the Excel document only for calculating the time difference between the start and end time of a case. The resulting time difference is used later on for filling the project hour journal. The Excel formula used for this purpose is *ROUND(((XLS_C160_ClosedDateTime-XLS_C170_StartDateTime)*24),2)*.

226

The next ER-model-configuration setup consists of creating the Excel-based format configuration and importing the Excel template. Those setup steps can be made in the same way as exemplified in chapter 3. Please see figure 3.16 and figure 3.17 for details.

After those setups have been made, the Excel template elements can be mapped with the ER-model elements. Figure 5.13 exemplifies this mapping process, which is identical to what has been shown in figure 3.19 in chapter 3.

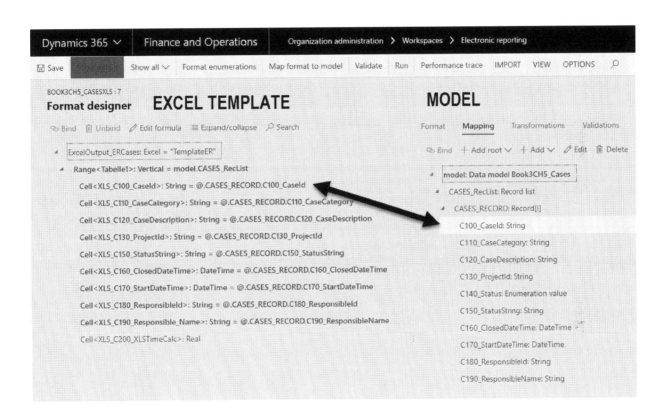

Figure 5.13 *ER-model configuration*

The last setup that has to be made for the ER report to be used is changing the ER-model configuration status from *draft* to *completed*. As this status change has also been exemplified before, refer to figure 3.20.

5.3.3.3.   SharePoint

The previous ER model and configuration-related setup steps ensure the general usability of the process that extracts all case-related data from MSDyn365FO. What the previous setups do not ensure, however, is the provisioning of the extracted data in a cloud-based storage—such as SharePoint—that can be accessed by MS-Flow for a subsequent processing of the data. To ensure this required provisioning of the data, a document type that points to the respective SharePoint site needs to be set up. This is illustrated in figure 5.14.

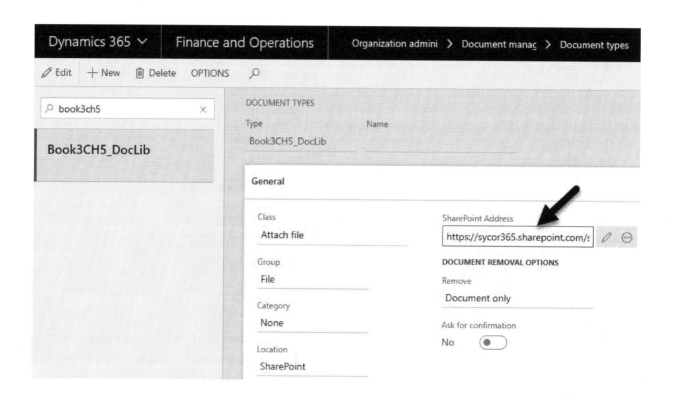

Figure 5.14 *Document-type specification with linkage to SharePoint*

Once the setup of the document type is completed, the ER-output destination can be configured. Making this configuration requires that a reference to the previously set up document type is made. For details, please see figure 5.15 below.

228

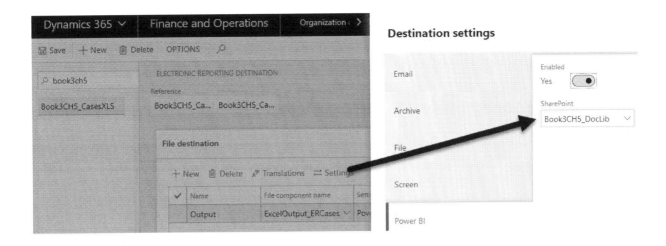

Figure 5.15 *Setup of ER-output destination*

With the output destination defined, the ER report can be processed by selecting the *run* button, which is shown in figure 5.16.

An important aspect that needs to be taken into account when processing the ER report is the filter that is applied when running the report. In the example shown in figure 5.16, a date-range filter—*((DayRange(-7,0))*—that extracts only those cases that have been closed within the last seven days is used. The idea underlying the usage of this filter is to avoid extracting and recording work time for cases that have already been closed weeks or month ago.

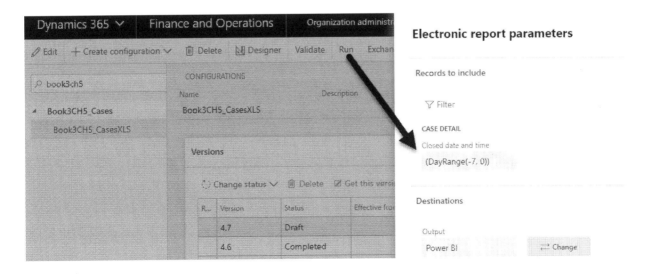

Figure 5.16 *Processing the ER report*

An implicit assumption that is made with the application of the date-range filter criteria shown in figure 5.16 is that closed cases are not reopened. Rather than that, it is assumed that new dependent cases are created if additional work for an already-existing case arises.

Using a date-range filter similar to the one shown in the previous figure necessitates that the ER report is processed in regular time intervals that are aligned with the selected date-range filter. Applied to the example shown above, the selection of a seven-day date-range filter requires that the ER is processed once a week. This weekly processing can be achieved by specifying a recurrence similar to the one shown in figure 5.17.

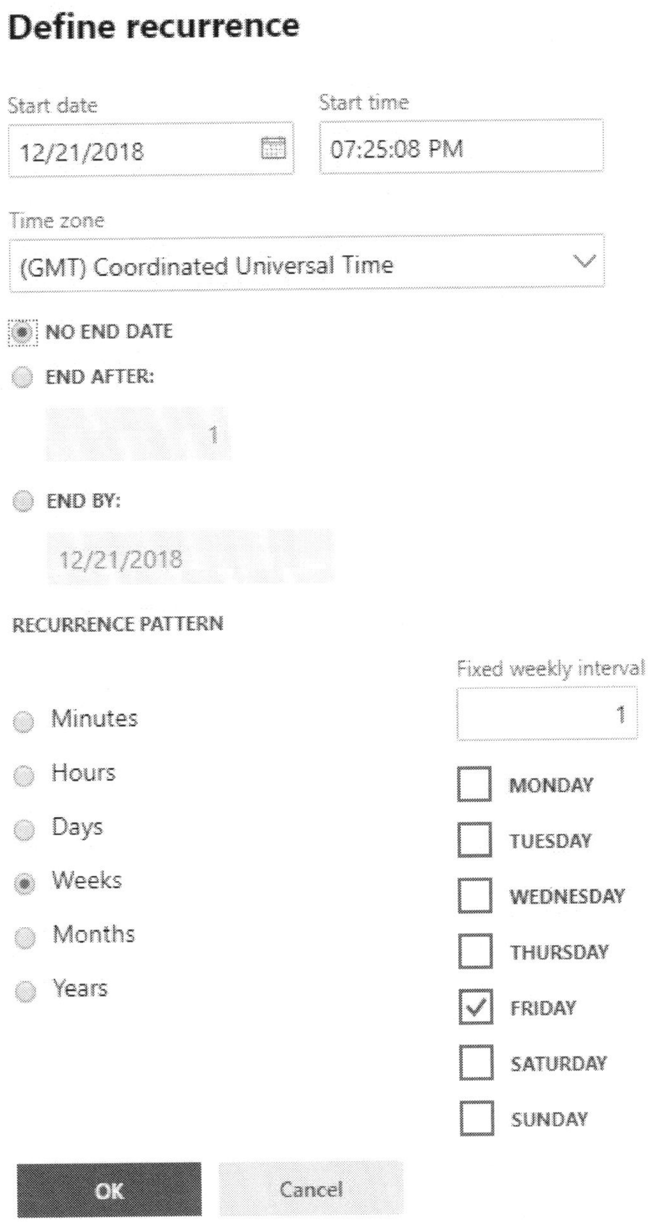

Define recurrence

Start date

| 12/21/2018 | 📅 |

Start time

| 07:25:08 PM |

Time zone

| (GMT) Coordinated Universal Time | ⌄ |

◉ NO END DATE

◯ END AFTER:

| 1 |

◯ END BY:

| 12/21/2018 |

RECURRENCE PATTERN

Fixed weekly interval

| 1 |

◯ Minutes

◯ Hours

◯ Days

◉ Weeks

◯ Months

◯ Years

☐ MONDAY

☐ TUESDAY

☐ WEDNESDAY

☐ THURSDAY

☑ FRIDAY

☐ SATURDAY

☐ SUNDAY

| OK | | Cancel |

Figure 5.17 *ER-processing recurrence*

Once the ER report has been processed, the created Excel output document can be identified in the configured SharePoint site. Please see figure 5.18 for an example.

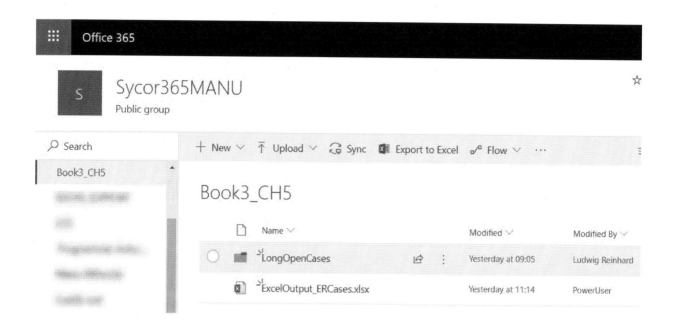

Figure 5.18 *ER report—Excel output document on SharePoint*

5.3.4. MS-Flow

With all of the previous elements set up, MS-Flow can be used for the next major process step that is illustrated in figure 5.3. In the following, the MS-Flow setup used for the process demonstration in chapter 5.3.6. will be explained in detail.

The MS-Flow used starts with a recurrence trigger (step 1) that needs to be aligned with the ER-report processing recurrence that is shown in figure 5.17. Alignment in this context means that the MS-Flow needs to be started after the ER report has been processed and saved to SharePoint.

Note The following MS-Flow steps 2 to 14 are optional steps and are used only because case-related financial dimensions need to be filled in in the author's MSDyn365FO system before case-related times can be posted.

To ensure that the case financial dimension value that is required for recording the case-related working time exists, the existing case financial dimensions are extracted in the second MS-Flow step. This extraction is made by using a filter query that extracts only those financial dimension values that belong to the *case* financial dimension. Please see figure 5.19 for details.

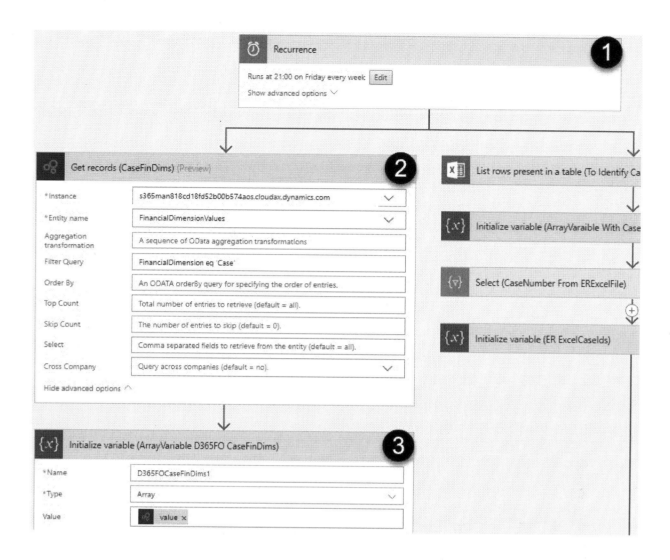

Figure 5.19 *Case management—MS-Flow (1)*

After all case financial dimension values have been extracted, they are included in an array variable denominated *D365CaseFinDims1*. This inclusion in MS-Flow step 3 is necessary for the subsequent selection of the financial dimension value numbers in step 4. The main purpose of the fourth MS-Flow step is excluding all financial dimension metadata, such as the financial dimension owner and alike, that are related to a financial dimension value. Once all case-related financial dimension numbers have been selected, they are bound into another array variable denominated *D365CaseFinDims2* in MS-Flow step 5. Please see figure 5.20 for details. This second array variable is needed later on for comparing the existing financial dimension numbers with the case numbers that are listed in the ER report.

Before this comparison can be made, the case numbers from the ER report are needed. This need is fulfilled in MS-Flow step 6, which lists all case data that have been processed in the ER report. The following MS-Flow steps 7 to 9 are *de facto* identical to the MS-Flow steps 3 to 5 and are required for listing all case IDs. Please see figure 5.20 for details.

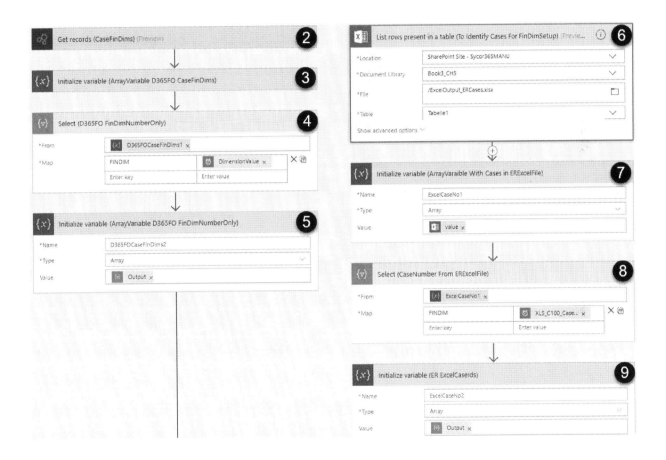

Figure 5.20 *Case management—MS-Flow (2)*

Note The MS-Flow expressions used in step 4 and step 8 are as follows:

- Step 4: *Item()['DimensionValue']*

- Step 8: *Item()['XLS_C100_CaseId']*

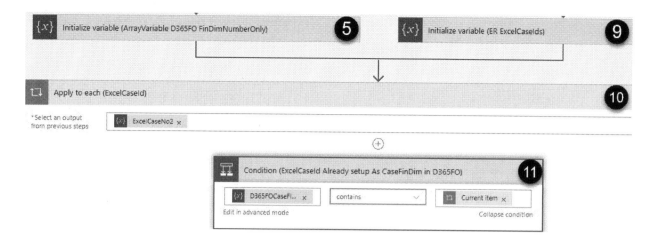

Figure 5.21 *Case management—MS-Flow (3)*

With two array variables that hold the case financial dimension values (step 5) and the case IDs used in the CM (step 9), a comparison of the two can be made to ensure that all cases that have been worked on are set up with a case financial dimension value. This comparison is made in the MS-Flow steps 10 and 11 where case IDs from CM are compared with the case financial dimension values.

If a case that has been worked on does not have a corresponding financial dimension value setup, the conditional MS-Flow step 11 ends in the *if no* branch and sets up the missing financial dimension values. This setup process is realized in the MS-Flow steps 12 to 14 that are illustrated in figure 5.22 below.

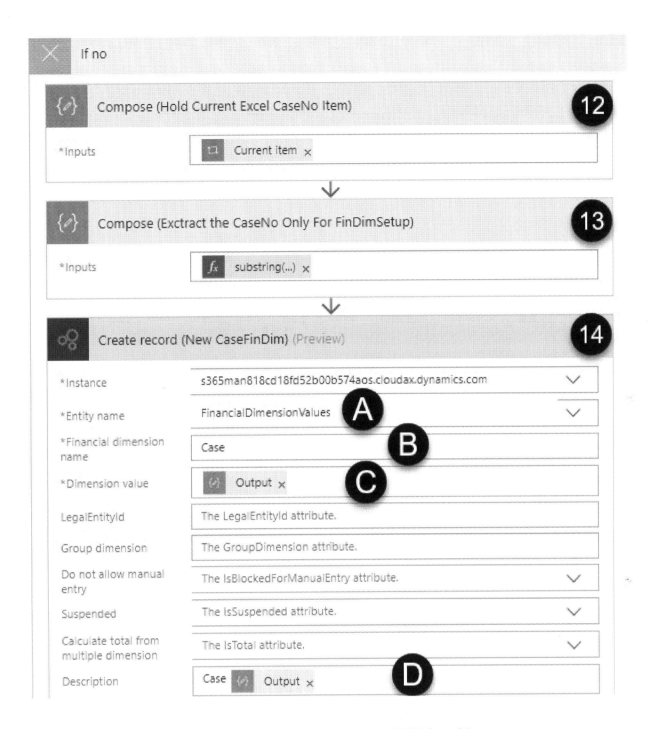

Figure 5.22 *Case management—MS-Flow (4)*

The expression used in MS-Flow step 13 is used to get rid of the curly brackets and spaces that are used in the array variable in MS-Flow step 9 and is defined as *substring(string(outputs('Compose_(Hold_Current_Excel_CaseNo_Item)')),11,5)*.

The output from MS-Flow step 13 is used in MS-Flow step 14 to create a new financial dimension value with the case ID used. The respective fields that have to be filled for this purpose are highlighted with the letters *A* to *D* in figure 5.22.

After the set up of the required financial dimension values for the posting of the case-related working time has been taken care of, the extraction of the closed cases can be started in MS-Flow step 15 by referring to the status of the case. Please see the filter query used in figure 5.23.

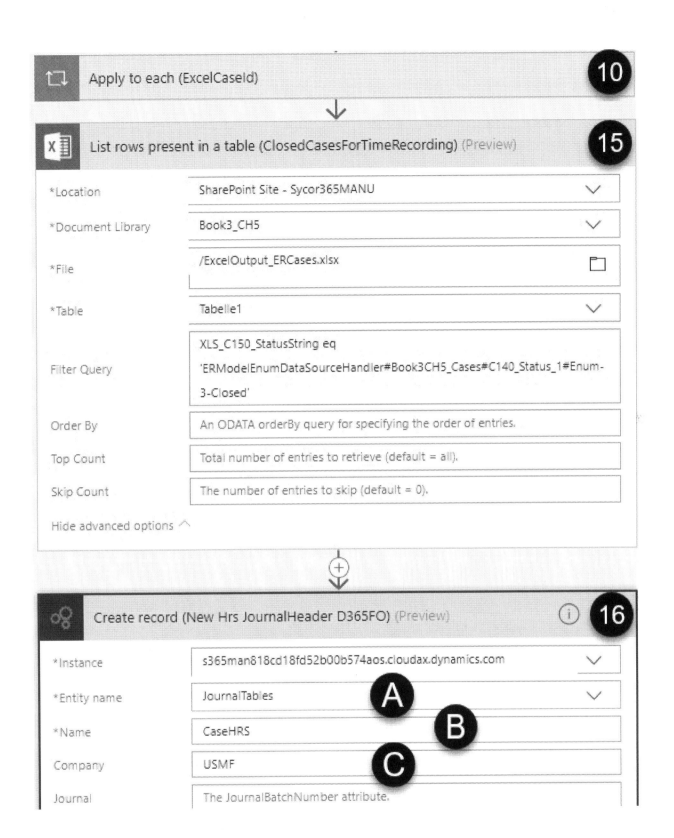

Figure 5.23 *Case management—MS-Flow (5)*

The filter query shown in MS-Flow step 15 filters only those cases that have a status that is *eq* (equal) to *closed.*

If closed cases exist, a new hour journal is created in MS-Flow step 16. This journal creation is realized by making use of the JournalTables data entity (*A*), the journal name (*B*) that has been set up before (please see figure 5.7), and the demo company USMF (*C*).

The next MS-Flow steps 17 to 30 are required for completing the hour-journal lines. This completion starts in MS-Flow step 18, which holds the calculated working time from the ER report. This calculated value is converted into a floating-number value in step 19 by making use of the following expression: *float(outputs('Compose_(TimeInHrs)')).*

MS-Flow steps 20 to 22 make a similar conversion that start with the composition of an MS-Flow element that holds the closed date-time value from the ER report. This value is then converted into an integer value in MS-Flow step 21.

The MS-Flow expression used in step 21 is *int(first(split(outputs('Compose_(ClosedDateTime)'), '.'))).*

The resulting integer value is finally used in MS-Flow step 22 for the definition of a date value, which defines the project and posting date that is used in the journal. Please see figure 5.24 for details.

The MS-Flow expression used in step 22 is *formatdatetime(adddays('12-30-1899',outputs('Compose_(Integer_Conversion_ClosedDateTime_ For_Calc_NextStep)')), 'yyyy-MM-dd')*.

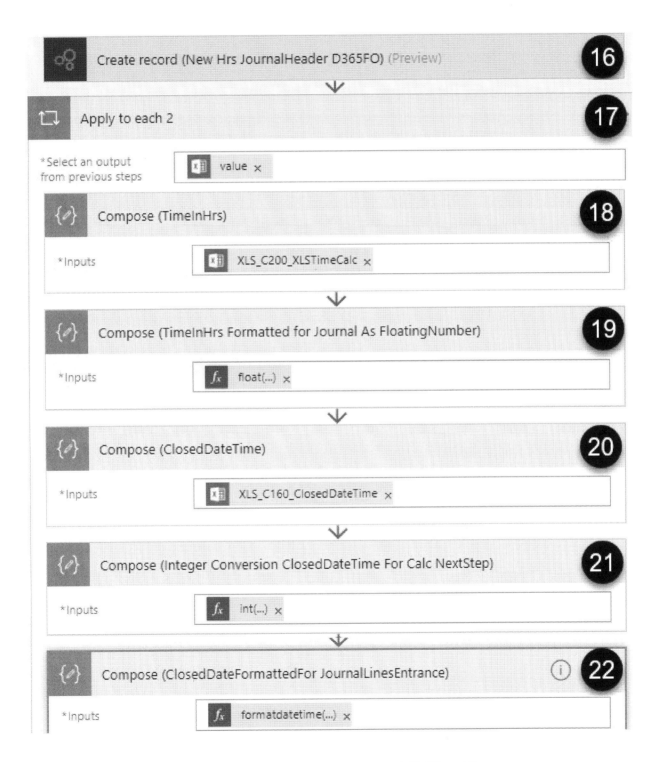

Figure 5.24 *Case management—MS-Flow (6)*

Once the Excel time and date values have been converted into a format that can be processed in the MSDyn365FO hours journal, the financial dimension values needed for making the posting of the working-time lines have to be provided.

Note
In addition to the aforementioned case financial dimension, a project financial dimension and the cost center and department financial dimensions (assigned to the employees) are used for posting case-related work times.

Provisioning the project financial dimension necessitates an extraction of the default-dimension values that are defined for the project that has been linked to the case. This extraction is illustrated in MS-Flow steps 23 to 25 and can be identified in figure 5.25.

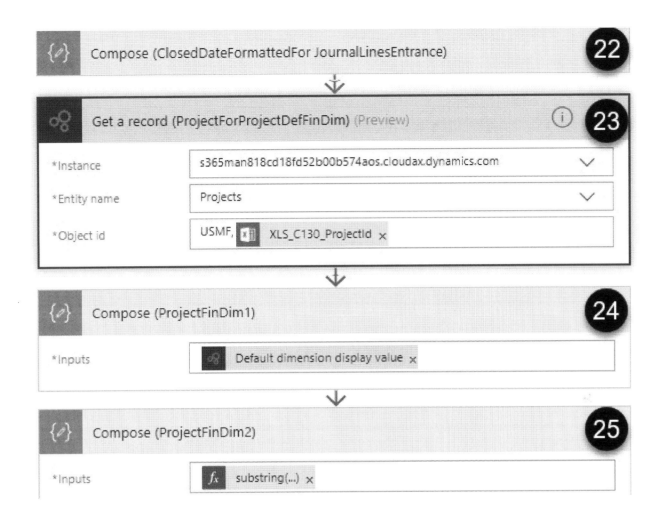

Figure 5.25 *Case management—MS-Flow (7)*

The MS-Flow expression used in step 25 is *substring(string(outputs*

('Compose_(ProjectFinDim1)')),8,12).

After the project financial dimension value has been extracted in step 25, the employee-related

cost center and department-financial dimension values need to be identified. This identification is made

in MS-Flow steps 26 to 30, which are exemplified in figures 5.26 and 5.27.

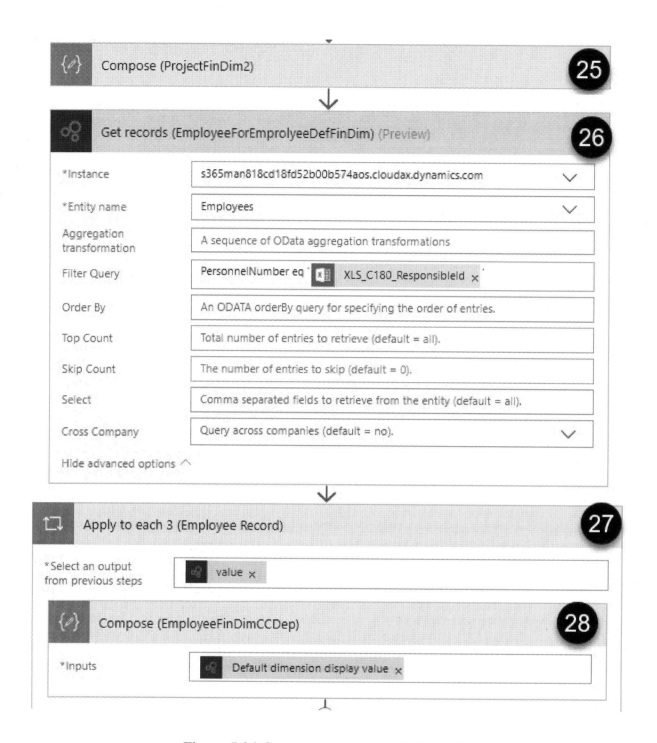

Figure 5.26 *Case management—MS-Flow (8)*

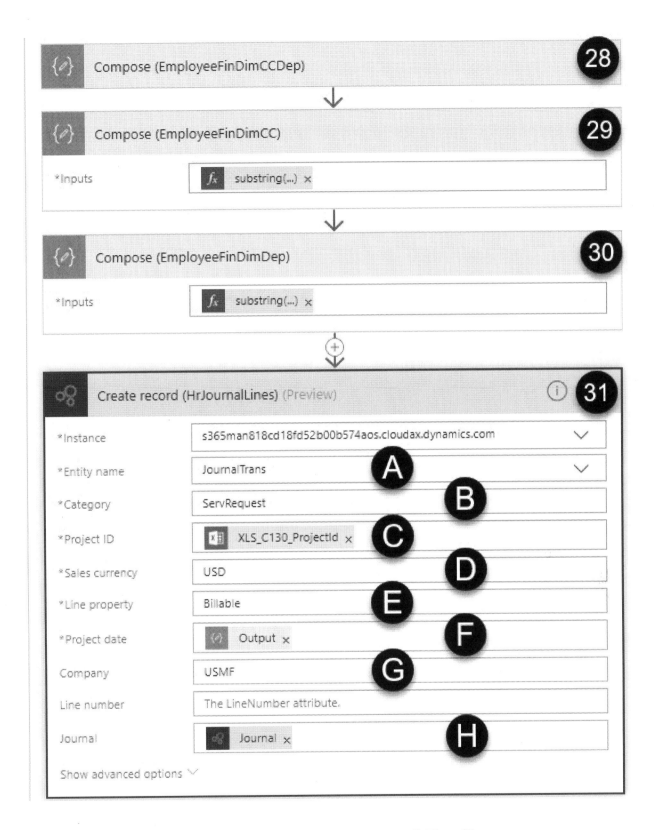

Figure 5.27 *Case management—MS-Flow (9)*

The MS-Flow expression used in step 29 is *substring(string(outputs('Compose_(Employee FinDimCCDep)')),2,3)*. In step 30, the following expression is used: *substring(string(outputs ('Compose_(EmployeeFinDimCCDep)')),6,3)*.

With all the information prepared, the project-hour journal lines can finally be filled. Filling the different journal-line elements—which are identified by the letters *A* to *L* in figures 5.27 and 5.28—is mainly self-explanatory. For that reason, only those elements that require special attention are explained in more detail below.

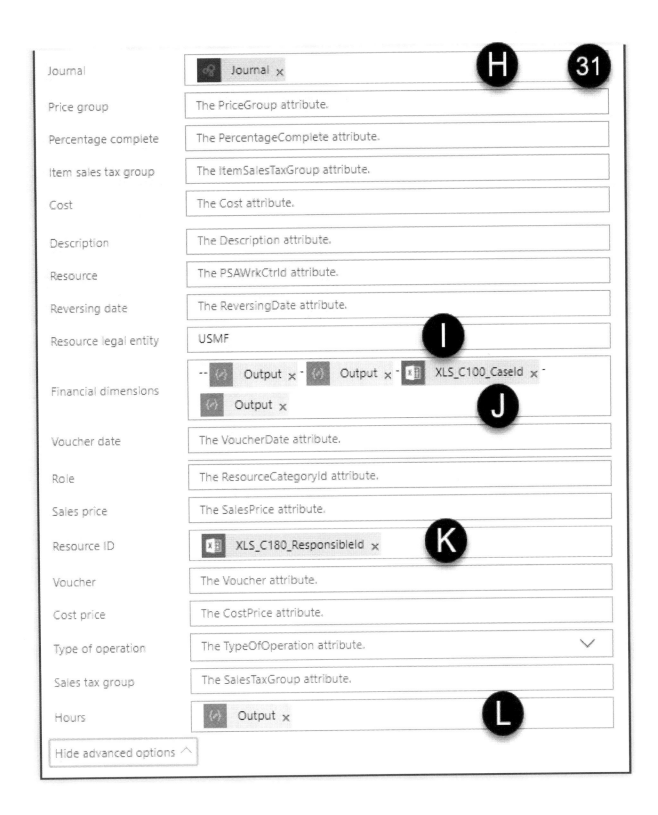

Figure 5.28 *Case management—MS-Flow (10)*

Figures 5.27 and 5.28 illustrate that a number of elements have been hard coded. As an example, the category (*B*), sales currency (*D*), line property (*E*), and company (*G* and *I*) are not dynamically extracted from the case-related information held either in the ER Excel document or in MSDyn365FO. While a dynamic insertion of those field values can be realized, it is not made here for reasons of simplicity and conservation of space.

Another journal-line element that deserves special attention is the financial dimension element that can be identified by the letter *J* in figure 5.28. This element is made up of the financial dimensions for the case, the cost center and department-related to the employee who worked on the case, and the billing project linked to the case. To get those financial dimension values correctly incorporated, one has to ensure that the financial dimensions are sequenced in the same way that is specified in MSDyn365FO.

Note
The sequence specified in MSDyn365FO can be identified in the *financial-dimension-configuration-for-integration-applications* form, which can be accessed from the general ledger module.

The MS-Flow does not end with filling the hour journal lines. What is needed in addition is for respective management to be informed that a case-related hours journal has been created and is ready for review and posting. This step is realized in MS-Flow step 32, which is shown in figure 5.29.

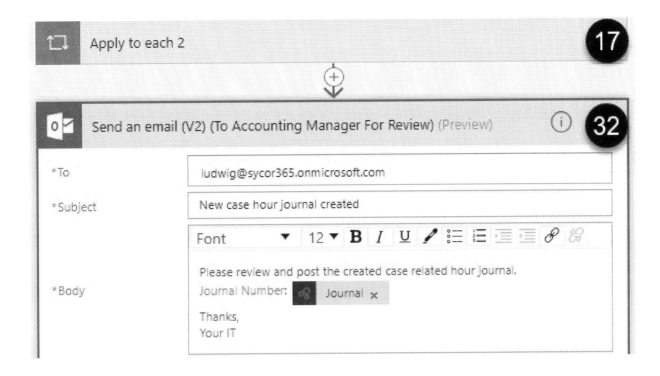

Figure 5.29 *Case management—MS-Flow (11)*

Filling and recording the hour journal lines overcomes two of the three finance-related issues that have been identified in chapter 5.2. What has not been addressed so far is the issue of following up long-running open cases.

Following up long-running open cases can be realized by applying the same technique that has been used in chapter 5.3.3. and chapter 5.3.4.—that is, by creating a separate ER report that filters all open cases, exports them in an Excel format to a cloud-based SharePoint drive, and applying MS-Flow for identifying and reporting those long-running cases. As the process steps and technique required for this reporting is *de facto* identical to what has been shown in the previous chapters, the setup and configuration of the necessary elements is left as an exercise for the reader.

5.3.5.   Project Management

The last step illustrated in the CM process in figure 5.3 relates to the project-management module where the hours journal is created. From a financial perspective, the only thing required in this process step is validating and posting the hours journal, which will be demonstrated in the following subchapter.

5.3.6.   Process Demonstration

After all configurations and setups have been completed, let us have a look at the process that is realized with those specifications in place.

The process starts in MSDyn365FO with the completion of the work on a case. The completion of the work on the case is documented by changing the case status to *closed,* which updates the *status* and *closed-date-and-time* fields that are shown in figure 5.30.

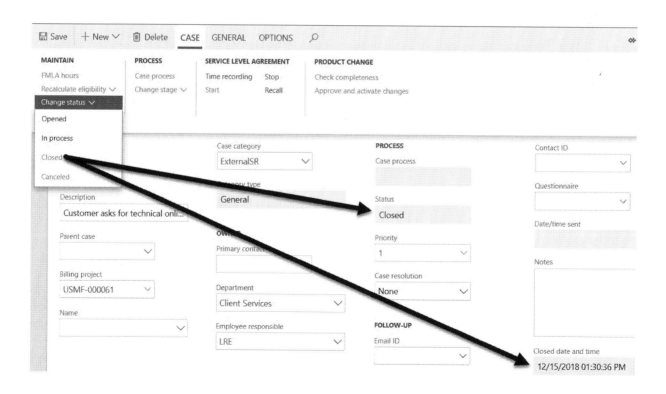

Figure 5.30 *Complete work for case*

The updated status and time field are the prerequisite for the identification of the completed case in the next process step: the generation of the ER. To generate this report, no human interaction is required, because a regular ER generation interval has been specified (please see figure 5.17 above for details). Figure 5.31 highlights this autogeneration of the ER report and ensures that the ER report is stored in the SharePoint document library (see figure 5.32) that has been defined as the ER output destination.

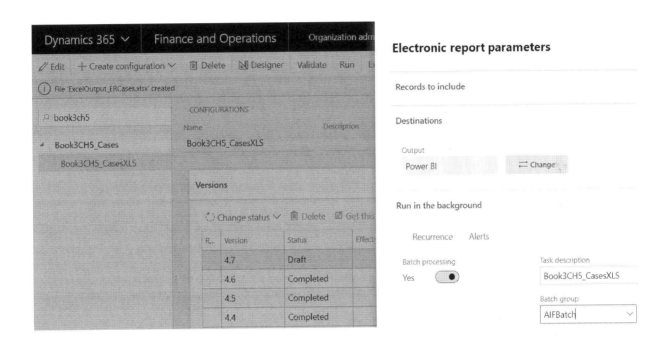

Figure 5.31 *Autoprocessing ER (1)*

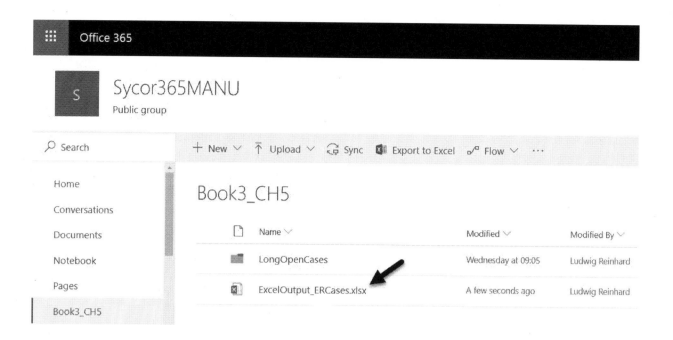

Figure 5.32 *Autoprocessing ER (2)*

Shortly after the ER has been generated, MS-Flow starts processing the ER reporting data that have been saved on SharePoint. This process also does not require a human interaction but is rather started automatically with the help of the MS-Flow recurrence trigger that has been shown in figure 5.19.

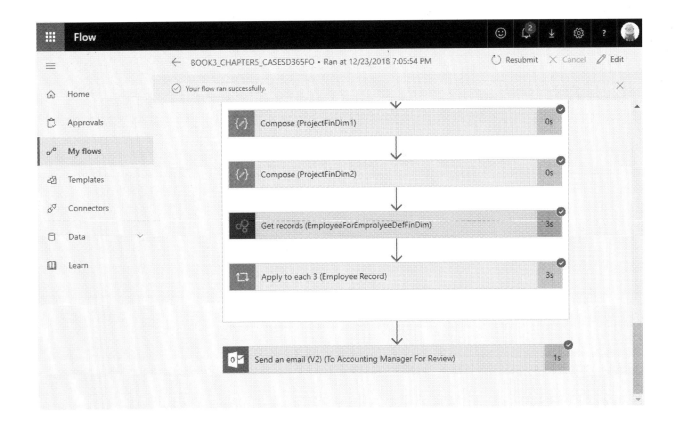

Figure 5.33 *Autoprocessing MS-Flow*

Once the MS-Flow process is completed, the management is informed about the creation of a new hour journal that needs to be reviewed and posted. This information is transmitted in the form of an email notification that is shown in figure 5.34.

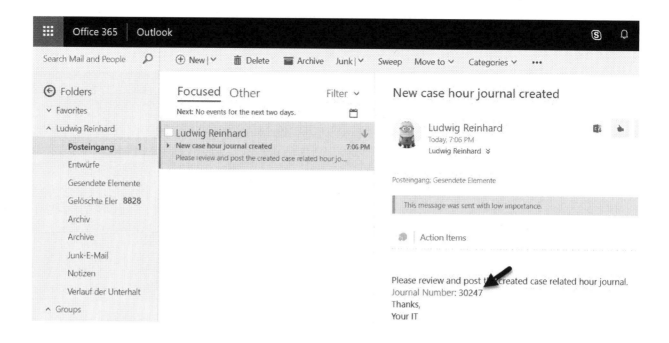

Figure 5.34 *Email for management journal review*

The next process step consists of a review of the created journal and the related journal lines before the journal can be posted. The next two figures exemplify this review and posting process.

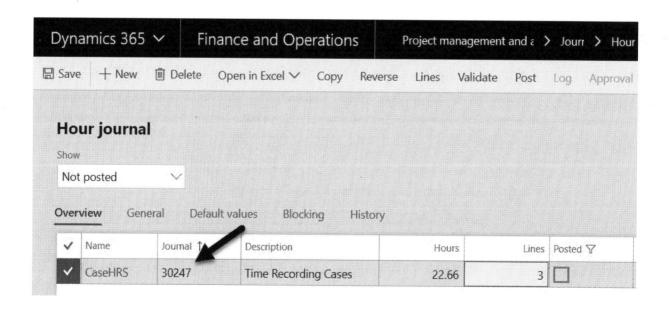

Figure 5.35 *Management review of autocreated hour journal (1)*

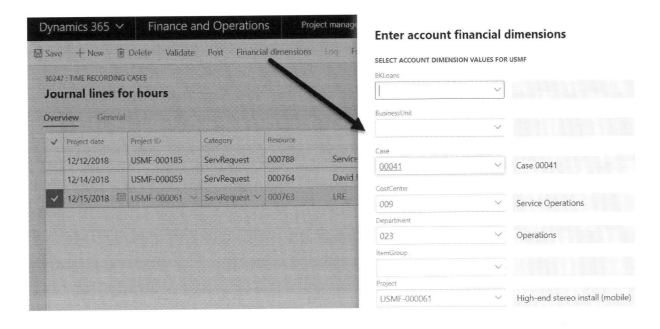

Figure 5.36 *Management review of hour journal (2)*

Note Figure 5.36 highlights the financial dimension values that have been extracted and filled in to the journal lines with the help of MS-Flow.

Posting the case hour journal creates vouchers similar to the one shown in the following figure and ends the operative CM process.

J...	V...	Date ↑	Ledger account	Account name	Currency	Amount i...	Posting layer
0...	7...	12/15/2...	618300-002-023-009--00041-USMF-000061	Consulting Service Expense	USD	1,122.50	Current
0...	7...	12/15/2...	600300-002-023-009---USMF-000061	Payroll Allocation	USD	-1,122.50	Current

Figure 5.37 *Sample hour-related voucher transaction CM*

The dollar amount shown in figure 5.37 is the result of a multiplication of the hours recorded and the cost-price that has been specified for the project category. As an example, the $1,122.50 that can be identified in the figure above is calculated by multiplying the $50 cost-price that has been specified for the *ServRequest* category and the 22.45 work time that has been recorded in the hours journal.

Once the operative CM is completed, the analytical part of the process can start. Due to the lack of sufficient sample data processed in the demo MSDyn365FO system of the author, the analytical CM part is presented from a conceptual perspective in the following.

Making this conceptual presentation requires an assumption about the salary expense of the employees working in the operative service department. In the following, it is assumed that these workers earn $10,000 a week. This salary expense is recorded in MSDyn365FO with a reference to the operations department 023 and the service-operations cost center 009. Figure 5.38 shows the respective voucher where the positive amount indicates a debit (DR) and the negative amount a credit (CR) transaction.

Account	Business Unit	Department	Cost Center	Case	Project	Amount
602100 - Salary expense [P&L]		023	009			$ 10,000.00
110110 - Bank account [BS]						$ -10,000.00

Figure 5.38 *Weekly salary expense for service-operation personnel*

The transaction illustrated in figure 5.38 debits a salary-expense account—in other words, a profit-and-loss (P&L) account that influences the company's profit. As the credit transaction is made on a balance sheet (BS) account, no profit effect arises from this second transaction line.

Let us now add the transaction that is posted for the case-related working time. This transaction can be identified from the last two lines in figure 5.39.

Account	Business Unit	Department	Cost Center	Case	Project	Amount
602100 - Salary expense [P&L]		023	009			$ 10,000.00
110110 - Bank account [BS]						$ -10,000.00
618300 - Project costs [P&L]	002	023	009	00041	USMF-000061	$ 1,122.50
600300 - Payroll allocation [P&L]	002	023	009		USMF-000061	$ -1,122.50

Figure 5.39 *Weekly salary expense for service-operation personnel and project hour posting*

The transactions listed in figure 5.39 show that the total costs of the operational service personnel is not changed by the case-related hour posting. This can be identified by adding all amounts that are recorded in combination with department 023 and cost center 009.

Analyzing the salary expense and the payroll-allocation accounts for the respective department and cost center shows, however, that not all salary expenses were allocated to cases. In other words, the operational service workers were not working at full capacity. This can be identified by the total amount that remains in the department and the cost center of the service employees and is highlighted in the gray cells in figure 5.40.

Account	Business Unit	Department	Cost Center	Case	Project	Amount
602100 - Salary expense [P&L]		023	009			$ 10,000.00
110110 - Bank account [BS]						$ -10,000.00
618300 - Project costs [P&L]	002	023	009	00041	USMF-000061	$ 1,122.50
600300 - Payroll allocation [P&L]	002	023	009		USMF-000061	$ -1,122.50
Total (grey highlighted cells)						$ 8,877.50

Figure 5.40 *Analysis resource usage*

An alternative resource-usage calculation can be made by building the quotient of the project costs and the total salary expense. Applied to the example used, this would result in a capacity-use percentage of ($1,122.50 / $10,000 * 100% =) 11.22%.

Another analysis that can be made from the transactions recorded in MSDyn365FO is the identification of the total costs required for providing the CM services. This cost amount can easily be identified by the case ID 00041 in figure 5.40 and can be used for making a comparison with the costs that an external service provider would request. Making this comparison can be a first indicator of (*a*) inefficiencies that might exist in the CM process and (*b*) which service processes should be outsourced.

5.4.   Summary

This chapter demonstrated the manifold functionalities that are available for the standard CM tool. Despite its inherent weaknesses (automatic time recordings, analysis of long-running cases, and the financial analysis of cases), standard MS process tools were introduced that allowed overcoming those weaknesses for making use of the full potential and power of the CM tool.

6. Conclusion

This book covered a number of special finance- and accounting-related topics that one often comes across in practice. Even though not all topics might be relevant for a specific MSDyn365FO environment, I hope that you found some new ideas and concepts in this book that you can apply for similar finance and accounting scenarios in your company.

Acknowledgments

This book would not have been possible without the help of the following people: Jan Timphaus and Karlin Reinhard, who helped me by reviewing and improving the different parts of this book.

At this point, I would also like to express special thanks to my employer, who provided me the time, support, and means to finish this book.

The Sycor Group is an international full-service partner and solution integrator (SI) for Microsoft Dynamics 365 (AX & CRM) and is a Microsoft Cloud Solution Provider. The experts consult, implement, optimize, and operate cloud on premises and in hybrid scenarios. For major implementation and rollout projects, the Sycor Group is a reliable partner, based on expertise in over eighty countries and with large systems up to five thousand users. Seven hundred fifty employees and twentynineteen locations worldwide (Europe, Asia, and America) assure international delivery capabilities.

As an ISV, Sycor is a Microsoft Strategic Development Partner for rental, trade, service, and maintenance of mobile goods and fleet management. Its industry solutions, Sycor.Rental and Sycor.Fleet, are genuine Microsoft Dynamics 365 solutions and are available at the Microsoft AppSource. The comprehensive Microsoft Dynamics 365 portfolio is backed by extensive hosting services (full Microsoft stack) and is complemented by solutions and services for Microsoft Azure, Microsoft Cortana Intelligence Suite, Power BI, Microsoft Office 365, Microsoft SharePoint, Skype for Business, and other online Microsoft products. In addition to that, Sycor offers software-asset management and license consulting. In the fields of manufacturing, retail, and professional services,

Sycor has consulting and development teams with many years of Microsoft Dynamics AX and industry expertise. Sycor is a member of the Microsoft Dynamics Industry Partner Program EMEA in the areas of professional services and manufacturing.

About the Author

Dr. Ludwig Reinhard is a senior Microsoft Dynamics 365 consultant from Germany specializing in the finance and project area. Dr. Reinhard holds a bachelor's degree in business administration, an MBA, and a PhD in finance, as well as a number of Microsoft Dynamics certificates. He is an active member in the Microsoft Dynamics community and has his own Dynamics blog (https://dynamicsax-fico.com). In 2017 and 2018, he was awarded the Microsoft MVP award and, in 2018, the D365UG/AXUG granite award. More information about Dr. Reinhard can be found on his blog and on LinkedIn.

About the Reviewer

Jürgen Weber

Jürgen Weber is a senior Dynamics 365 consultant from Germany working mainly in the supply-chain-management, production, and project-accounting sector. With more than twenty-five years of industrial background in logistics and controlling, he furthermore implemented different ERP systems on customer sites serving as project manager. More information about Jürgen Weber can be found on LinkedIn.

Made in the USA
Middletown, DE
24 July 2023

35643758R00152